GLOBAL VALUE CHAINS AND GEOPOLITICAL UNCERTAINTY

This book offers a timely and insightful look at how political tensions, economic disruptions, and technological advances are reshaping the way goods and services move across borders. At a time when global trade faces mounting pressure, this book explores how businesses, governments, and communities can adapt to an increasingly uncertain world.

Spanning diverse geographic areas and themes, the book delves into the evolving trade dynamics between developed and developing countries, the involvement of governments alongside international partnerships, as well as the impact of emerging digital technologies such as automation and artificial intelligence. Additionally, it addresses how companies are reevaluating their business models to enhance resilience, adopt sustainable practices, and meet rising demands for ethical conduct. Rich case studies from recent years bring these themes to life, highlighting real-world examples of innovation, adaptation, and strategic thinking.

This volume serves as a vital resource for students, researchers, policymakers, and business executives aiming to comprehend and tackle the intricate challenges currently confronting global value chains. Whether engaged in international trade studies or overseeing a multinational enterprise, readers will find practical advice and forward-looking strategies essential for navigating a period characterized by transformation.

Imran Ali is a globally ranked researcher and senior lecturer at Central Queensland University. His expertise spans digital transformation, logistics, and sustainable supply chains. He has published in leading journals, received the Emerald Literati Award, and serves on editorial boards. His work bridges academic research and industry transformation.

William Ho teaches at the University of Melbourne and who studies supply chain risk, sustainability, and strategic sourcing. He has published 60+ articles, earned over 13,000 citations, and secured major international grants. He is the associate editor of *Decision Sciences* and OR Spectrum, promoting practice-oriented, job-ready graduate education.

Thanos Papadopoulos is a researcher who focuses on digital transformation, supply chains, and global value chains. He has published 150+ articles and serves on top-tier editorial boards. A Clarivate Highly Cited Researcher and British Academy Fellow, he is recognized among the world's top 2% of scientists (2021–2023).

"This book provides timely and interesting insights into global value chains amid geopolitical tensions. The real-world case studies and strategic insights make it a useful guide for researchers, students, and policymakers. It is a much-needed contribution to understanding how global trade networks are evolving in an era of uncertainty."

Sri Talluri, *John Hoagland—Richard Metzler Professor in Purchasing and Supply Management, Michigan State University, USA*

"This timely book offers a compelling synthesis of research and practical approaches for navigating global value chains during periods of geopolitical uncertainty. The editors have collected insights from a group of esteemed scholars to present valuable perspectives that are both theoretically sound and supported by practical examples. This volume is an indispensable resource for scholars, students, professionals, and policymakers."

Mark Stevenson, *Professor of Operations Management, Lancaster University, UK*

"This is a timely and well-curated book to understand the evolving dynamics of global value chains in an era marked by geopolitical uncertainty. With its blend of theoretical depth and practical relevance, the book offers fresh insights into resilience, innovation, and strategic adaptation. It is a must-read for scholars, practitioners, and policymakers seeking to navigate today's complex global landscape."

Angappa Gupta Gunasekaran, *Professor of Supply Chain Management, Pennsylvania State University at Harrisburg, USA*

GLOBAL VALUE CHAINS AND GEOPOLITICAL UNCERTAINTY

Disruption and Transformation

Edited by Imran Ali, William Ho and Thanos Papadopoulos

Routledge
Taylor & Francis Group
LONDON AND NEW YORK

Designed cover image: © Getty Images

First published 2026
by Routledge
4 Park Square, Milton Park, Abingdon, Oxon OX14 4RN

and by Routledge
605 Third Avenue, New York, NY 10158

Routledge is an imprint of the Taylor & Francis Group, an informa business

British Library Cataloguing-in-Publication Data
A catalogue record for this book is available from the British Library

ISBN: 978-1-032-74358-5 (hbk)
ISBN: 978-1-032-74357-8 (pbk)
ISBN: 978-1-003-46889-9 (ebk)

DOI: 10.4324/9781003468899

Typeset in Galliard
by Apex CoVantage, LLC

CONTENTS

ABOUT THE EDITORS

Imran Ali is a globally ranked researcher, academic leader, and innovative educator, recognized as a thought leader in business management, specifically in information systems, logistics, operations, and supply chain management. According to the 2023 rankings of Stanford University, Dr. Ali is among the top 2% of the most cited researchers in business and management globally. Currently, Dr. Ali serves as a senior lecturer in operations and innovation management at the School of Business and Law, Melbourne Campus, Central Queensland University, Australia. He earned a PhD in business management from the University of South Australia, specializing in logistics and supply chain management. Dr. Ali's research covers a wide range of contemporary topics, including digital transformation of businesses, global value chains, supply chain risk and resilience, the circular economy, and sustainable supply chain performance. Dr. Ali brings these research insights into the classroom, teaching closely related subjects at both undergraduate and postgraduate levels. His scholarly contributions have been widely recognized, with publications in several high-quality journals, such as the *International Journal of Operations & Production Management, International Journal of Production Economics, IEEE Transactions on Engineering Management, Transportation Part E: Logistics and Transportation Review, Journal of Business Research, International Journal of Information Management, and Supply Chain Management: An International Journal.* He has also coauthored two books. In 2023, one of his papers was honored with the prestigious Emerald Literati Award for Outstanding Paper. Dr. Ali serves as Regional Editor at Asia Pacific Business Review and an editorial board member of the *Journal of Business Research and Production Planning & Control*, and the *International Journal of Logistics*

Management. His consulting experience encompasses driving digital transformation and cultivating resilience in the food and beverage industry.

William Ho is a professor of operations and supply chain management in the Department of Management and Marketing at the University of Melbourne, Australia. Professor Ho's research expertise includes supply chain risk management, sustainable supply chain management, and strategic sourcing and supplier performance management. He has published over 60 articles in a variety of top-tier academic journals, such as the *Journal of Operations Management*, *Operations Research*, *Decision Sciences*, *European Journal of Operational Research*, *IEEE Transactions on Engineering Management*, and many others. He has over 13,000 citations for his work and a h-index of 37. He has won several research awards and received five large competitive research grants funded by the Australian government's Cooperative Research Centre Program, the UK's Economic and Social Research Council (two grants), the European Regional Development Fund, and the National Natural Science Foundation of China. He currently serves as the associate editor of *Decision Sciences* and OR Spectrum and is an editorial review board member of *IEEE Transactions on Engineering Management*.

Professor Ho teaches a wide range of subjects related to operations, supply chain, logistics, and value chain at both the undergraduate and postgraduate levels. He is a fervent proponent of industry-led, innovative education, which equips graduates with the skills necessary to secure employment.

Thanos Papadopoulos is a professor of management (information systems/operations management) and Deputy Dean of Department at the Department of "Analytics, Operations, and Systems" of Kent Business School, University of Kent, UK. His teaching and research focus on the problems that are at the nexus of operations, supply chain management, global value chains, and digital transformation. He has published over 150 articles in peer-reviewed journals and conferences, including, among other things, the *British Journal of Management*, *Decision Sciences*, *European Journal of Operational Research*, *International Journal of Operations and Production Management*, *European Journal of Information Systems*, *International Journal of Production Research*, *IEEE Transactions on Engineering Management*, *International Journal of Production Economics*, *Technological Forecasting and Social Change, and Production Planning and Control.*

Thanos successfully led multiple special issues in top-tier journals and holds tremendous editorial experience as an associate editor for the *British Journal of Management*, *Decision Sciences*, *International Journal of Operations and Production Management*, as well as departmental editor for *IEEE Transactions on Engineering Management*. He sits on the editorial board of Production Planning and Control and is a distinguished editorial board member of the

International Journal of Information Management and *International Journal of Information Management Data Insights.* Thanos is a Fellow of the British Academy of Management. He has recently been included in the Clarivate list of Highly Cited Researchers 2023 for a third time in a row, as well as in Stanford University's Top 2% of Scientists in the world for the single year 2023, marking three consecutive years of inclusion (2023, 2022, 2021).

CONTRIBUTORS

Tage Andersson is a lecturer and head of course for the Master of Management for Engineers at Central Queensland University. His research focuses on strategic project management and innovation in supply chains, drawing from extensive industry experience with firms like Nokia.

Ahmad Arslan is a professor at the Department of Marketing, Management, and International Business, University of Oulu, Finland. He is a visiting academic at InnoLab, University of Vaasa, Finland, and holds an honorary chair position at the Business School, University of Aberdeen, Scotland, UK.

Nasrin Asgari is an associate professor of supply chain management at Anglia Ruskin University. Her research interests include operations management, humanitarian logistics, supply chain sustainability, and circular economy. Her research outputs are published in some distinguished journals like *Production and Operations Management*, *Management Science—Operations Management*, *Harvard Business Review*, *European Journal of Operational Research*, and *Transportation Research Part E: Logistics and Transportation Review*.

Abhishek Behl is a senior lecturer at Keele Business School, Keele University, UK. He holds more than 10 years of experience in teaching, research, and consulting. Abhishek is a fellow of the Spatial Data Lab at Harvard University, USA, and an affiliate member of the Gamification and Systems Thinking Lab at the University of Edinburgh, UK.

Donella Caspersz is an associate professor at the University of Western Australia. Donella's research focuses on how family business management, operations, and governance influence firm sustainability and the significance of temporary labor migration for society and the economy.

Dolly Gaur is an academic and researcher specializing in finance, with a PhD from Amity University. She has teaching experience at institutions like the Symbiosis Centre for Management Studies and Lloyd Business School. Her research focuses on Fintech, banking, and nonperforming assets, with publications in Scopus-indexed journals.

Kanishka Gupta is an assistant professor at Vivekananda Institute of Professional Studies—Technical Campus, New Delhi. Awarded PhD in Intellectual Capital and earned a Gold Medal for exceptional academic performance during her masters. Her research focuses on intellectual capital, Fintech, and accounting.

David M. Herold is a supply chain researcher with a focus on the mechanisms and dynamics of digital and sustainable operations. In 2018, he was awarded a PhD from Griffith University and is currently a senior lecturer at the Queensland University of Technology in Brisbane, Australia.

Anas Iftikhar is an assistant professor at Lancaster University who conducts research on the capabilities of supply chains in complex and disruptive environments, with a focus on resilience and emerging technologies. He has published in leading operations management journals, contributing valuable insights to both academic understanding and practical application.

Waqas Khan is working as deputy treasurer at Government College University, Lahore, Pakistan. He is specialized in financial and business management within entrepreneurial contexts. His research explores enterprise development, with several publications in high-impact SSCI, SCIE, ABS, ABDC, and Scopus-indexed journals at both national and international levels.

Renata Klafke is a lecturer at Central Queensland University, Australia. Her research explores global value chains, digital innovation in supply chains, and service ecosystems. She draws on over 16 years of international industry experience to bridge theory and practice in higher education.

Huashan (Jason) Li is a senior lecturer at Deakin Business School, Deakin University. His research focuses on how firms adapt their global supply chains and business models to enhance resilience against risk events, such as product recalls and geopolitical disruptions.

Arnoldus (Ron) Maas is a lecturer at the Business School of the University of Western Australia. His research focuses on how organizations strategically respond to and are structurally affected by their institutional environment across the international business context.

Qasim Ali Nisar has over 10 years of experience in academia and is passionate about conducting and teaching management research that contributes to the advancement of knowledge and practice in the field of management. His research endeavors span the domains of management, digitalization at the workplace, supply chain management, and sustainable enterprise.

Abhinav Pal is a postgraduate in economics. He has approximately 10 years of teaching experience at Symbiosis International (Deemed University). He cleared UGC-NET in Economics in 2014. His research interests lie in areas of personal finance, macroeconomics, and applications of blockchain in finance, economics and public policy.

Sanjoy Kumar Paul is an associate professor of operations and supply chain management at the University of Technology, Sydney, Australia. He has published more than 130 papers in top-tier journals and conferences. He is also an editor and reviewer of many reputed journals. Dr. Paul has received several recognitions and awards in his career, including the top 2% of scientists in author databases of standardized citation indicators since 2020.

Arza Faldy Prameswara is a PhD candidate at the University of Western Australia. His research focuses on how firms strategically respond to an increasingly de-globalized world, with particular attention to the political, economic, and institutional shifts that shape global business environments.

Towfique Rahman is a lecturer in logistics and supply chain management at Griffith University, Australia. He holds a PhD from the University of Technology, Sydney, Australia, and over a decade of experience in operations and supply chain management. His research focuses on supply chain risk, resilience, digital twins, and sustainability, with publications in top journals and contributions as a peer reviewer and editor.

Rashida Salmani is associated with the Asian School of Business in the capacity of an assistant professor in the area of human resource management and organizational behavior. She holds a PhD in commerce. She is also a UGC-NET JRF (Junior Research Fellowship) awardee.

Said Usman is a lecturer in Business Management at the University of Wales Trinity Saint David. He holds a PhD in supply chain management. His research focuses on sustainable supply chain management, supply chain integration, and the role of technology in organizational performance and operations.

Ilias Vlachos is a professor of supply chain management, has published over 300 journal articles, conference presentations, and studies, including those in top *AJG/ABS* journals. He advises the European Union on various issues. He is ranked among the 1,000 best scholars in the business and management field.

Cait White is a specialist in organizational communication with a focus on rhetoric and discourse analysis. She received her BA in Communication from the University of California, San Diego, and her MA and PhD, again in Communication, from the University of Washington.

Agus Wicaksana is a lecturer in business analytics at the Adelaide Business School, Australia. His research interests focus on risk management in firm operations and supply chains. Prior to his academic career, Agus worked as operations and supply chain professional in multinational companies.

Wantao Yu is a professor of supply chain management at the University of Roehampton, UK. His research interests include digital supply chain management, supply chain sustainability, and lean, agile, resilient, and green (LARG) supply chain management. His work has been published in prestigious academic outlets.

1

INTRODUCTION TO GLOBAL VALUE CHAINS AND GEOPOLITICAL TURMOIL

Imran Ali, William Ho, Thanos Papadopoulos and Cait White

Introduction

In the present interconnected world, global value chains (GVCs) have emerged as a pivotal aspect of the international economic framework, influencing the movement of goods, services, and capital across borders. Unlike earlier production methods confined to individual countries, contemporary manufacturing is spread across various nations, creating complex networks that utilize comparative advantages in labor, technology, and resources. For example, the journey of smartphone production typically involves research and design in the United States (U.S.), component manufacturing in South Korea and Taiwan, assembly in China, and distribution to global markets. This division of labor enables nations and companies to focus on specific functions, leading to increased productivity, lower costs, and enhanced economic growth (World Bank, 2020).

Nevertheless, the effective operation of these networks is increasingly jeopardized by a turbulent geopolitical climate. Trade conflicts, diplomatic strains, economic sanctions, and military confrontations have disrupted established supply chain frameworks, compelling businesses to reevaluate their global strategies. A prominent illustration is the U.S.–China trade war, which led companies to diversify their suppliers, relocate production, or bring operations back to their home countries to counteract tariff effects. Similarly, the Russia-Ukraine conflict has impacted energy and agricultural exports and disrupted transportation routes, highlighting the susceptibility of GVCs to geopolitical shocks with extensive implications (Ali et al., 2024; Magableh et al., 2023). Lastly, there remains a risk that the tariffs imposed by the American President, Donald Trump, will affect global trade, introduce supply chain risks, and have potential broader economic impacts (Ticha, 2025).

DOI: 10.4324/9781003468899-1

Amid this instability, three significant megatrends are transforming GVCs and altering the priorities of global trade: technological advancement, environmental sustainability, and the restructuring of globalization. These trends not only address emerging challenges but also reflect proactive measures taken by businesses and policymakers to create GVCs that are more robust, fair, and environmentally sound.

Innovative technologies, such as artificial intelligence (AI), blockchain, the Internet of Things (IoT), and advanced analytics are fundamentally changing supply chain design and operations. For instance, blockchain technology enhances traceability and security within networks, ensuring product authenticity and minimizing fraud. Likewise, AI aids in demand forecasting, inventory control, and risk management. These advancements facilitate the shift from linear supply chains to digitally integrated ecosystems that can better adapt to disruptions. However, their adoption brings challenges concerning digital infrastructure, cybersecurity, and workforce preparedness (Wamba et al., 2020).

At the same time, environmental sustainability has emerged as a critical issue for GVCs. As consumers, investors, and regulators increasingly demand action, companies are urged to lower emissions, reduce waste, and implement ethical sourcing practices. Industries such as fashion and electronics are facing greater scrutiny, prompting a move toward circular economy models and more transparent supply chains. Embracing sustainable practices is not merely about compliance; it also fosters innovation, bolsters brand reputation, and enhances long-term competitiveness (Kumar & Srai, 2019).

Additionally, the framework of globalization is experiencing considerable transformation. The COVID-19 pandemic, geopolitical conflicts and rising protectionist sentiments have exposed the vulnerabilities of overextended supply chains. Consequently, there is a growing trend toward reshoring, nearshoring, and regionalization strategies, as companies aim to lessen reliance on distant suppliers and strengthen local resilience. These shifts are redefining the creation of value, compelling businesses to find a balance between efficiency and robustness (McKinsey Global Institute, 2024).

Given these developments, understanding and responding to the changing structure and strategic implications of GVCs is more crucial now than ever. For scholars, industry leaders, and policymakers, there is an urgent need to investigate how GVCs function under pressure, adapt to technological advancements, and achieve sustainability objectives while also navigating escalating geopolitical uncertainties.

This chapter seeks to lay a thorough groundwork for comprehending the evolution and current dynamics of GVCs. It begins with a definition of the concept and historical progression of global value chains, followed by an analysis of their economic importance and structural changes. It then explores the disruptive effects of geopolitical instability and how the three interconnected megatrends—technological innovation, sustainability, and the reconfiguration of globalization—are transforming the global production landscape. Through this perspective, the chapter prepares the foundation for a more in-depth examination of how companies and governments can develop more resilient, agile, and inclusive value chains in an era characterized by complexity and uncertainty.

Defining Global Value Chains

GVCs encompass all activities necessary to bring a product or service from its initial idea to final consumption and beyond. These activities include design, production, marketing, distribution, and post-sale services. Within a GVC, different phases of production are spread across various countries, enabling firms to focus on specific tasks that align with their comparative advantages. This international division of labor allows companies to enhance efficiency, cut costs, and improve product quality. For example, producing a consumer electronic device might involve design and research in the U.S., component manufacturing in East Asia, assembly in China, and global market distribution. This modular approach to production enables firms to capitalize on regional strengths and capabilities. The expansion of GVCs has resulted in a remarkable degree of economic interdependence, as companies now operate within integrated transnational networks rather than isolated national economies. Such interconnectedness offers firms opportunities to scale their operations and access new markets, while simultaneously introducing new risks linked to global disturbances and political uncertainties (Antràs, 2020).

The Transformation from Traditional Supply Chains to GVCs

The shift from traditional supply chains to GVCs has been driven by several interconnected factors over the past few decades. Traditional supply chains were primarily characterized by vertically integrated firms managing production processes within a single country, retaining control over most production aspects. However, advancements in technology, trade liberalization, and changes in corporate strategies have fundamentally altered supply chain structures, enabling businesses to leverage cost efficiencies and expertise across diverse regions. A significant catalyst for the evolution of supply chains into GVCs has been improvements in transportation and communication technologies. Innovations, such as containerized shipping, real-time inventory management, and digital supply chain integration, have permitted companies to distribute their production processes across multiple geographic locations while maintaining efficiency. The advent of the internet and cloud computing has further hastened this transition, facilitating seamless communication and collaboration among global suppliers, manufacturers, and distributors (Kinkel & Maloca, 2009).

Additionally, trade liberalization policies and regional trade agreements have been key drivers of this transformation. In recent decades, reductions in trade barriers through agreements like the North American Free Trade Agreement (NAFTA), the European Union's (EU) single market, and the Regional Comprehensive Economic Partnership (RCEP) have enabled the cross-border movement of goods, services, and capital, making it more feasible for companies to diversify production across various regions to take advantage of competitive benefits (Kowalski et al., 2015). Moreover, the rise of outsourcing and offshoring strategies among multinational enterprises (MNEs) has significantly fueled the emergence of GVCs. Instead of maintaining in-house production for all product components, firms have increasingly relied on specialized suppliers for different production stages. This trend has been driven by cost considerations, particularly in labor-intensive sectors such as textiles, electronics, and automotive manufacturing. Nations with lower labor costs, like China, Vietnam, and Bangladesh, have emerged as vital players in global supply chains due to their capacity to provide high-volume, cost-effective production capabilities (Pietrobelli & Rabellotti, 2011). Of course, the influence of President Trump's economic policies on GVCs is yet to be determined.

Furthermore, the principles of lean manufacturing and just-in-time (JIT) production have reinforced the fragmentation of supply chains. Originally developed by Japanese firms, such as Toyota, JIT focuses on minimizing inventory levels and maximizing efficiency by ensuring that components arrive exactly when needed. While this strategy has significantly enhanced cost efficiency and reduced waste, it has also rendered supply chains more susceptible to disruptions caused by natural disasters, geopolitical conflicts, and pandemics (Christopher, 2016). The transition from traditional supply chains to GVCs has also introduced new challenges, including increased complexity, greater exposure to risks, and ethical issues regarding labor standards and environmental sustainability. The reliance on numerous international suppliers means that disruptions occurring in one region—such as factory shutdowns due to geopolitical tensions or trade disputes—can have cascading effects across entire industries. Consequently, companies are increasingly investing in more resilient supply chain models, adopting multi-sourcing strategies, embracing digital transformation, and exploring nearshoring options to mitigate these risks (Gereffi & Lee, 2016).

Role in Global Economic Integration

GVCs have played a crucial role in enhancing global economic integration by fostering interdependence among nations. Currently, around 70% of international trade is linked to GVCs, where services, raw materials, components, and parts cross borders multiple times before reaching consumers. This interconnectedness has opened doors to new markets, facilitated technology transfers, and spurred economic growth, especially in developing countries that engage in particular segments of the value chain (OECD, n.d.). One of the primary ways GVCs contribute to economic integration is through improving the efficiency of international trade. By enabling countries to focus on specific production tasks rather than trying to produce entire products domestically, GVCs have significantly lowered production costs and boosted competitiveness. This, in turn, has led to increased cross-border trade and foreign direct investment (FDI), reinforcing economic connections between countries.

For example, economies in East Asia have emerged as significant centers for electronics and semiconductor production, with nations like South Korea and Taiwan specializing in high-value technological components. Concurrently, European countries, such as Germany, have utilized their advanced engineering skills to dominate the automotive industry within GVCs. These regional clusters allow companies to access global markets while promoting economic interdependence among nations (Baldwin, 2016). Furthermore, participation in GVCs has enabled developing nations to industrialize by integrating into established global production networks rather than starting entire industries from scratch. This involvement can lead to job creation, skill enhancement, and improvements in infrastructure. However, the benefits of engaging in GVCs depend on the nature of the activities performed and the value retained domestically. Participating in higher value-added processes, such as design and marketing, tends to yield more significant economic benefits compared to lower value-added activities like basic assembly (Kowalski et al., 2015).

Additionally, GVCs have facilitated the transfer of technology and innovation across borders. Companies in developing nations gain access to advanced technologies and management practices through their involvement in GVCs, which can boost productivity and competitiveness. This transfer of knowledge occurs through interactions between local firms and multinational corporations within the value chain. However, this process is not always straightforward, as domestic firms must possess the necessary capacity to absorb and effectively apply new knowledge (Pietrobelli & Rabellotti, 2011). While GVCs have undeniably promoted economic integration, they have also revealed vulnerabilities concerning supply chain disruptions, labor rights issues, and environmental challenges. The COVID-19 pandemic, for instance, exposed the fragility of global production networks, prompting many companies to rethink their dependence on offshore suppliers. As a result, some firms have transitioned toward regional supply chains, reshoring, and digitalization strategies to create more resilient and adaptable value chains for the future (Gereffi, 2020).

GVCs as a Cornerstone of Global Economic Architecture

GVCs are now a fundamental aspect of the contemporary global economy, shaping the framework and operation of international trade and production systems. Their importance as a foundational element of global economic architecture is increasingly clear in how goods and services are produced, assembled, and delivered across borders. By enabling the fragmentation of production across various countries, GVCs allow firms and nations to specialize in different segments of the value creation process, thus improving overall efficiency and competitiveness. This distributed production model is particularly evident in complex sectors, such as electronics, automotive, and agribusiness, where numerous countries contribute distinct components or services to a final product.

The scale and reach of GVCs are substantial. Recent estimates indicate that over 50% of global trade in goods operates through GVCs, with some sources suggesting that as much as 70% of global trade involves intermediate goods and services exchanged within supply chains before final consumption (World Bank, 2020). This trading pattern illustrates that national economies are no longer isolated but are deeply integrated into cross-border production networks. For example, the World Trade Organization (WTO) has noted that a single completed car may involve the movement of parts across borders more than 30 times before it is finished, highlighting the depth of global integration in high-value manufacturing sectors (WTO, 2019).

The electronics sector serves as a prime illustration of the complexity and extent of GVCs. The production process for a smartphone usually entails design and research and development in the U.S. or Europe, semiconductor fabrication in Taiwan or South Korea, assembly in China, and global distribution networks that span multiple continents. Each phase contributes varying types and levels of value, typically captured by firms with technological or operational advantages. Similarly, the automotive industry relies heavily on a network of suppliers spread across various regions. European car manufacturers procure engine components from Germany, electrical systems from Eastern Europe, and upholstery from North Africa, creating a dense network of interdependencies that support employment and economic growth across borders (Sturgeon et al., 2008).

Agribusiness, despite being more geographically anchored due to agricultural limitations, is also becoming increasingly globalized. Multinational food companies often manage supply chains that link smallholder farmers in regions like Latin America or Southeast Asia to processing facilities and distribution centers in North America or Europe. These connections not only enable the global availability of a wide range of food products but also integrate rural economies into global trade systems. However, this integration presents challenges, exposing local farmers to the volatility of international markets and fluctuating regulatory environments (Lee et al., 2012).

The worldwide expansion of GVCs has intensified economic interdependence among nations. This interdependence fosters cooperation and the exchange of knowledge but also generates shared vulnerabilities. Disruptions in any part of the chain—whether due to natural disasters, pandemics, or geopolitical tensions—can have widespread repercussions across entire industries globally. The COVID-19 pandemic, for instance, illustrated the fragility of GVCs when lockdowns and transportation restrictions in manufacturing hubs led to significant delays and shortages. This exposure has sparked renewed interest in strategies for supply chain resilience, reshoring, and diversification to minimize overreliance on specific nodes within the global production system (Miroudot, 2020).

In conclusion, GVCs are not merely logistical frameworks but integral components of the global economy that shape trade dynamics, influence industrial strategies, and determine the allocation of economic value. Their widespread impact underscores the necessity for coordinated governance and robust institutional structures to ensure inclusive and sustainable engagement in global trade.

Understanding Geopolitical Turmoil and Its Impacts on GVCs

Geopolitical turmoil refers to instability or conflict arising from political decisions, military actions, diplomatic tensions, or strategic rivalries among states, which can significantly disrupt international relations and economic activities. In the context of GVCs, such geopolitical risks emerge through various avenues, including trade disputes, territorial conflicts, sanctions, and shifts in foreign policy, all of which collectively affect the flow of goods, services, capital, and information across borders. These risks are diverse and dynamic, often evolving unpredictably, and can be categorized into types, such as interstate conflict, economic nationalism, regulatory unpredictability, and extraterritorial enforcement of domestic policies. Each of these categories can cause delays, uncertainty, or disruptions within international production networks, making GVCs increasingly susceptible to external shocks (Manuj & Mentzer, 2008).

In recent years, several geopolitical incidents have highlighted the vulnerability of GVCs to such risks. A prominent example is the U.S.–China trade war, which began in 2018 and illustrates how protectionist measures and political tensions between major economies can impact global supply chains. The introduction of tariffs on hundreds of billions of dollars' worth of goods led companies to reassess sourcing strategies, relocate production facilities, and reconfigure logistics networks. Consequently, some businesses moved operations to other Southeast Asian nations, while others opted to reshore production back to domestic markets to avoid tariff implications. This trade dispute created volatility not only for U.S. and Chinese firms but also for MNEs dependent on components or inputs from either country. Additionally, uncertainty regarding the duration of tariffs and trade agreements further complicated planning and investment decisions (Bown, 2020).

Another critical example is the conflict between Russia and Ukraine, which escalated into a full-scale war in 2022. This war and the ensuing sanctions against Russia disrupted energy supplies, agricultural exports, and transport routes across Europe and Asia. Russia, a significant exporter of natural gas, oil, and essential raw materials like palladium and nickel—key inputs for industries, such as automotive, aviation, and electronics—experienced profound economic shifts. Meanwhile, Ukraine is a leading exporter of grain and sunflower oil. The conflict not only curtailed regional exports but also led to increased commodity prices and global supply shortages. Companies with ties to Eastern Europe had to swiftly diversify sourcing strategies, reroute logistics, and adapt to new compliance requirements amid evolving sanctions. The uncertainty and intricacy introduced by this crisis underscore the growing interconnection between geopolitics and supply chain management (Manuj & Mentzer, 2008).

The ways in which geopolitical turmoil disrupts GVCs are multifaceted. Sanctions are among the most frequently employed tools of economic statecraft, aimed at limiting access to specific markets, technologies, or financial systems. These sanctions can target specific firms, sectors, or entire economies. For example, U.S. sanctions imposed on Huawei resulted in a significant reconfiguration of the telecommunications supply chain, compelling suppliers to sever ties with the company or face secondary sanctions. Similarly, trade restrictions and export controls on semiconductors and advanced technology to China have reshaped the global technology landscape, prompting Chinese firms to localize production and invest in domestic alternatives. Tariffs, as seen during the U.S.-China trade conflict, serve both as a revenue-generating tool and as a strategic barrier, increasing the cost of imported goods and thereby altering sourcing patterns. Other mechanisms include investment restrictions grounded in national security considerations, such as limitations on foreign acquisitions in strategic sectors like critical minerals, data infrastructure, or defense technologies (Bown, 2020).

Geopolitical risks introduce long-term uncertainty into GVC operations, influencing decisions at the firm level regarding location, investment, and supplier relationships. The increasing frequency of such disruptions indicates that businesses can no longer afford to regard geopolitics as a peripheral issue. Instead, geopolitical awareness must become a fundamental capability of supply chain strategy, integrating political risk assessments into operational resilience planning. As companies navigate a more fragmented and politically charged global environment, adaptability, diversification, and scenario planning will be vital for maintaining competitiveness and continuity (Manuj & Mentzer, 2008).

Three Transformative Megatrends Influencing GVCs

Emerging Technologies Reshaping GVCs

The GVC landscape is experiencing swift changes influenced by three interrelated megatrends: the advent of emerging technologies, the emphasis on environmental sustainability, and the restructuring of globalization. These dynamics are not only altering the framework of international production networks but are also transforming the competitive landscape, governance structures, and overall resilience. As geopolitical risks and global crises reveal the vulnerabilities inherent in highly globalized production systems, these megatrends present both challenges and opportunities for businesses and policymakers aiming to secure the future of GVCs.

Emerging technologies, including AI, blockchain, the IoT, and 3D printing, are fundamentally changing the design, management, and optimization of GVCs. AI facilitates predictive analytics for demand forecasting, automates procurement decisions, and allows for real-time logistical adjustments, thereby enhancing supply chain visibility and enabling more responsive actions during disruptions. Likewise, blockchain offers secure, decentralized data systems that enhance transparency, improve traceability, and mitigate fraud, particularly in industries such as food, pharmaceuticals, and high-value consumer goods. IoT technologies enable real-time monitoring of goods, machinery functionality, and environmental conditions, promoting operational efficiency and compliance with regulations. Additionally, 3D printing fosters decentralized manufacturing, decreasing reliance on long-distance shipping and large stockpiles. In fields like aerospace and medical devices, additive manufacturing has already enabled the swift production of intricate components with minimal waste. These technologies are increasingly establishing the foundation for digital supply networks that supplant conventional, linear value chains with interconnected, data-driven ecosystems (Ivanov et al., 2019).

The Environmental Sustainability Imperative

The necessity for environmental sustainability has emerged as a pivotal factor in the transformation of GVCs, especially as consumers, investors, and regulators intensify their demands to combat climate change and resource depletion. The pursuit of carbon neutrality compels companies to not only curtail their direct emissions but also evaluate the environmental impact of their suppliers and logistics partners. Given that supply chains represent a substantial portion of a firm's total emissions, decarbonization initiatives now encompass auditing the entire value chain, including upstream raw material extraction and downstream distribution. This shift has resulted in the rise of sustainability standards and certifications, heightened demand for renewable energy, and efforts to enhance transportation and warehousing efficiencies.

The concept of a circular economy is also gaining prominence in GVC design. It challenges the conventional linear model of take-make-dispose by advocating for reuse, remanufacturing, recycling, and closed-loop systems. Companies are reevaluating product designs to facilitate component recovery, developing reverse logistics capabilities, and forming partnerships that promote material circularity. For example, within the fashion sector, several global brands (e.g., Uniqlo) are piloting recyclable textiles and take-back programs, while electronics companies are redesigning products for easier disassembly and repair. These strategies not only reduce environmental impacts but also open avenues for value recovery, cost savings, and brand differentiation (Montabon et al., 2016).

Reconfiguration of Globalization

The reconfiguration of globalization represents a significant and immediate change affecting GVCs, particularly in the aftermath of recent disruptions, such as the COVID-19 pandemic, trade conflicts, and geopolitical fragmentation. The expectation that globalization would continue to expand without interruption has been challenged by the rise of economic nationalism, supply chain disruptions, and an increasing awareness of overreliance on specific regions, notably East Asia. In response, businesses are progressively adopting reshoring, nearshoring, and regionalization strategies to enhance supply chain resilience and responsiveness.

Reshoring entails relocating production back to the company's home country, while nearshoring involves moving production to adjacent countries with similar time zones, lower risks, and more straightforward logistical coordination. These strategies aim to lessen vulnerability to global shocks, shorten lead times, and improve alignment with local regulations and consumer preferences. For example, manufacturers in the pharmaceutical, semiconductor, and critical mineral sectors of the U.S. and Europe are reevaluating their dependence on distant suppliers and investing in domestic or regional manufacturing capabilities. Regionalism is further bolstered by new trade agreements and regional supply chain coalitions, such as the EU's Green Deal, the African Continental Free Trade Area (AfCFTA), and the RCEP, which are reshaping the competitive landscape of GVCs (Barbieri et al., 2020).

However, reconfiguration comes with trade-offs. While reshoring and nearshoring may enhance resilience, they can also lead to increased production costs and diminished economies of scale. Companies must therefore find a balance between efficiency and flexibility, as well as between short-term cost considerations and long-term strategic benefits. Additionally, regionalization may result in fragmented standards and regulations, complicating coordination across borders. Despite these challenges, the transition toward a more regionally balanced and digitally enabled GVC structure reflects an adaptation to a world marked by systemic risks and growing sustainability demands.

Interconnectedness of the Megatrends

These three megatrends—technological advancement, environmental sustainability, and restructuring of global production—are intricately linked. Emerging technologies serve as critical enablers of sustainability objectives, providing tools necessary for measuring, reporting, and minimizing emissions, as well as supporting product lifespan extension. Similarly, regional supply chain strategies often utilize digital technologies to maintain visibility and coordination across shorter, yet still complex networks. Environmental considerations also affect reshoring decisions, especially when local production offers access to greener energy sources or stricter environmental governance. Collectively, these trends indicate a shift from cost-focused to value-centric GVCs, where resilience, sustainability, and adaptability are becoming essential strategic priorities. As firms and governments navigate this transformation, their ability to embrace innovation while integrating ethical and environmental considerations will dictate future success in the global economic landscape.

Structural Vulnerabilities and Power Asymmetries in GVCs

GVCs have transformed international trade by dispersing production processes across borders, allowing companies to optimize costs and efficiencies. However, this globalization of production has also introduced structural vulnerabilities and power imbalances that impact economic stability, labor markets, and governance standards. These challenges create an uneven playing field where leading firms, typically based in developed economies, exert control over production networks, while smaller suppliers and labor-intensive enterprises in developing countries face significant vulnerabilities to economic shocks, changing regulations, and technological disruptions. As businesses continue to adjust their sourcing and manufacturing strategies to mitigate risks, these structural disparities have become increasingly pronounced.

One major vulnerability within GVCs stems from the ongoing reconfiguration of production networks. Companies frequently shift manufacturing and sourcing operations in response to changing economic conditions, labor costs, and geopolitical factors. While such relocations can enhance operational efficiencies, they often transfer vulnerabilities to new regions rather than eliminating them. For example, production has increasingly shifted from China to alternative sites in Southeast Asia, Latin America, and Eastern Europe as companies seek to diversify their supply bases and diminish reliance on a single manufacturing hub. However, many of these emerging locations lack the institutional infrastructure, regulatory maturity, and technological capabilities necessary to support complex manufacturing, exposing firms to operational risks, such as inconsistent regulatory enforcement, political instability, and logistical challenges. Furthermore, the reliance on JIT production systems has increased the fragility of GVCs, making it difficult for them to adapt to sudden disruptions caused by geopolitical conflicts, pandemics, or environmental catastrophes (Gereffi, 2020).

Labor availability and skill mismatches represent another significant challenge within GVCs. While relocating production to low-cost countries may yield immediate financial advantages, many of these regions struggle with limited skilled labor pools and outdated vocational training systems. The growing divide between workforce capabilities and the technological demands of contemporary production systems hampers firms' ability to implement automation, AI-driven supply chain management, and data analytics effectively. In high-tech sectors, such as semiconductors and pharmaceuticals, a deficiency of skilled labor in certain areas creates bottlenecks that affect production continuity and overall competitiveness. This issue is further complicated by demographic changes, particularly in developed nations, where aging populations are diminishing the availability of skilled workers. Additionally, as automation and digitalization reshape manufacturing and logistics, workers in developing countries who depend on traditional production methods are at risk of obsolescence, exacerbating labor market imbalances between advanced and developing economies (Dallas et al., 2019).

Social and governance challenges, particularly regarding environmental, social, and governance (ESG) standards, human rights, and labor conditions, have become central to evaluating the sustainability of GVCs. Pressure on leading firms to cut costs often translates into fierce price competition among suppliers, resulting in downward pressure on wages, labor conditions, and environmental standards, especially in the lower tiers of the chain. This dynamic raises significant concerns about exploitative labor practices, insufficient enforcement of health and safety regulations, and human rights violations, particularly in sectors, such as garment manufacturing, electronics, and mining. While multinational corporations based in high-income countries may adopt ESG principles and demand compliance from their suppliers, the enforcement and monitoring of these standards remain inconsistent, particularly in regions with weak governance and regulatory oversight. Additionally, suppliers in developing countries often lack the financial means to meet stringent ESG standards, leading to circumstances where they either struggle to comply or risk exclusion from lucrative contracts. This disparity underscores the challenges of implementing uniform sustainability standards across diverse regulatory contexts (Locke, 2013).

Technological and institutional disparities further intensify power imbalances within GVCs. Leading firms from developed nations typically control design, branding, intellectual property, and market access, whereas suppliers in developing countries engage in routine manufacturing or assembly tasks with limited influence over decision-making. This results in an unequal distribution of value, where a some companies capture the majority of economic benefits, while others remain confined to low-margin, high-risk roles. Moreover, firms in technologically advanced countries benefit from superior infrastructure, regulatory environments, and access to capital and innovation ecosystems, allowing them to dictate industry standards and shape the strategic direction of GVCs. These disparities also hinder knowledge and technology transfer, as leading firms often safeguard proprietary information to maintain competitive advantages, restricting the ability of local suppliers to enhance their capabilities or ascend the value chain. The digital divide exacerbates these discrepancies, as firms and regions lacking digital infrastructure and expertise are excluded from participating in new, digitally integrated GVCs. This structural inequality reinforces the concentration of power among multinational corporations, making it challenging for smaller firms and developing economies to fully engage in high-value segments of GVCs (Dallas et al., 2019).

Addressing these structural vulnerabilities and power imbalances necessitates comprehensive strategies that encompass policy reform, capacity building, and collaborative governance. Developing nations must invest in education, vocational training, and workforce development to align labor skills with the requirements of modern production systems. This would not only bolster their competitiveness but also create pathways for economic advancement within GVCs. Concurrently, multinational corporations must assume greater responsibility in ensuring equitable labor practices, fair value distribution, and mechanisms for knowledge sharing that empower suppliers and workers throughout the supply chain. Implementing robust ESG frameworks requires not only corporate commitment but also supportive institutional infrastructures that facilitate compliance and sustainability. Furthermore, bridging the digital divide through targeted investments in digital infrastructure, technology transfer initiatives, and public-private partnerships can promote greater inclusivity in GVC participation.

By recognizing and addressing these multifaceted challenges, policymakers, businesses, and international organizations can work toward establishing more resilient, equitable, and sustainable GVCs. Ensuring that GVCs serve as engines of inclusive growth rather than perpetuating structural inequities is crucial in shaping the future of global trade and production. As GVCs continue to evolve in response to technological advancements, geopolitical shifts, and sustainability imperatives, tackling these structural weaknesses will be vital for fostering long-term supply chain resilience and economic stability.

Conclusion and Transition to Subsequent Chapters

This chapter has provided a crucial foundation for comprehending the development, intricacies, and strategic significance of GVCs amid the escalating geopolitical volatility and global transformations. We initiated our discussion by defining GVCs and illustrating how their advancement has altered the landscape of international trade, linking businesses and economies across different regions through complex production and service networks. The chapter highlighted the increasing economic relevance of GVCs in sectors such as electronics, automotive, and agribusiness, while also emphasizing the interdependence they foster between developed and developing nations.

Next, we examined the repercussions of geopolitical instability, pinpointing the ways in which trade disputes, regional conflicts, sanctions, tariffs, and national security issues are disrupting the conventional dynamics and frameworks of GVCs. These disruptions are not solely political or diplomatic; they significantly influence corporate decision-making, strategic planning, and operational effectiveness across various industries. In this context, we discussed three transformative megatrends—emerging technologies, sustainability imperatives, and the evolution of globalization—that are fundamentally altering the organization, governance, and stakeholder experiences within GVCs. These megatrends are interconnected and reflect broader changes in the global political economy and institutional expectations.

The chapter also discussed the inherent structural vulnerabilities within GVCs, such as labor shortages and skill mismatches, the uneven distribution of power and value among supply chains, and the governance challenges related to enforcing ESG principles and labor rights. Technological and institutional disparities further complicate these issues, resulting in unequal access to innovation and participation in high-value segments of the supply chain.

Collectively, these insights lay the groundwork for the in-depth analyses that will follow in the subsequent chapters.

- Chapter 2 directly builds on this foundation by exploring the shifting trade and investment dynamics in GVCs between developed and developing economies, offering a critical perspective on evolving trade policies and how emerging players are navigating and reshaping the global trade landscape.
- Chapter 3 broadens the discussion by investigating the historical and current impacts of geopolitical turmoil on globalization, tracing the rise of protectionist sentiments and the realignment of global economic alliances.
- Chapter 4 emphasizes the human aspect, analyzing how GVCs affect labor markets, employment, wages, and working conditions in both high- and low-income settings, particularly in light of automation and digitalization.
- Chapters 5 and 6 delve into how technological innovations are transforming production networks and facilitating new business models, while also improving adaptability in the face of disruptions.

- Chapter 7 highlights the essential role of governments and public policy in influencing GVC trajectories, focusing on the interplay between industrial strategies, trade agreements, and regulatory frameworks.
- Chapter 8 presents tools for risk assessment and management, while Chapter 9 offers practical strategies for enhancing supply chain resilience through digital solutions, redundancy, and stakeholder collaboration.
- Chapter 10 shifts the focus to ESG and sustainability, emphasizing the rising expectations surrounding ethical, environmental, and socially responsible practices in value chains.
- Chapter 11 assesses the impact of regional blocs and economic alliances on GVC integration, and Chapter 12 concludes the book by outlining a strategic roadmap for navigating the future of GVCs in a landscape characterized by complexity, uncertainty, and opportunity.

By introducing these key themes, this chapter has not only established the analytical framework for the remainder of the book but also highlighted the necessity of viewing GVCs—previously regarded solely as instruments for cost optimization—through a broader perspective that encompasses resilience, equity, sustainability, and geopolitical awareness. The forthcoming exploration will delve deeper into each of these themes, supported by empirical data, theoretical frameworks, and contemporary case studies that provide valuable insights for academics, business leaders, and policymakers aiming to reimagine GVCs in a turbulent environment.

References

Ali, I., Gligor, D., Balta, M., Bozkurt, S., & Papadopoulos, T. (2024). From disruption to innovation: The importance of the supply chain leadership style for driving logistics innovation in the face of geopolitical disruptions. *Transportation Research Part E: Logistics and Transportation Review*, *187*, 103583.

Antràs, P. (2020). Conceptual aspects of global value chains. *The World Bank Economic Review*, *34*(3), 551–574. https://doi.org/10.1093/wber/lhaa006

Baldwin, R. (2016). *The great convergence: Information technology and the new globalization*. Harvard University Press.

Barbieri, P., Elia, S., Fratocchi, L., & Golini, R. (2020). What can we learn about reshoring after Covid-19? *Operations Management Research*, *13*(3–4), 131–136. https://doi.org/10.1007/s12063-020-00160-1

Bown, C. P. (2020). The US–China trade war and phase one agreement. *Journal of Policy Modeling*, *42*(4), 805–819. https://doi.org/10.1016/j.jpolmod.2020.06.002

Christopher, M. (2016). *Logistics & supply chain management* (5th ed.). Pearson.

Dallas, M. P., Ponte, S., & Sturgeon, T. J. (2019). Power in global value chains. *Review of International Political Economy*, *26*(4), 666–694. https://doi.org/10.1080/09692290.2019.1608284

Gereffi, G. (2020). What does the COVID-19 pandemic teach us about global value chains? The case of medical supplies. *Journal of International Business Policy*, *3*(3), 287–301. https://doi.org/10.1057/s42214-020-00062-w

Gereffi, G., & Lee, J. (2016). Economic and social upgrading in global value chains and industrial clusters: Why governance matters. *Journal of Business Ethics*, *133*(1), 25–38. https://doi.org/10.1007/s10551-014-2373-7

Ivanov, D., Dolgui, A., & Sokolov, B. (2019). The impact of digital technology and industry 4.0 on the ripple effect and supply chain risk analytics. *International Journal of Production Research*, *57*(3), 829–846. https://doi.org/10.1080/00207543.2018.1488086

Kinkel, S., & Maloca, S. (2009). Drivers and antecedents of manufacturing offshoring and backshoring—a German perspective. *Journal of Purchasing and Supply Management*, *15*(3), 154–165. https://doi.org/10.1016/j.pursup.2009.05.007

Kowalski, P., Gonzalez, J. L., Ragoussis, A., & Ugarte, C. (2015). *Participation of developing countries in global value chains: Implications for trade and trade-related policies* (OECD Trade Policy Papers No. 179). OECD Publishing. https://doi.org/10.1787/5js33lfw0xxn-en

Kumar, M., & Srai, J. S. (2019). Sustainable supply chains: Challenges and opportunities. *Production Planning & Control*, *30*(5–6), 373–376. https://doi.org/10.1080/09537287.2019.1582100

Lee, J., Gereffi, G., & Beauvais, J. (2012). Global value chains and agrifood standards: Challenges and possibilities for smallholders in developing countries. *Proceedings of the National Academy of Sciences*, *109*(31), 12326–12331. https://doi.org/10.1073/pnas.0913714108

Locke, R. M. (2013). *The promise and limits of private power: Promoting labor standards in a global economy*. Cambridge University Press.

Magableh, G. M., Mahfouz, A., & Al-Jarrah, I. M. (2023). Geopolitical risks and supply chain resilience: A systematic literature review. *International Journal of Production Research*, *61*(1), 1–18. https://doi.org/10.1080/00207543.2022.2099704

Manuj, I., & Mentzer, J. T. (2008). Global supply chain risk management. *Journal of Business Logistics*, *29*(1), 133–155. https://doi.org/10.1002/j.2158-1592.2008.tb00072.x

McKinsey Global Institute. (2024). *Geopolitics and the geometry of global trade*. McKinsey & Company.

Miroudot, S. (2020). Resilience versus robustness in global value chains: Some policy implications. *VoxEU.org—CEPR Policy Portal*. https://cepr.org/voxeu/columns/resilience-versus-robustness-global-value-chains

Montabon, F., Pagell, M., & Wu, Z. (2016). Making sustainability sustainable. *Journal of Supply Chain Management*, *52*(2), 11–27. https://doi.org/10.1111/jscm.12077

OECD. (n.d.). *Global value and supply chains*. https://www.oecd.org/en/topics/policy-issues/global-value-and-supply-chains.html

Pietrobelli, C., & Rabellotti, R. (2011). Global value chains meet innovation systems: Are there learning opportunities for developing countries? *World Development*, *39*(7), 1261–1269. https://doi.org/10.1016/j.worlddev.2010.05.013

Sturgeon, T. J., Van Biesebroeck, J., & Gereffi, G. (2008). Value chains, networks and clusters: Reframing the global automotive industry. *Journal of Economic Geography*, *8*(3), 297–321. https://doi.org/10.1093/jeg/lbn007

Ticha, V. (2025). As Trump's tariffs take effect, UNSW business school's Dr Scott French examines the impact on Australia and why policy responses should not include protective tariffs of our own. *UNSW, Sydney Newsroom*. https://www.unsw.edu.au/newsroom/news/2025/03/how-us-tariffs-impact-australia-and-what-policymakers-can-do

Wamba, S. F., Gunasekaran, A., Akter, S., Ren, S. J. F., Dubey, R., & Childe, S. J. (2020). Big data analytics and firm performance: Effects of dynamic capabilities. *Journal of Business Research*, *70*, 356–365. https://doi.org/10.1016/j.jbusres.2016.08.009

World Bank. (2020). World development report 2020: Trading for development in the age of global value chains. *World Bank*. https://doi.org/10.1596/978-1-4648-1457-0

WTO. (2019). *Global value chains development report: Technological innovation, supply chain trade, and workers in a globalized world*. World Trade Organization.

2

THE CHANGING DYNAMICS OF TRADE IN GLOBAL VALUE CHAINS BETWEEN DEVELOPED AND DEVELOPING ECONOMIES

Agus Wicaksana and William Ho

Global Value Chains and Trade Policies

The concept of the global value chain (GVC) has emerged since the early '90s, along with the rise of globalisation. A GVC is defined as a network of activities that produce goods and services sequentially and simultaneously in different locations worldwide (Cohen & Kouvelis, 2021). The goal of GVC is to optimise the value in each stage of the production process by leveraging the competitive advantage of each country or region to provide necessary resources and execute the tasks. For example, Figure 2.1 shows a simplified GVC of a smartphone that includes mining rare minerals, manufacturing different components, and final assembly before distribution to the global market through offline and online channels. Those activities happen in different countries or regions. The GVC has enabled the integration of diverse expertise and economies in a network of value-added activities. As a result, companies and customers benefit from the enhancement of overall efficiency and innovation, which is reflected in lower costs and high-quality products.

In addition, Figure 2.1 implies that the GVC acts like a network influenced by many countries or regions. They are unique in their objective to participate in the network, which is reflected in their trade policies. Trade policies are defined as a set of rules and regulations imposed by the government of a country to manage its trade internationally (Gereffi et al., 2021). The most common trade policies are in the form of trade agreements and trade tariffs. A trade agreement is an agreement between two or more countries on managing trade among them (Gereffi et al., 2021). Trade tariffs are regulations in the form of a tax applied to products or services imported to a country (Shu & Steinwender, 2019). These policies influence the trade flows in terms

DOI: 10.4324/9781003468899-2

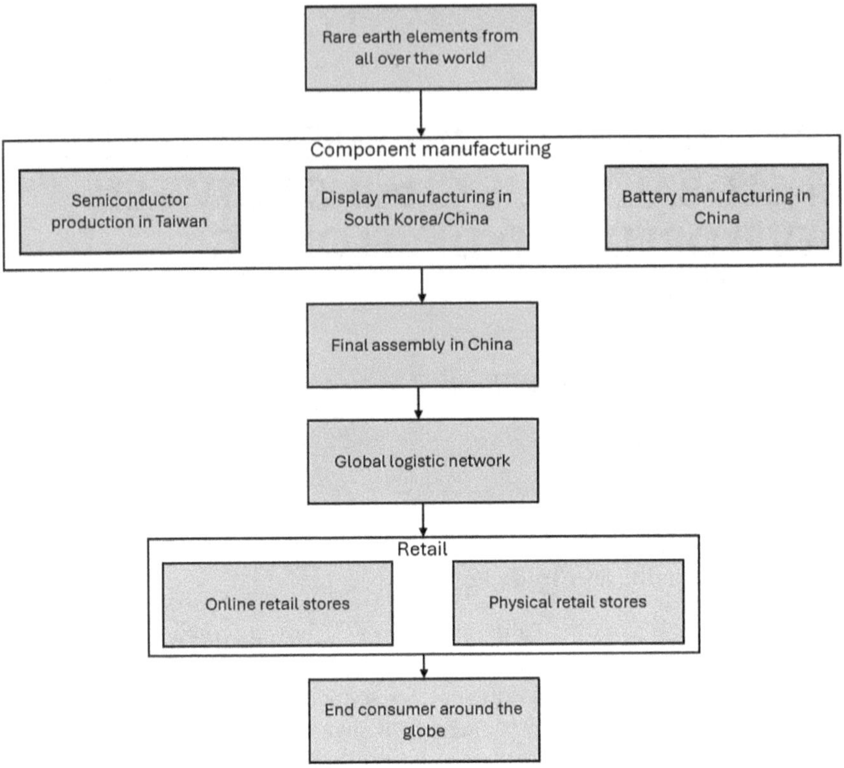

FIGURE 2.1 Illustration of smartphone GVC

of volume and direction between countries and regions, thus influencing economic collaborations worldwide (Amiti et al., 2019). In addition, trade policies also enable a country to protect its domestic industries, economic stability, and geopolitical dominance (Amiti et al., 2019). This point implies that trade policies are interrelated with GVCs in that they can either facilitate or obstruct the flow of products and services. For example, reducing tariffs and non-tariff barriers makes it cheaper and easier to move goods and services between countries and enhances the efficiency of GVC, whereas protectionist measures, such as increased tariffs and import restrictions, can raise costs and reduce the availability of products and services within GVC (Shu & Steinwender, 2019). Further, other policies indirectly influence the GVC as well. These policies include regulations that address intellectual property rights, environmental standards, and labour practices. Together, trade policies influence how and where production activities are carried out, which shapes the GVC.

The discussion above implies that trade policies influence how goods, services, and investments flow across the GVC. For example, Figure 2.2 shows

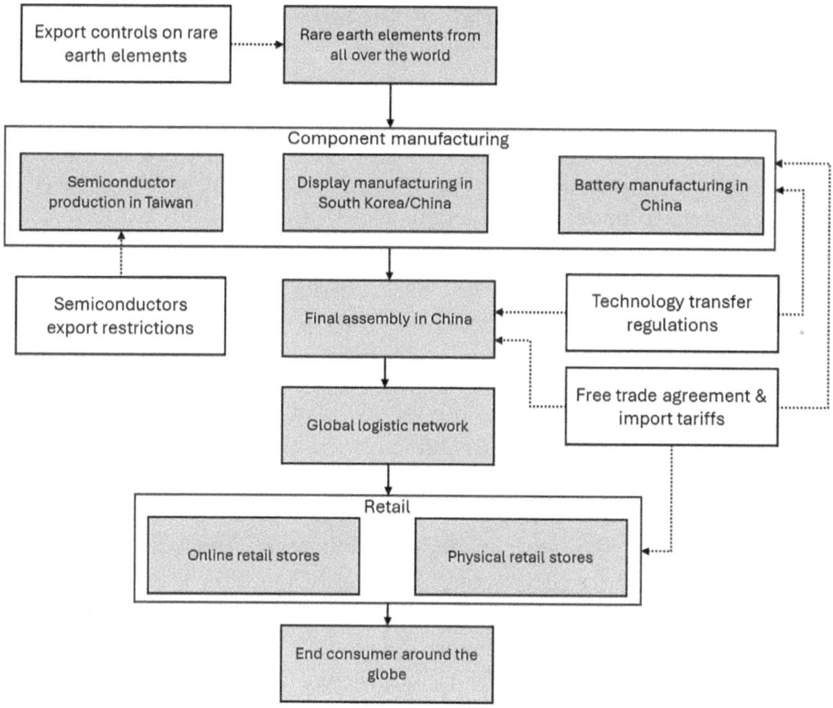

FIGURE 2.2 Illustration of trade policies surrounding smartphone's GVC

that at least four major trade policies influence the smartphone's GVC effectiveness. First, countries may impose export controls on rare minerals, potentially affecting the raw materials' extraction stage and influencing the availability and price of raw materials for smartphone components. Second, countries may impose semiconductor export restrictions that potentially impact the semiconductor supply in the smartphone's GVC. For example, as a semiconductor powerhouse, Taiwan has deployed a semiconductor export restriction to protect national interests and maintain technological advantages over China (Pao, 2024).

Third, countries may also impose technology transfer regulations dictating how and where specific technologies are shared or implemented in manufacturing and assembly. This policy may impact the component manufacturing and final assembly stages of the smartphone's GVC. Finally, the most influential and popular trade policies are free trade agreements and import tariffs among countries, which influence multiple stages of the smartphone's GVC. The free trade agreements may ease the movement of components and finished products across borders, facilitating smoother trade between countries in the smartphone's GVC. However, the imposition of import tariffs may increase costs in the smartphone's GVC, which can affect sourcing, distribution, and pricing decisions throughout the value chain.

In the end, the complexities and interrelationships of trade policies surrounding the GVC can affect the costs and availability of materials and technologies to produce goods. Eventually, it affects the selling price and availability in different markets. Due to its far-reaching implications, it is critical for business leaders to understand the dynamics of trade policies worldwide and how organisations can navigate without jeopardising the benefits of the GVC.

Major Powers in the GVCs

The criticalities of trade policies on GVC and the uniqueness of trade policies in each country or region lead to the following question: Which country's or region's trade policies significantly influence the GVC? This question can be answered by understanding countries with high influence and dominance in the GVC. Since its emergence in the 1990s, the GVC has been dominated by developed economies, such as the United States of America (USA), Japan, and European countries (Alves et al., 2022). Overall, they lead the GVC due to their advanced technological capabilities, substantial capital resources, and well-established infrastructure (Figure 2.3).

Technological capabilities refer to knowledge and know-how to develop and utilise technology to gain competitive advantages. Anecdotal evidence has shown that developed countries possess high technological capabilities, reflected in their research and development (R&D) intensity and innovation

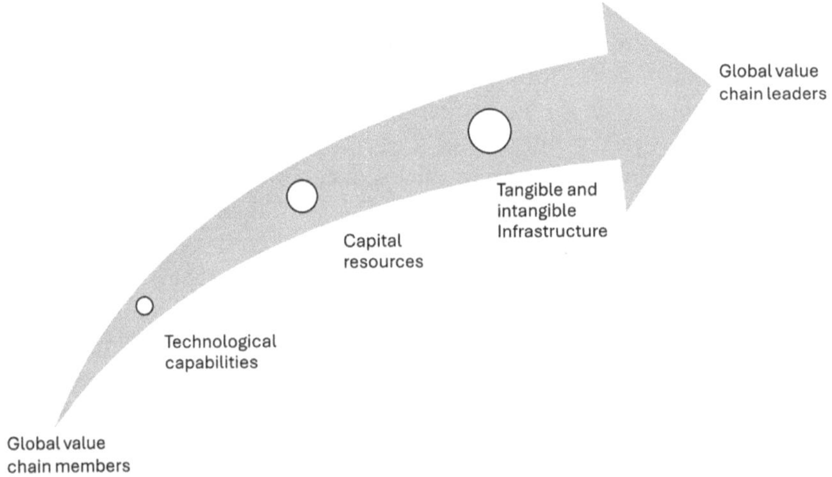

FIGURE 2.3 Key factors influence the dominance of developed countries as GVC leaders

in developing and applying new technology. For example, the USA is a leader in developing quantum computing technologies (Kim & Monroe, 2024), while Germany excels in precision engineering and automotive manufacturing (Bluth, 2018). These advanced technological capabilities have enabled developed countries to lead high value-added activities and put them at the forefront of the GVC.

In addition, developed countries also possess substantial capital resources that facilitate large-scale investments in state-of-the-art equipment and facilities (Meier et al., 2012). This financial strength has also enabled them to fund R&D processes to continuously increase the efficiency and innovation of their manufacturing capabilities. For instance, Japan has invested heavily in their supply chains and production facilities since the early globalisation stage to achieve efficiency and innovation that reinforce its leadership in the GVC for the automotive industry (Kawahara, 2012).

Finally, developed countries are typically equipped with well-established tangible and intangible infrastructures supporting their dominance in the GVC. Developed countries' notable tangible infrastructure is robust transportation networks and communication systems, which facilitate efficient logistics operations (Luo & Xu, 2018). Moreover, intangible infrastructure, such as regulatory framework and government policies, has also created a conducive setting for the business environment (Coen et al., 2010). Together, both the tangible and intangible infrastructures in developed countries have enabled them to reduce transaction costs and facilitate better integration across various stages of the production process to retain significant value in the GVC activities.

Overall, the above discussion implies that advanced technological capabilities, substantial capital resources, and well-established infrastructure have enabled developed countries to lead and define standards for quality and efficiency in the GVC. They are the USA, Japan, the European Union (EU), the United Kingdom (UK), Canada, and South Korea. Based on a combination of indicators, including gross domestic product (GDP), trade volume, and global economic influence, they can be grouped into three groups in the GVC pyramid (Figure 2.4). First, the superpower group consists of countries that dominate global trade in volume, such as the USA. The EU and Japan are two major power countries/regions that rank below superpowers in terms of influence on GVC due to their sizable economies and significant regional trade volumes. The third group is labelled as significant power countries, such as the UK, Canada, and South Korea, as they play essential roles in niche areas of the GVC. For example, South Korea leads the GVC for the consumer electronic sector, whereas Canada specialises in the natural resources sector.

As a result of their domination in the GVC, those developed countries and their trade policies have significant implications. For instance, the USA has significantly influenced the development of GVC in the North and South American countries through agreements like the North American Free Trade

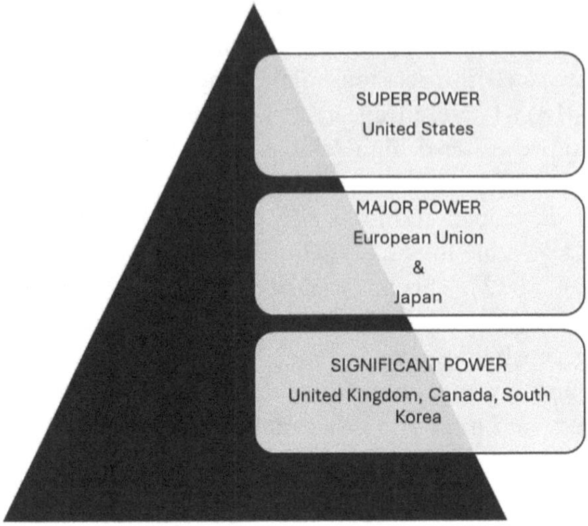

FIGURE 2.4 The GVC pyramid before the emergence of developing countries

Agreement (NAFTA), which is substituted by the USA-Mexico-Canada Agreement (USMCA). Similarly, as a collective economic bloc, countries in the EU have been shaping GVCs through stringent regulatory standards that emphasise sustainability. In conclusion, the power dynamic in GVC has been dominated by developed countries.

The Shift of the GVCs from Developed to Developing Countries

A recent development in the GVC shows the emergence of developing countries that have replaced the domination of developed countries. This shift is due to five major factors that allow developing countries to generate attractive contributions for the GVC. Those factors are the rise of manufacturing capabilities, the democratisation of technology, regional integration, the emergence of consumer markets, and government incentives in developing countries (Figure 2.5).

Manufacturing capability and efficiency have been the primary drivers for companies moving their production facilities to developing countries. This is evident in regions like Asia and Latin America, where labour costs are almost half of the cost in developed countries (Coates et al., 2022). Many electronics firms have relocated their production to these countries to take advantage of competitive costs and quality. In the process, technology and knowledge are shared, which helps developing countries enhance their manufacturing capabilities. This pattern is common in various industries, where GVC has benefited both developing countries and the companies that capitalise on it. For

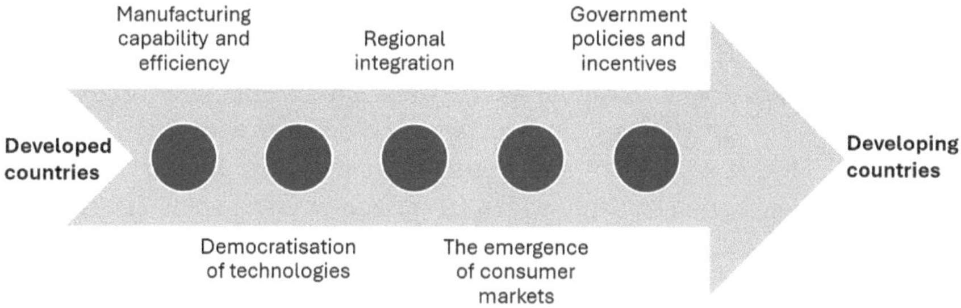

FIGURE 2.5 Key factors influencing the shift of GVC power from developed to developing countries

example, Samsung has invested over $17 billion in Vietnam since 2008 (Reuters, 2024a). The company now produces about half of its smartphones in Vietnam in addition to China. Samsung also develops a network of local suppliers, which boosts Vietnam's overall electronics manufacturing capabilities. This development, in turn, benefits Samsung's efficiency (Reuters, 2024a).

Second, technology democratisation has also significantly influenced the emergence of developing countries in GVC. Technology democratisation refers to reducing barriers to accessing technology. For example, internet penetration in Asia has been remarkable, where the number of users has tripled in the last decade (Seong et al., 2023). This process has benefitted individuals and businesses in developing countries as they become increasingly connected to the global market, resources, and knowledge. This condition, in turn, improves their innovation. The decreasing cost of technology due to democratisation has also made it easier for businesses in developing countries to adopt advanced tools that enhance productivity and efficiency. This point is evident in the rapid automation and digitalisation in manufacturing sectors in developing countries. Investments in smart factories and advanced production systems are increasingly common in countries like India, Vietnam, and Mexico. For instance, Tata Motors of India has been transforming its manufacturing processes by utilising artificial intelligence and robotics to enhance production efficiency and quality control across its plants (Haritas, 2022). These initiatives result in improved operational efficiency. Therefore, technology democratisation has supported the emergence of developing countries in the GVC, as these countries have become highly productive and innovative in their manufacturing.

From a governance perspective, trade agreements and regional integration have also played a crucial role in the emergence of developing countries in the global value chains. For example, the ASEAN Free Trade Area (AFTA), the Mercado Común del Sur (MERCOSUR/Southern Common Market), and the African Continental Free Trade Area (AfCFTA) agreements have facilitated cross-border trade in the Southeast Asia, South America, and Africa regions, respectively (AfCFTA, 2021; Meng-Kng, 2012; Mercosur, 2014). Global companies have also capitalised on these agreements. For instance, the automotive sector, particularly in Thailand, has seen growth due to AFTA. Toyota and Honda are two of many companies that have increased production and exports from Thailand to take advantage of lower trade tariffs in the region (Warr & Kohpaiboon, 2017).

From a downstream supply chain perspective, the shift in consumer markets and demand from developed to developing countries has also contributed to their emergence in the GVC. Specifically, the growth of the middle class in developing countries means a rising demand for goods and services (Kharas, 2010), which is an opportunity that companies need to capitalise on. One way to do that is by localising their production and supply chain activities to make the products or services as close as possible to the potential market. This localisation strategy helps firms cater to local requirements and reduce logistical costs. For example, the expanding middle class in China and its manufacturing capabilities have led Tesla to establish manufacturing facilities in that country so that the product can be closer to this emerging market (Weijia, 2024). Therefore, the ability of developing countries to provide cost optimisation and market access has made them critical in the GVC network.

Finally, government incentives have also been critical in supporting the emergence of developing countries in the GVC. Governments in developing countries have been incentivising companies to move their production facilities to this region by offering tax incentives, loans, or even subsidies. For instance, India's "Make in India" initiative incentivises foreign companies to invest in the manufacturing sector through capital expenditure reimbursement of up to 25% (Department for Promotion of Industry and Internal Trade, 2019). Those incentives are attractive and have been capitalised by multinational companies to set up their production base in developing countries. For example, Toyota has benefited from tax holidays, reduced import duties on machinery, and investment promotion incentives in Thailand and Indonesia. As a result, Toyota has designated Thailand and Indonesia as production hubs for both domestic sales and export markets (Akama & Jibiki, 2023).

As a result of excellence in the above key factors, developing countries have been increasingly attractive to companies expanding their GVC. Countries like China, India, Vietnam, Thailand, and other Southeast Asian countries (i.e., Malaysia, Indonesia, and the Philippines) are establishing themselves as emerging players in the GVC. Accordingly, these countries can be positioned in the GVC pyramid as emerging players (Figure 2.6) based on their economic significance in terms of trade volume and geopolitical influence.

First, China has become a dominant force in the manufacturing sector due to its vast workforce, competitive labour costs, technology, and infrastructure. It is often referred to as the "factory of the world". Similarly, India has become

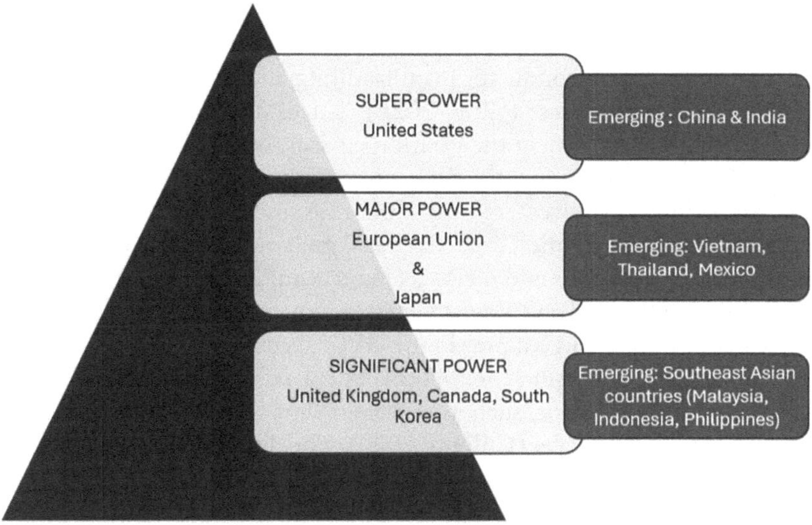

FIGURE 2.6 Emerging players in the GVC pyramid

an essential player by leveraging its large, English-speaking, and technically skilled workforce to support its role in the global manufacturing and outsourcing sectors (IBEF, 2024). These two countries have emerged as members of the superpower group in the GVC pyramid due to their increasingly large economic size and significance.

Below the superpower group, three developing countries have emerged as members of the major power group in the GVC. They are Vietnam, Thailand, and Mexico. Vietnam has emerged as a new player in the GVC due to its participation in various trade agreements, such as the Comprehensive and Progressive Agreement for Trans-Pacific Partnership (CPTPP) and the European Union–Vietnam Free Trade Agreement (EVFTA). Those agreements have opened the gate to new markets for Vietnam and also attracted investment from multinational companies (Samuel, 2024). Similarly, Thailand has diverse manufacturing capabilities, ranging from automotive to electronics sectors, making Thailand increasingly attractive as an alternative to the current GVC in those sectors. Mexico has also emerged as a significant new player in the GVC in the South American region due to its automotive manufacturing capability and access to the North American market (i.e., the USA and Canada). In fact, companies like Ford, Volkswagen, and General Motors have developed their production facilities there to capitalise on Mexico's emergence (Pelaez-Fernandez, 2023). Those three countries have emerged as the new major powers in the GVC pyramid.

Finally, below the major power group are countries that can be considered a significant power group in the GVC. Most of them are Southeast Asian countries, such as Malaysia, Indonesia, and the Philippines, which have benefitted from the economic development in the region. For instance, Malaysia is well known for its semiconductor manufacturing and is even dubbed the next semiconductor powerhouse (WEF, 2024). This is due to a combination of a skilled workforce, stability in the political environment, and sound economic policies. In the case of Indonesia, the emergence of this country in the GVC is much more driven by the emergence of the consumer market and government incentives. With a population exceeding 270 million, Indonesia presents a significant market for goods and services (Jin & Kim, 2022). In the Philippines, a large pool of educated and English-speaking professionals has been supporting the emergence of this country in the GVC, specifically in the service sector (Culvera, 2023). As a result, the Philippines has been a leader in the business process outsourcing sector, such as customer support, information and technology, and finance services (Culvera, 2023). The discussion implies that these countries have emerged as significant powers in the GVC, thanks to their role in specialised and niche areas.

The Dynamic of the GVC

Overall, we have discussed some key factors that influence the emergence of developing countries as leaders in the GVC and which countries they are. However, it is worth noting that there is a dynamic that determines GVC leadership. For example, Vietnam has recently lost significant potential investment from LG Chemical and Intel because the Vietnamese government does not provide sufficient incentives (Reuters, 2024b). This condition has limited Vietnam's advancement to being the GVC leader for petrochemical products and semiconductors. This case indicates that the landscape of GVC continues to evolve, meaning that multinational corporations must continuously adapt to maintain their competitiveness, as illustrated in the following case studies.

Hyundai's and Audi's Value Chain

Hyundai Motor Company is a South Korean automotive manufacturer. Hyundai relied solely on South Korean manufacturing capabilities before the globalisation era. With the emergence of the Indian consumer base and competitive labour cost, the company entered the Indian market in 1996 and has since become one of the largest car manufacturers in the country. It was started by the establishment of its wholly owned subsidiary, Hyundai Motor India Limited (HMIL). Two years after that, Hyundai opened its first manufacturing plant in Irungattukottai in 1998. After enjoying stellar growth in India, Hyundai opened its second plant in 2008, which has been doubling its production capacity to date. In addition, the company has established its R&D centre in Hyderabad, India. Hyundai has also developed a network of local suppliers and introduced modern manufacturing techniques and technologies, improving India's competitiveness in the automotive manufacturing sector. This case implies that Hyundai has continuously capitalised on access to a large and growing domestic market, lower production costs, and a skilled workforce offered by India. As a result, India has been deeply integrated into Hyundai's GVC and is projected to be Hyundai's global export hub to emerging markets in Asia, the Middle East, and Africa (Hyundai, 2024).

A second case of companies adapting to the dynamic of GVC is shown by Audi AG, a German luxury vehicle manufacturer and member of the Volkswagen Group. The company has capitalised on the emergence of Mexico's automotive manufacturing sector. It was started in 2012, when the company began its significant investment to build a new plant in San José Chiapa, Puebla, Mexico. The $1.3 billion plant was finally opened in 2016 and became Audi's first North American manufacturing facility. As a European car brand, the move was unpopular because the majority of other car brands still adhere to the tradition of "made in Europe" to represent engineering excellence, high quality, and luxurious products. However, Audi AG has successfully retained those values in Mexico by developing a local supplier network and introducing modern manufacturing techniques and technologies that improve Mexico's competitiveness in the automotive manufacturing sector. In that process, Audi AG has also benefited from the lower labour costs compared to Germany, the proximity to the USA, and the free trade agreements between the USMCA that provide greater access to other markets. In fact, Audi has moved a significant portion of its Audi SUV-Q5 production from Germany to Mexico, making it an export hub for markets worldwide, including Europe (Audi, 2024). This case implies that even companies that target specific markets, such as Audi AG, with its position as a luxury car brand, can also benefit from the shift of the GVC from developed to developing countries.

Insights

The above case studies illustrate the GVC strategies of two major automotive companies to maintain their competitive advantages amid the changing dynamic in the automotive GVC. Both companies have leveraged the competitive advantages of each host country to maximise the GVC benefits. Importantly, both companies have made their respective countries (i.e., India and Mexico) essential parts of their GVC. In the process, both companies have also contributed significantly to the growth of the automotive sectors in the host country. Hyundai and Audi AG have proactively been involved in workforce development, technology and knowledge transfer, and supply chain ecosystem development. This process provides a snowball effect where improvements in those countries' automotive manufacturing capabilities make them increasingly attractive and lead the automotive's GVC.

However, it is also worth noting that Hyundai's presence in India and Audi AG's presence in Mexico are actually two slightly different strategies in GVC management. Hyundai's approach in India focuses on capturing a large domestic market (i.e., India's market), whereas Audi's strategy in Mexico is primarily to leverage the country's position for easy access to North American markets (i.e., not for Mexico's domestic market) and cost-effective production of luxury cars. As a result, the impact on host countries is also slightly different. For India, the presence of Hyundai in the last 20 years has significantly contributed to creating thousands of direct and indirect jobs. In addition to manufacturing facilities, Hyundai in India has also developed a network of dealerships and service centres, which has contributed to the development of the country's base workforce in the automotive sector. Meanwhile, the presence of Audi in Mexico in the last decade has infused specialised skills into the workforce and boosted Mexico's position in the global luxury car market. These cases demonstrate how global automotive companies manage their value chains to remain competitive while significantly contributing to the host countries' economies.

Geopolitical Tensions that Threaten the Benefits of GVCs

The USA–China Trade War and Brexit

Overall, the shift of power from developed to developing countries in the GVC can be seen as an optimisation process that increases the benefit of the GVC itself. Specifically, the rearrangement in the GVC is driven by the search for expertise and efficiency. In the end, it leads to an increase in the welfare of customers through lower costs and high-quality products. However, this benefit has been threatened recently by geopolitical tension, reflected in the changing trade policies among countries. There is a shift towards protectionist trade policies that involve a significant increase in trade tariffs, increasing the cost of global trade and even leading to a trade conflict. Based on trade data worldwide, trade openness, defined as the ratio of trade and GDP, has increased since the development of GVC in the 1990s. Unfortunately, this upward trend has flattened since 2008, indicating lower enthusiasm for GVC expansion and optimisation (Cappariello et al., 2020).

The most recent example of geopolitical tension in the GVC is shown in the dynamic of trade relationships between the USA and China. The escalation in geopolitical tensions between the two largest economies since 2018 has led to the imposition of tariffs on each other's goods, export controls that restrict the flow of critical technologies, and stringent regulations on technology transfer (Fajgelbaum & Khandelwal, 2022). The USA government has portrayed these policies as precautious measures to address the threat of intellectual property theft and national security from China's domination in the GVC (Fetzer & Schwarz, 2021). However, research has shown that the policy has also introduced significant disruptions to the global supply chain and economic stability (Fajgelbaum & Khandelwal, 2022). For instance, the semiconductor industry has been particularly hard-hit by the trade tensions and restrictions imposed during the USA–China trade war. This condition has caused delays and increased costs for industries depending on semiconductors, such as consumer electronics and automotive manufacturing.

Another example of geopolitical tension is shown in the case of the British Exit (Brexit), where the UK left the EU in 2020. This case is slightly different from the USA–China trade war because Brexit was motivated by reasons other than trade. The UK voters for Brexit have portrayed the goal of this event as improving immigration and sovereignty (Kren & Lawless, 2024). Unfortunately, Brexit also has significant implications for trade flow. The separation of the UK from the EU means new trade barriers through tariffs and customs checks on goods traded between them. Prior to Brexit, the UK was an integral component in the EU's supply chains, with many industries operating on a highly integrated basis across the EU and UK. Post-Brexit, companies that previously benefitted from seamless supply chains face increased administrative burdens and logistical challenges (Kren & Lawless, 2024). This condition is particularly evident in the European automotive industry, which relies heavily on just-in-time supply chains and cross-border components. Manufacturers in the UK and the EU face increased costs and delays due to these trade barriers, which impact their ability to produce and distribute their products efficiently. In addition, Brexit has introduced complexities related to standards and compliance because cars that are marketed in the UK or the EU have to follow different regulatory frameworks in the respective regions. Customers will feel an accumulation of these issues either by delayed delivery, an increase in product price, or potentially lower quality products.

Impact of Geopolitical Tensions on GVCs Structure and Efficiency

In addition to the impact on customers, geopolitical tensions, such as the USA–China trade war, also impact the GVC structures (Figure 2.7). Stringent protectionist policies have significantly impacted companies operating in developed economies because their GVC structure, which is concentrated in China, become increasingly costly and less attractive. Accordingly, as trade disputes between major economies like the USA and China escalate, many multinational corporations reevaluate their supply chains and move production out of China to alternative locations such as Vietnam and India (Fajgelbaum et al., 2023).

Further, geopolitical tensions have also motivated companies to adopt reshoring and nearshoring strategies. By definition, reshoring refers to bringing manufacturing activities back to the home country, while nearshoring involves

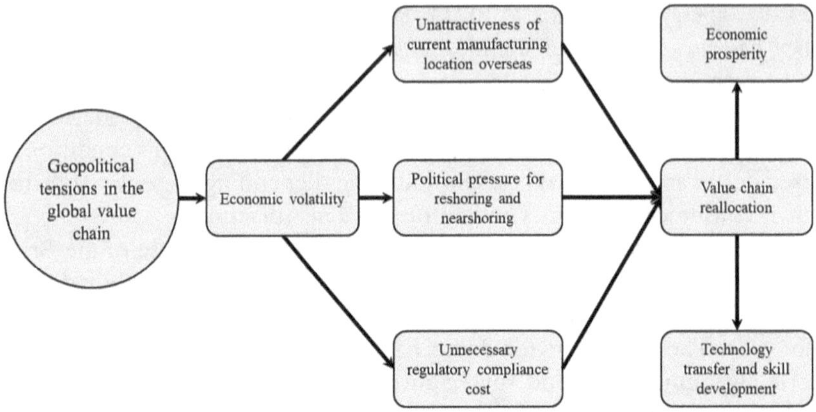

FIGURE 2.7 The relationship between geopolitical tensions and GVC reallocation

relocating production to nearby regions (Ellram et al., 2013). Both strategies can be seen as a way to maintain proximity to key markets while avoiding some of the complexities associated with geopolitical tensions in global supply chains. For example, the USA and several European countries are investing in domestic manufacturing capabilities and encouraging companies to relocate production closer to home as a response to the USA–China trade war and the Brexit event, respectively (Fajgelbaum et al., 2024; Moradlou et al., 2022). In the long run, reshoring and nearshoring strategies are expected to enhance control and reduce reliance on distant and potentially unstable supply chains.

In addition to the structure of the GVC, geopolitical tension also leads to unnecessary costs that influence efficiency. This is because geopolitical tension tends to break the regulatory framework among countries that unify the standard of products or services. For example, before Brexit, cars sold in both EU and UK markets had the same standards to be fulfilled. This is not the case after Brexit. Cars now have to pass two types of approval, Great Britain (GB) type approval and EU type approval, to be marketed in each region (Bailey & De Propris, 2017). As a result, a report from the Society of Motor Manufacturers and Traders (SMMT) shows that UK-based car manufacturers and traders have to absorb additional costs, measured in time and resources, to trade with customers in the EU and vice versa (SMMT, 2023). This case implies that geopolitical tensions can exacerbate the costs associated with maintaining adherence to diverse standards across different markets, which can impact the competitiveness of UK and EU-based manufacturers.

On the bright side, all the above consequences of geopolitical tensions (i.e., unattractiveness of current GVC, reshoring or nearshoring, and unnecessary costs) have led to a notable increase in value chain relocations to developing countries, particularly in Southeast and South Asian regions

(Fajgelbaum et al., 2024). Multinational companies in developed economies seeking to diversify their supply chains and reduce reliance on Chinese manufacturing increasingly establish their production facilities in developing countries, such as Vietnam, India, and Thailand. This influx has provided developing countries with opportunities for economic growth, infrastructure development, and job creation. For example, Vietnam's electronics sector has seen significant investment from major tech companies since 2023 amid the USA–China trade war. This investment enhances Vietnam's presence in the global supply chain and boosts its domestic economy, with at least 6.98% growth in the processing and manufacturing sector in the first quarter of 2024 (Vietnam Briefing, 2024). This trend reflects that geopolitical tension leads to global value chain relocation through a shift of capital to developing countries as companies adapt to geopolitical tension. This is evident in the export values of bystander countries, which are dominated by developing countries that are not involved in the geopolitical tension between the USA and China. These countries reduce their exports to China and increase their exports to the USA as the tariff rate increases, which indicates GVC reallocation (Fajgelbaum et al., 2024). In other words, tariff rate increases have made developing countries evolve from indirect suppliers of the USA market through China (indicated by decreased exports to China) to direct providers of products in USA markets (indicated by increased exports to the USA).

Moreover, the value chain relocation also brings opportunities for technology transfers and skill development in developing countries, leading to economic prosperity in developing countries. As multinational companies set up operations in developing countries, they also bring advanced technologies and expertise, contributing to the development of local workforce and manufacturing capabilities. For instance, a significant increase in technology export products from Vietnam indicates the massive establishment of manufacturing plants for technology-related products in the country (Reuters, 2024a). This condition has led to the development of technical skills among local workers and the transfer of cutting-edge technologies. This skill enhancement helps developing countries build more competitive industries, dominate the GVC, and improve their overall economic prosperity. In fact, this cycle has happened in other countries, such as Taiwan, where they started as low-technology manufacturers and then advanced to the GVC leader in the semiconductors industry (Huang, 2024).

Company Strategies for Managing Geopolitical Tensions

To manage the geopolitical tensions in the GVC, companies have developed various strategies to mitigate risks and maintain operational stability. The strategies can be grouped into three parts, along with the timeline of geopolitical tensions. They are value chain reintegration, diversification, and localisation.

This section will discuss several case studies from companies worldwide that illustrate those strategies.

The first example is coming from USA companies in the technology sector, such as Apple, Intel, and Tesla. As a consequence of the ongoing USA–China trade war, Apple has decided to diversify and localise its production facilities. The company has intensively expanded its manufacturing base to countries like Vietnam and India. This strategy aims to reduce reliance on China while expanding its presence to emerging middle-class consumers in developing countries. As a result, Apple has successfully maintained the risks in their GVC due to geopolitical tensions, which is reflected in its ability to maintain product availability in the market (Horwitz, 2022).

A slightly different strategy is shown by Intel Corporation, which has responded to geopolitical uncertainties under the USA–China trade war through a reshoring strategy. Intel has significantly increased its investment in domestic manufacturing. Specifically, the company is committed to building new semiconductor fabrication facilities in Arizona to bring back its domestic production capabilities in the USA. Like Apple, this strategy aims to reduce Intel's reliance on overseas manufacturing and shield the company from potential disruptions caused by geopolitical tensions. Moreover, Intel claims that the process of bringing back the manufacturing process in the USA also benefits local job creation and technological leadership (Nellis, 2021).

Another strategy is shown by Tesla, which focuses on localising its value chains. Tesla's approach to managing geopolitical risks includes the establishment of gigafactories in multiple countries outside the USA, such as China and Germany. By establishing a significant production facility in China, Tesla mitigates the impact of trade barriers and tariffs that could affect its exports from the USA to China and vice versa. Similarly, establishing the production facility in Germany has helped Tesla secure access to the growing electric vehicle market in the EU. Specifically, localising production helps Tesla better align with local regulations and market preferences. The initial objective of this strategy is to improve Tesla's supply chain efficiency and help companies integrate more closely with regional markets. At the same time, the strategy has also successfully helped Tesla adapt to geopolitical tensions (Zhang, 2024).

The second group of examples comes from companies in the European and UK automotive sectors affected by the Brexit event. These companies are BMW, Jaguar Land Rover (JLR), and Volkswagen. They have adopted proactive strategies focusing on operational planning and collaborative approaches to navigate trade barriers and regulatory uncertainties in the EU and UK post-Brexit. For example, the BMW Group has implemented a proactive production strategy by moving out the engine production process from the UK to South Africa, even before Brexit, to manage the uncertainties. This flexibility enables BMW to continue meeting demand across Europe and the UK while minimising the impact of Brexit-related challenges on its operations (Pitas,

2019a). BMW's approach underscores the importance of proactive planning to mitigate geopolitical tensions.

JLR, which is a UK-based car manufacturer, has also developed a comprehensive strategy to enhance its supply chain resilience in response to Brexit. Although JLR only exports 20% of its products to the EU, the company imports 40% of its raw materials from upstream supply chain partners located in the EU. Accordingly, the company has focused on diversifying its supply base and collaborating with suppliers to ensure components' availability and smooth flow (Pitas, 2019b). JLR's approach has highlighted the importance of adaptability and collaboration in navigating geopolitical tensions in the GVC.

The latest example is Volkswagen Group, which has employed a localisation strategy to address trade challenges posed by Brexit. To maintain its presence in the UK market post-Brexit, the company has proactively optimised the inventory of their products in the UK before Brexit. After that, the company increases its focus on local production and sourcing within the EU to reduce reliance on cross-border supply chains. For example, the Volkswagen electric vehicles lineup will be supported by a localised supply chain within European countries such as Germany, Sweden, Spain, the Czech Republic, Hungary, and Poland (Steitz & Amann, 2024). Therefore, Volkswagen's approach highlights the importance of aligning production and sourcing strategies with regional market conditions through a localisation strategy to effectively manage the impact of geopolitical tensions.

In summary, the above examples illustrate how companies across different industries and regions are strategically navigating the challenges posed by geopolitical tensions. Overall, the strategies can be grouped into three stages, along with the advancement of GVC disruption due to geopolitical tension (Figure 2.8). When a disruption due to geopolitical tension occurs for the first time, the fastest response that can be given is through reintegration of the supply chain. This means companies have to re-optimise their current supply chain by increasing strategic planning and collaboration with supply chain partners. As the geopolitical tension continues, companies may plan for diversification of their supply chain, including supply base diversification and production facilities dispersion to non-affected regions. Finally, to mitigate future

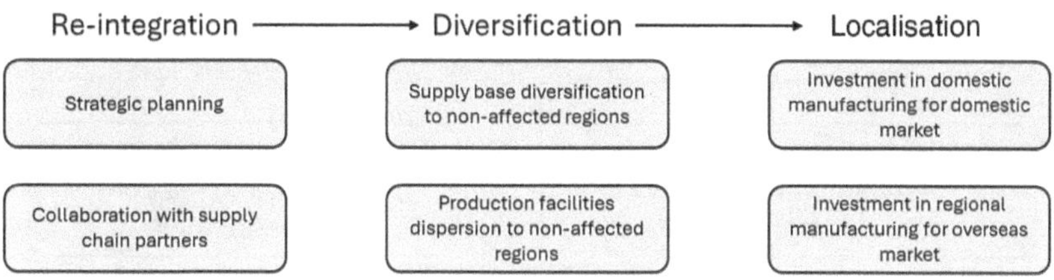

FIGURE 2.8 Strategies to mitigate geopolitical tension in GVCs

geopolitical tension in the GVC, companies may adopt localisation strategies by investing in domestic and regional manufacturing capabilities. These strategies enable companies to mitigate geopolitical risks, ensure supply chain stability, and maintain their competitive positions in rapidly changing GVCs.

Conclusion

Looking ahead, the evolving dynamics of the GVC between developed and developing countries present both positive and negative outlooks for the future (Figure 2.9). From a positive perspective, this shift leads to the diversification of GVCs. The diversification process may seem counterproductive with the efficiency. However, in the long run, this diversification will benefit the GVC overall because it reduces reliance on a single GVC member and provides protection from disruption. For instance, the ongoing shift of manufacturing activities from China to other countries like Vietnam and India helps create a second layer of global supply networks for companies worldwide. This additional layer can be used as a shield if companies experience disruption in one of the two regions, and can also boost the production capacity to serve emerging markets.

Further, the shift of power in the GVC from developed to developing countries fosters a more balanced trade and stimulates economic growth in developing countries. The shift offers substantial economic benefits for these countries, including job creation and infrastructure development. In the end, this process helps wealth distribution and drives balanced economic progress around the world. In fact, we have noticed that the income per capita in

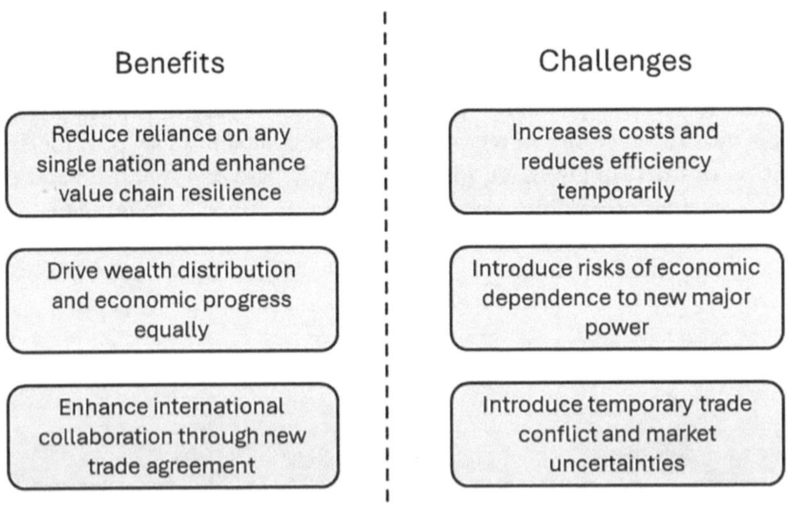

FIGURE 2.9 The outlook for the changing dynamic of GVCs

developing countries has been rising steadily. For example, Vietnam's income per capita has seen average annual growth rates of around 6%–7% over the past decade, which has dropped Vietnam's poverty rate from over 58% in the 1990s to around 5% in 2023 (World Bank, 2024).

Furthermore, the power shift from developed to developing countries in the GVC enhances international collaboration through new trade agreements. As developed countries seek to mitigate the risks associated with geopolitical tensions and see the potency of collective contribution from developing countries to the GVC, they increasingly engage in trade agreements and regional partnerships. These agreements facilitate smoother trade flows and promote cooperation between developed and developing countries. For instance, the CPTPP includes several developing countries and aims to enhance trade and economic integration in the Asia-Pacific region. Ultimately, trade agreements involving both developed and developing countries foster greater collaboration and economic growth worldwide.

However, there are also notable negative implications associated with the changing trade dynamics in global value chains between developed and developing economies. In the short term, disruptions in the GVC due to shifting dynamics between developed and developing countries can lead to increased costs and reduced efficiency. Assuming that a company's current supply chain arrangement has been optimised, the transition of supply chains from one country to another can involve logistical challenges, higher production costs, and temporary inefficiencies. This condition will be worsened if the company that makes the transition has limited familiarity with the new country or region. In fact, it can introduce new risks due to supply base complexity and information asymmetry. For example, a company that moves its supply base from China to Vietnam may need to engage with a middleman to navigate new territory or even take more time to establish the most efficient supply base. This process may temporarily affect both businesses and consumers through higher prices and delays in product availability.

Finally, the shift in the GVC from developed to developing countries potentially introduces hidden risks to the stability of the GVC. The first risk is coming from economic dependence on developing countries in the GVC. As these developing countries become increasingly influential to the GVC, any disruption in them might create vulnerabilities in the global economic system. This point is critical because the political and business environment in developing countries is naturally less stable than in developed countries. For instance, the political risk in Vietnam is considered moderate, whereas that of the USA is considered low (Export Finance Australia, 2024). This condition means that Vietnam is more likely to experience political instability, which in turn disrupts the country's business environment. It will massively disrupt the GVC, given that many companies have moved their manufacturing facilities there in response to the USA–China trade war. Moreover, the second risk also comes from potential trade conflicts between countries that want to defend their dominance and countries that would like to advance their dominance in the GVC. As developing countries gain prominence, they may face increased scrutiny and competition from developed countries. This condition might result in frequent trade disputes and regulatory challenges.

In summary, the changing dynamic of trade in GVCs between developed and developing economies poses some benefits and challenges. While the dynamic between developed and developing countries in the GVC offers promising opportunities for diversification, economic growth, and enhanced collaboration, it also presents challenges related to short-term inefficiencies, economic dependence, and potential trade conflicts. Therefore, a holistic perspective is crucial for maintaining a stable and resilient global trading system in the future.

References

AfCFTA. (2021). *About the AfCFTA*. Retrieved September 23, from https://au-afcfta.org/about/

Akama, K., & Jibiki, K. (2023). *Indonesia challenges Thailand's title as the 'Detroit of Asia'*. Retrieved September 21, 2024, from https://asia.nikkei.com/Business/Automobiles/Indonesia-challenges-Thailand-s-title-as-the-Detroit-of-Asia

Alves, L. G., Mangioni, G., Rodrigues, F. A., Panzarasa, P., & Moreno, Y. (2022). The rise and fall of countries in the global value chains. *Scientific Reports*, *12*(1), 9086.

Amiti, M., Redding, S. J., & Weinstein, D. E. (2019). The impact of the 2018 tariffs on prices and welfare. *Journal of Economic Perspectives*, *33*(4), 187–210.

Audi. (2024). *Audi in Mexico*. Retrieved September 26, 2024, from https://www.audi.com/en/company/strategy/locations/mexico.html

Bailey, D., & De Propris, L. (2017). Brexit and the UK automotive industry. *National Institute Economic Review*, *242*(1), R51–R59.

Bluth, C. (2018). *German key industries in a global value chains network*. Retrieved October 3, 2024, from https://globaleurope.eu/globalization/german-key-industries-in-a-global-value-chains-network/

Cappariello, R., Franco-Bedoya, S., Gunnella, V., & Ottaviano, G. I. (2020). *Rising protectionism and global value chains: Quantifying the general equilibrium effects* (Working Paper No. 1263). Bank of Italy Temi di Discussione.

Coates, R., Gherman, M., & Ferraz, R. (2022). *Global labor rate comparisons: The impact on manufacturing location decisions and reshoring*. https://reshoringinstitute.org/wp-content/uploads/2022/09/GlobalLaborRateComparisons.pdf

Coen, D., Grant, W., & Wilson, G. (2010). *The Oxford handbook of business and government*. OUP.

Cohen, M. A., & Kouvelis, P. (2021). Revisit of AAA excellence of global value chains: Robustness, resilience, and realignment. *Production and Operations Management*, *30*(3), 633–643.

Culvera, R. (2023). *The steady growth of the Philippine BPO sector*. Retrieved September 26, from https://www.jll.com.au/en/trends-and-insights/research/the-steady-growth-of-the-philippine-bpo-sector

Department for Promotion of Industry and Internal Trade. (2019). *Schemes for electronics manufacturing in India*. Retrieved September 27, from https://www.makeinindia.com/schemes-electronics-manufacturing-india

Ellram, L. M., Tate, W. L., & Petersen, K. J. (2013). Offshoring and reshoring: An update on the manufacturing location decision. *Journal of Supply Chain Management, 49*(2), 14–22.

Export Finance Australia. (2024). *Country profiles.* Retrieved October 5, 2024, from https://www.exportfinance.gov.au/resources/country-profiles/

Fajgelbaum, P., Goldberg, P., Kennedy, P., Khandelwal, A., & Taglioni, D. (2023). *The 'bystander effect' of the US-China trade war.* Retrieved March 21, 2024, from https://cepr.org/voxeu/columns/bystander-effect-us-china-trade-war

Fajgelbaum, P., Goldberg, P., Kennedy, P., Khandelwal, A., & Taglioni, D. (2024). The US-China trade war and global reallocations. *American Economic Review: Insights, 6*(2), 295–312.

Fajgelbaum, P. D., & Khandelwal, A. K. (2022). The economic impacts of the US–China trade war. *Annual Review of Economics, 14*, 205–228.

Fetzer, T., & Schwarz, C. (2021). Tariffs and politics: Evidence from Trump's trade wars. *The Economic Journal, 131*(636), 1717–1741.

Gereffi, G., Lim, H.-C., & Lee, J. (2021). Trade policies, firm strategies, and adaptive reconfigurations of global value chains. *Journal of International Business Policy, 4*(4), 506–522.

Haritas, B. (2022). *Tata Motors digitises its manufacturing ecosystem.* Retrieved September 8, 2024, from https://cio.economictimes.indiatimes.com/news/strategy-and-management/tata-motors-digitises-its-manufacturing-ecosystem/94310396

Horwitz, J. (2022). *Apple supply chain data shows receding exposure to China as risks mount.* Retrieved October 3, 2024, from https://www.reuters.com/technology/apple-supply-chain-data-shows-receding-exposure-china-risks-mount-2022-11-30/

Huang, L.-M. (2024, May 10). *A short history of semiconductor technology in Taiwan during the 1970s and the 1980s.* Retrieved October 2, from https://taiwaninsight.org/2024/05/10/a-short-history-of-semiconductor-technology-in-taiwan-during-the-1970s-and-the-1980s/

Hyundai. (2024). *Milestones of Hyundai Motor India since 1996 until now.* Retrieved October 2, from https://www.hyundai.com/in/en/hyundai-story/hyundai-motor-india/history-1996–2000

IBEF. (2024). *Manufacturing sector in India.* Retrieved October 2, from https://www.ibef.org/industry/manufacturing-sector-india

Jin, B. E., & Kim, G. (2022). Assessing Malaysia and Indonesia as emerging retail markets: An institution-based view. *International Journal of Retail & Distribution Management, 50*(6), 692–707.

Kawahara, A. (2012). *The origin of competitive strength: Fifty years of the auto industry in Japan and the US.* Springer Science & Business Media.

Kharas, H. (2010). *The emerging middle class in developing countries.* Retrieved August 14, 2024, from https://www.truevaluemetrics.org/DBpdfs/Economics/OECD/OECD_EmegingMiddleClass.pdf

Kim, J., & Monroe, C. (2024). America is the undisputed world leader in quantum computing even though China spends 8x more on the technology–but an own goal could soon erode U.S. dominance. *Fortune.* https://fortune.com/2024/04/12/america-undisputed-world-leader-quantum-computing-even-though-china-spends-technology-us-dominance/

Kren, J., & Lawless, M. (2024). How has Brexit changed EU–UK trade flows? *European Economic Review, 161*, 104634.

Luo, X., & Xu, X. (2018). *Infrastructure, value chains, and economic upgrades* (World Bank Policy Research Working Paper No. 8547). World Bank.

Meier, H. B., Marthinsen, J. E., & Gantenbein, P. A. (2012). *Swiss finance: Capital markets, banking, and the Swiss value chain.* John Wiley & Sons.

Meng-Kng, C. (2012). *Regional business development in ASEAN: AFTA*. Retrieved September 12, from https://asean.org/regional-business-development-in-asean-afta/

Mercosur. (2014). *Mercosur in brief.* Retrieved September 23, from https://www.mercosur.int/en/about-mercosur/mercosur-in-brief/

Moradlou, H., Fratocchi, L., Skipworth, H., & Ghadge, A. (2022). Post-Brexit back-shoring strategies: What UK manufacturing companies could learn from the past? *Production Planning & Control*, *33*(14), 1319–1336.

Nellis, S. (2021, September 25). Intel breaks ground on $20 bln Arizona plants as U.S. chip factory race heats up. *Reuters*. https://www.reuters.com/technology/intel-breaks-ground-20-bln-arizona-plants-us-chip-factory-race-heats-up-2021-09-24/

Pao, J. (2024). Taiwan considering new chip export ban against China. *Asia Times*. https://asiatimes.com/2024/02/taiwan-considering-new-chip-export-ban-against-china/#:~:text=Last%20December%2C%20Taiwan's%20National%20Science,not%20want%20Beijing%20to%20obtain.

Pelaez-Fernandez, A. (2023, March 22). Mexico makes lots of electric cars, but few Mexicans drive them. *Reuters*. https://www.reuters.com/business/autos-transportation/mexico-makes-lots-electric-cars-few-mexicans-drive-them-2023-03-21/

Pitas, C. (2019a, July 9). BMW has moved some engine output from UK due to Brexit. *Reuters*. https://www.reuters.com/article/us-britain-eu-bmw/bmw-has-moved-some-engine-output-from-uk-due-to-brexit-idUSKCN1U41E5/

Pitas, C. (2019b, April 8). Jaguar Land Rover begins Brexit-linked UK plant shutdowns. *Reuters*. https://www.reuters.com/article/business/jaguar-land-rover-begins-brexit-linked-uk-plant-shutdowns-idUSKCN1RK11F/

Reuters. (2024a). Samsung plans to invest $1.8 bln more in Vietnam for OLED manufacturing. *Reuters*. https://www.reuters.com/technology/samsung-invests-18-billion-more-vietnam-oled-manufacturing-plant-2024-09-23/

Reuters. (2024b). Vietnam misses out on Intel, LG Chem investments due to lack of incentives, ministry document shows. *Reuters*. https://www.reuters.com/markets/asia/vietnam-misses-out-intel-lg-chem-investments-due-lack-incentives-ministry-2024-07-05/

Samuel, P. (2024). *Vietnam's international free trade agreements*. Retrieved October 2, 2024, from https://www.vietnam-briefing.com/doing-business-guide/vietnam/why-vietnam/vietnam-s-international-free-trade-and-tax-agreements

Seong, J., Bradley, C., Leung, N., Woetzel, L., Ellingrud, K., Kumra, G., & Wang, P. (2023). *Asia on the cusp of a new era*. Retrieved August 24, 2024, from https://www.mckinsey.com/mgi/our-research/asia-on-the-cusp-of-a-new-era

Shu, P., & Steinwender, C. (2019). The impact of trade liberalization on firm productivity and innovation. *Innovation Policy and the Economy*, *19*(1), 39–68.

SMMT. (2023). *Open roads: Driving Britain's global automotive trade*. https://www.smmt.co.uk/wp-content/uploads/SMMT-Automotive-Trade-Report–2023.pdf

Steitz, C., & Amann, C. (2024, May 29). Volkswagen to develop low-cost electric car to tackle Chinese rivals. *Reuters*. https://www.reuters.com/business/autos-transportation/volkswagen-develop-entry-level-electric-vehicles-around-20000-euros-2024-05-28/

Vietnam Briefing. (2024, April 3). *Vietnam's state of the economy: Q1 2024 report*. Retrieved September 28, from https://www.vietnam-briefing.com/news/vietnams-state-of-the-economy-q1–2024-report.html/

Warr, P., & Kohpaiboon, A. (2017). *Thailand's automotive manufacturing corridor* (ADB Economics Working Paper No. 519). https://www.adb.org/sites/default/files/publication/411926/ewp-519-thailand-automotive-manufacturingc-corridor.pdf

WEF. (2024). *Malaysia is emerging as a new semiconductor powerhouse*. Retrieved September 30, 2024, from https://www.weforum.org/videos/malaysia-semiconductors/

Weijia, H. (2024, September 10). Tesla's Shanghai plant running at max capacity shows China market irreplaceable. *Global Times*. https://www.globaltimes.cn/page/202409/1319597.shtml#:~:text=For%20Tesla%2C%20China%20is%20indispensable,first%20Gigafactory%20outside%20the%20US

World Bank. (2024, April 19). *The world bank in Viet Nam*. Retrieved October 5, from https://www.worldbank.org/en/country/vietnam/overview

Zhang, M. (2024, May 2). *The geopolitics of Tesla's China breakthrough*. Retrieved October 3, from https://www.uts.edu.au/acri/research-and-opinion/commentary/geopolitics-teslas-china-breakthrough

3

GEOPOLITICAL TURMOIL AND THE CHANGING NATURE OF GLOBALIZATION

Arza Faldy Prameswara, Huashan (Jason) Li, Donella Caspersz and Arnoldus (Ron) Maas

Introduction

For decades, the world has experienced a process of globalization characterized by the increasing flow of goods, services, and capital. However, significant disruptions due to recent geopolitical turmoils, such as Brexit, the United States (US)–China trade war, and the Russia-Ukraine conflict, are challenging this status quo. These events have introduced new challenges to the global system, with political instability, trade disputes, and tension between countries becoming increasingly common. This corresponds with a shift toward a more inward-looking focus among nations, reflected in the rise of protectionism at the country level and a more fragmented and complex international environment globally.

The tensions between the US and China highlight how geopolitical turmoil can disrupt international trade and the global supply chain. The growing rivalry between the two largest economies in the world has created uncertainty for businesses and fuelled a broader trend of global fragmentation. In recent years, both countries have introduced policies and regulations such as tariffs and trade barriers, which have hindered cross-border trade and investment activities not only between the US and China but also among their allies. This situation has prompted multinational enterprises (MNEs) to reconfigure their global supply chains by adopting strategies such as relocating their international operations to reduce their dependence on particular countries. For instance, semiconductor manufacturers from the US are increasingly shifting their production back to their home country to mitigate the risks, such as increasing costs from tariffs associated with the US-China tensions in the advanced technology industries.

The influence of geopolitical factors on globalization is reflected in the emergence of protectionism in several countries, as protectionist policies have

DOI: 10.4324/9781003468899-3

become more common and fundamentally reshaped the world's economic dynamics. According to the World Trade Organization (2024), the number of trade concerns related to restrictive policies on trade raised by members has increased from 159 cases in 2013 to 298 cases in 2023, an 87% increase in the past decade. Nations have become more inward-looking, prioritizing the protection of domestic industries and jobs. The focus on domestic interests has weakened the efficacy of multilateral institutions, as countries are reluctant to compromise on national priorities. This has resulted in a more fragmented and contentious global landscape.

The increase in geopolitical turmoil is partially driven by a shifting balance of power from developed countries to emerging markets. As emerging market economies such as China and India continue to grow, so does their demand for greater political influence and advocacy of their interests in global institutions such as the World Trade Organization (WTO). Developed countries are, however, often reluctant to meet those demands due to concerns that it would weaken their influence in global institutions. This tension between maintaining the status quo and adapting to the shifting global power structure has fuelled geopolitical turmoil, as reflected in the surge of trade disputes and retaliatory measures.

In sum, the rising tensions between nations, the surge of protectionism, the shifting balance of power, and disruptive events highlight the increasing concerns about the impact of geopolitical factors on the international business landscape. It is, therefore, important for governments to implement policies that counteract the uncertainty that arises from geopolitical turmoil and promote stability and resilience, while firms need to develop strategies that help them navigate these conditions of uncertainty.

This chapter is organized as follows. First, we examine how geopolitical turmoils have shaped and influenced the history of globalization, particularly its impact on the modern global economy. Next, we delve into the rise of protectionism, exploring its underlying rationale and the potential consequences for global business operations. Following this, we analyze the shifting balance of power from developed countries to emerging markets, highlighting the growing interdependencies and dynamics between these two groups of countries. We then provide insights into how geopolitical turmoils affect global value chain (GVC) configurations and the broader implications of geopolitical risk for firm supply chains. Finally, we explore strategies that firms can adopt to enhance resilience and adapt to these emerging geopolitical challenges.

Globalization and Geopolitical Turmoil

A Brief History of Economic Globalization

From an economic perspective, globalization refers to the process of increasing economic interdependence among countries (Fischer, 2003). This process is reflected in the growth in the cross-border movement of goods, capital flows, labor, technology, and knowledge. Although the concept of globalization gained prominence in the 1990s, the phenomenon has been present throughout economic history.

While global trade has existed for thousands of years, globalization accelerated during the age of discovery (15th–17th centuries), when European powers began exploring and colonizing new territories to extract resources. This period saw the creation of the world's first multinational and publicly listed companies, for example, the *Vereenigde Oostindische Compagnie* (Dutch East India Company), which facilitated the cross-border movement of goods, people, and information. Technological advancements during the Industrial Revolution of the 18th and 19th centuries, including railways, machinery, and the telegraph, further accelerated the movement of goods, people, and information while European colonial powers started to create global supply chains. Between the late 19th and early 20th centuries, globalization further intensified as new technologies and free market policies resulted in a surge in international trade, investments, and migration. However, the World Wars caused an abrupt halt to the increasing interdependence among nations. After the Second World War, globalization resumed its course, spurred by the establishment of the Bretton Woods system and supranational institutions such as the International Monetary Fund (IMF), WTO, and World Bank, which promoted increased international economic cooperation. The invention of shipping containers during this time also significantly reduced transportation costs, further boosting global business. Finally, the late 20th and early 21st centuries have marked the peak of modern globalization, with the Internet revolution and the development of digital technologies, alongside the expansion of free markets. This significantly enhances the connectedness of the world's economies and allows organizations to develop customer and supplier networks around the world.

The trend in global trade (i.e., the percentage of imports and exports to world gross domestic product [GDP]) is depicted in Figure 3.1 and demonstrates an upward trajectory of global imports and exports as a share of the global economy from 1970 to 2023. The shares of both imports and exports as percentages of global GDP have increased significantly from 1970 (12.68% and 12.77%, respectively) to 2023 (28.67% and 29.27%). This represents the growth of international trade and supports the notion of increasing globalization.

However, this long-term upward trend of globalization has experienced challenges in recent years, reflected in the stagnation of global trade flows between 2008 and 2020. This stagnation of global trade can be attributed to several events, such as the Global Financial Crisis of 2008, Brexit in 2016, the US–China trade war in 2018, and the COVID-19 pandemic.

FIGURE 3.1 Global export and import as a percentage of world GDP, 1970–2022

This trend has sparked ongoing debates on the emergence of de-globalization or reconfiguration of trade flows. Some argue that de-globalization has taken hold, with nations becoming less interdependent, as evidenced by the plateauing and even declining cross-border trade activities between 2008 and 2020. Others, however, contest this view, highlighting the rapid rebound in global trade flow in 2021 and 2022 following the COVID-19 pandemic. Recent studies argue that while globalization remains relevant, it is transforming, with trade flows increasingly shaped by divergent national agendas, shifting alliances, and the reconfiguration of supply chains.

Geopolitical Turmoil and Economic Activities

In recent years, geopolitical factors have played a key role in shaping the trajectory of globalization. Geopolitics refers to the study of how geographical context influences politics and relationships among nations (Caldara & Iacoviello, 2022). Based on this definition, geopolitical turmoil manifests as instability, conflict, and tension among nations caused by disruptive events, such as wars, interstate conflicts, and terrorism.

Events such as the US–China trade war have brought geopolitical concerns to the forefront of international relations and global business. The trade war between the two major countries has not only affected bilateral relations between these economies but also created ripple effects across global supply chains among their allies. Hence, understanding geopolitical turmoil is important in examining future global business.

Geopolitical turmoil is driven by factors like resource competition, territorial disputes, ideological differences, and technological rivalry. Resource competition often prompts tensions among nations to claim certain areas that contain essential natural resources, such as energy and commodities. Territorial disputes, such as disagreements over borders and territorial claims, drive geopolitical turmoil. This is reflected in the historical conflict of Israel-Palestine and Russia-Ukraine. Ideological differences contribute to tension between nations that leads to political or military conflicts. This is illustrated in the Cold War between the US and the Soviet Union, which was fuelled by ideological differences between the two economic blocs. Technological rivalries may transform into geopolitical tensions and influence the GVC, such as the US-China rivalry in the semiconductor industry.

Throughout history, geopolitical turmoil has repeatedly affected economic and international business activities. Key events such as World War I and II, the Cold War, the US–China trade war, Brexit, and the Russia-Ukraine conflict highlight the damaging impact of such instability. For example, World War II caused a significant loss of life and wealth that spurred severe economic problems in many countries, including high inflation, a surge in unemployment, and a rise in international debt. This further disrupted global trade and international business as firms faced challenges in accessing raw materials and financial resources across countries. In recent years, wars have continued to disrupt GVCs. The Russia-Ukraine conflict has led to pressure on global energy and commodity prices. In addition to outright conflict, political tensions and rivalries such as the US–China trade war have also contributed to a more fragmented global economy. These events have fuelled concerns about the emergence of de-globalization, where countries might be turning inward and limiting their international cooperation.

Geopolitical turmoil potentially harms the globalization process from multiple perspectives. From an international trade perspective, geopolitical turmoil causes a significant disruption in international trade flows. These disruptions increase trade costs and reduce the operational efficiency of the global business. Furthermore, from an institutional view, geopolitical turmoil represents conflicts between different political and economic systems that cause uncertainty in the business environment. For instance, the US–China trade war demonstrates friction between two political systems: the trade liberalization policies of the US and the state interventionist policies of China. This friction hinders the globalization process as firms face higher uncertainty in their international operations, such as the unpredictability of trade and investment regulations. These uncertainties complicate decision-making for firms to expand their international market.

Case Study 1. The Impact of the Russia-Ukraine Conflict on Energy and Food Security

The escalation of the Russia-Ukraine War in 2022 significantly altered the global business landscape. This conflict traces its roots to the collapse of the Soviet Union in 1991, which marked the emergence of Ukraine as an independent nation. Since then, the countries have had a territorial dispute over the Crimea region. In 2014, Russia invaded this area with the intent to integrate it into Russia, marking the beginning of the armed conflict between Russia and Ukraine.

One of the most significant consequences of the ensuing war has been the impact on the energy infrastructure in Ukraine and Russia. Pipelines and facilities that were crucial to transporting energy to various parts of Europe were damaged, causing significant disruptions in global energy trade flows and a massive reduction in natural gas and energy exports from the region. In response to Russia's invasion of Ukraine, both the US and European countries announced economic sanctions on Russia and a boycott of Russian products. While the goal was to punish Russia for its transgressions, the wider result was a surge in global energy prices. Guenette et al. (2022) show that natural gas prices have risen by around 40% since the beginning of the invasion in 2022. Figure 3.2 highlights that Brent crude oil prices reached a 10-year high of USD 133 per barrel at the beginning of March 2022.

FIGURE 3.2 Crude oil Europe Brent daily prices (USD per barrel) and wheat global daily prices (USD per bushel), January–June 2022

Source: Graphs developed using data from the US Energy Information and Administration (EIA) and www.macrotrends.net (2024)

This conflict also had ramifications for the global food supply chain. The war resulted in a sharp decline in agriculture and food production from these countries. The supply-side shock posed a threat to global price fluctuations and food security. Since Russia and Ukraine produce substantial shares of the wheat traded globally, the sudden shortage led to a surge in the global price of wheat. Figure 3.2 demonstrates the significant jump in global wheat prices from around USD 9 per bushel in February 2022 to USD 12.9 per bushel at the beginning of March 2022. Since wheat is an essential agricultural input with multiple downstream products, the rising cost of wheat has contributed to food shortages and increased food prices in many parts of the world, particularly in countries that are heavily reliant on wheat imports. This case illustrates how geopolitical turmoil can severely disrupt global supply chains and influence the shift toward a fragmented global economy.

Rise of Protectionism

Geopolitical tensions are not the only factor contributing to unrest in the global market. Another influential aspect is the rise of protectionism across various countries. According to Evenett (2019), protectionism is defined as all government interventions that discriminate against foreign companies and provide an advantage to domestic firms. These interventions can take various forms, such as tariff increases, regulatory restrictions, and local content requirements. One of the contributing factors of protectionism is that the country prioritizes its national interest through policies that promote domestic firm competitiveness, protect local jobs from immigrants, and prevent competition from foreign firms.

While globalization thrives in conditions of political stability, protectionism often emerges during geopolitical turmoil. In stable political environments, countries are more likely to engage in open trade policies, promoting international cooperation and fostering economic globalization. In contrast, during conditions of geopolitical turmoil, such as trade wars and military conflicts, countries may prioritize their domestic interests over global cooperation. During these times, governments often implement various protectionist policies to reduce their dependency on foreign economies. For example, during World War II, the war fuelled nationalist sentiments in conflicting countries and led to a shift to protectionism and isolationism.

The rise of protectionism is reflected in the growing number of trade concerns raised by WTO members related to barriers and restrictions on export and import. Figure 3.3 exhibits the growing number of trade concerns raised at the Council for Trade in Goods of WTO from 2005 to 2023. Overall, there

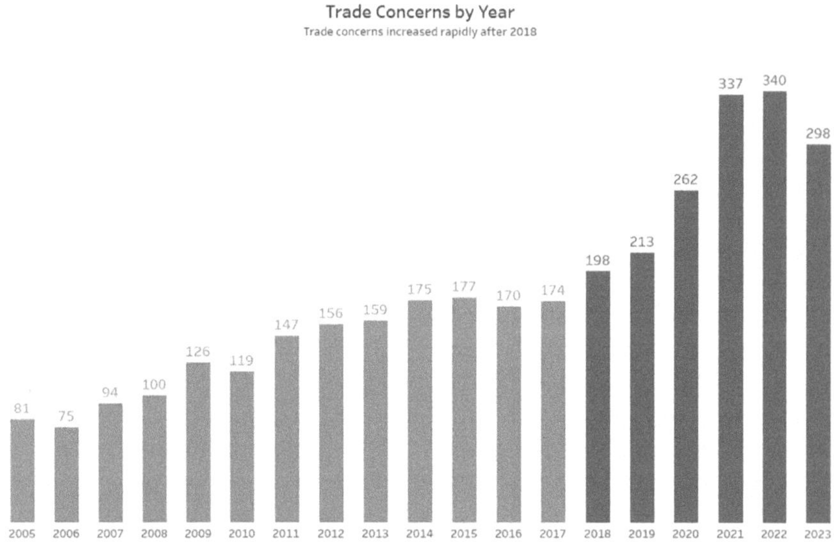

FIGURE 3.3 Number of trade concerns raised by WTO members in Council Trade meeting

has been a significant rise in the number of trade concerns, from around 81 in 2005 to 298 in 2023. The upward trend of trade concerns reached its highest point in 2022, with 340 cases and a slight decrease in 2023. The trend reflects the increasing trade measures in the form of import-export restrictions and technical barriers by WTO members.

Protectionism can also stem from an increasing concern for national sovereignty and security. While this is not a new phenomenon, it has gained significant momentum due to growing geopolitical tensions and uncertainty in the global market. In such an environment, countries are increasingly seeking to limit their risk exposure by tightening control over strategic industries and key technologies. Therefore, they impose regulatory restrictions on foreign investments and acquisitions in their strategic industries and limit the cross-border transfer of key technologies. For example, the Foreign Investment and National Security Act (FINSA) in 2007 has significantly influenced the decrease in foreign acquisitions in the national security industries in the US (Godsell et al., 2023). Another example is the US and European ban on Huawei, a leading mobile communication company from China, due to concern over potential espionage and risks to critical communication infrastructures. These examples highlight the increasing concern about national security and its implication on the rise of protectionism.

Traditionally, protectionism has manifested through the use of tariffs, which were employed to distort the flow of exports and imports from foreign countries. According to the World Trade Organization (2023) report, the average tariff for all products has decreased from 10% in 2006 to 8.9% in 2021. This tariff decline over the years seemingly indicates a trend toward greater globalization and market integration. However, the decline in tariff levels has coincided with a notable shift toward the use of nontariff barrier policies. Instead of increasing globalization, these shifts, therefore, underscore how the global trade landscape is evolving, with protectionist policies moving beyond traditional tariffs to more complex forms of trade restrictions.

According to WTO classification, examples of nontariff barriers include sanitary and phytosanitary & technical trade barriers (SPS & TBT), anti-dumping policies (ADP), countervailing (CV), and safeguards (SG). SPS & TBT represent standard and technical regulations imposed on foreign products related to safety, product quality, and packaging. ADP exhibits counteract policies to protect domestic industries from unfair competition from foreign producers that sell products below market price. CV represents the barriers imposed on imported products that are subsidized by foreign governments. SG exhibits targeted restrictions on imported products that are threatening the domestic industry.

Countries adopt these nontariff barriers because they can be particularly effective in undermining the low-cost manufacturing advantage that their trading partners possess, especially when they are from low-cost environments. Nontariff barriers in the form of higher standards for product safety, quality assurance, and environmental practices force companies from low-cost environments to increase their compliance level if they want to remain competitive in foreign markets. This leads to an increase in compliance costs and erodes their domestic position.

Figure 3.4 depicts the general trend of nontariff barriers from the past decades. The data shows the number of policies initiated and reported by WTO member countries annually. SPS & TBT are the most prominent types of barriers, with around 78% of the total nontariff barriers in 2020. ADP measures increased from 187 cases in 2005 to 344 cases in 2020. Furthermore, there is a surge in countervailing duties and SG, from 9 and 7 cases in 2005 to 55 and 23 cases in 2021, respectively.

A third form of protectionism is through government subsidies, which are offered to boost local industries and strengthen a country's competitive edge in certain sectors. Evenett and Fritz (2021) classify subsidies into inward and outward subsidies. Inward subsidies distort the domestic market by granting industries or firms advantages over competitors. This policy is often showcased as a defensive instrument to protect the domestic market from foreign exposure. Outward subsidies distort international markets by providing domestic firms with tax incentives or financial assistance to reduce costs and improve the competitiveness of exporters in foreign markets.

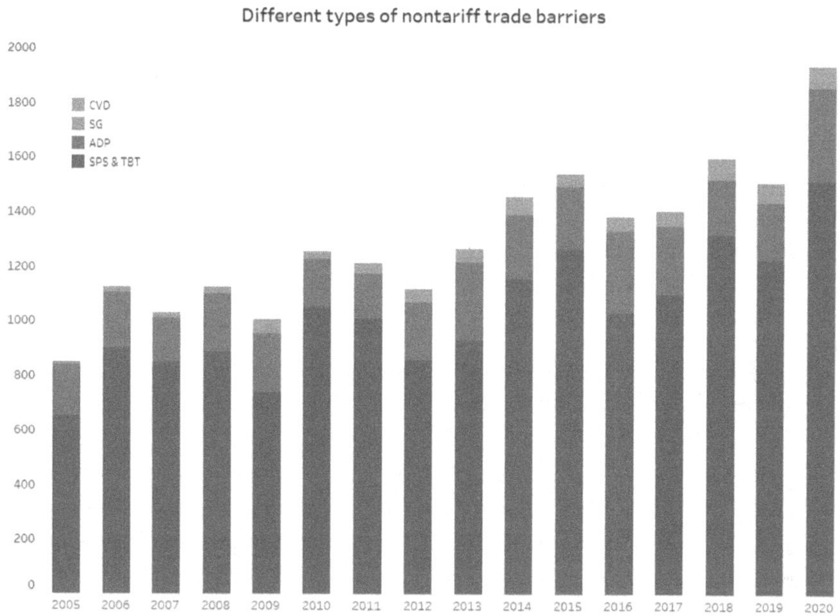

FIGURE 3.4 The number of nontariff barriers initiated worldwide, 2005–2020

While this practice may not directly align with protectionism, it often provokes retaliatory measures from trade partners. For example, the tit-for-tat policies, that is, a retaliatory trade strategy where the country counteracts the trade actions of another party, in the US–China trade wars illustrate how outward subsidies promoted by the Chinese government can trigger escalating protectionist measures. The report by Evenett and Fritz (2021) shows that two major economies (the US and China) have been actively engaged in both inward and outward subsidies since 2008.

Alongside nontariff barriers, a further form of protectionism has emerged with the use of restrictive industrial policies. The surge of restrictive industrial policies has contributed to the increase in geopolitical turmoil, especially between China and Western countries. This is because China's economic and political supremacy threatens the influence of the US and the European Union (EU) on the global economy. China aims to become a global leader in technology industries by establishing the "Made in China 2025" plan and the "Belt and Road Initiative". In response, the US and EU adopted restrictive industrial policies to reduce reliance on Chinese technologies and supply chains. A recent example is the ongoing EU vote on a potential tariff of up to 45% on Chinese electric vehicle (EV) producers. This measure is intended to address concerns over perceived unfair competition, as Chinese EV producers may benefit from state programs, posing a threat to European EV manufacturers.

The resurgence of protectionism in recent years has been characterized by a shift from traditional tariff barriers toward a more complex form of protectionism, such as nontariff barriers, government subsidies to domestic companies, political-driven industrial policies, and other restrictive regulations. Therefore, firms operating in the international market face increasing challenges in mitigating the impact of these policies. To navigate these complexities, firms need to develop a strong understanding of the regulation and geopolitical conditions in foreign markets.

Case Study 2. The US–China Trade War and Its Implications on Bilateral Trade

The US–China trade war has contributed to the resurgence of protectionism in several countries. The trade war started during the Trump presidency in mid-2018 with the US government's decision to impose tariffs on iron, steel, and aluminum imports from China. In March 2018, the US government announced a 12% import tariff on aluminum products and a 25% import tariff on iron and

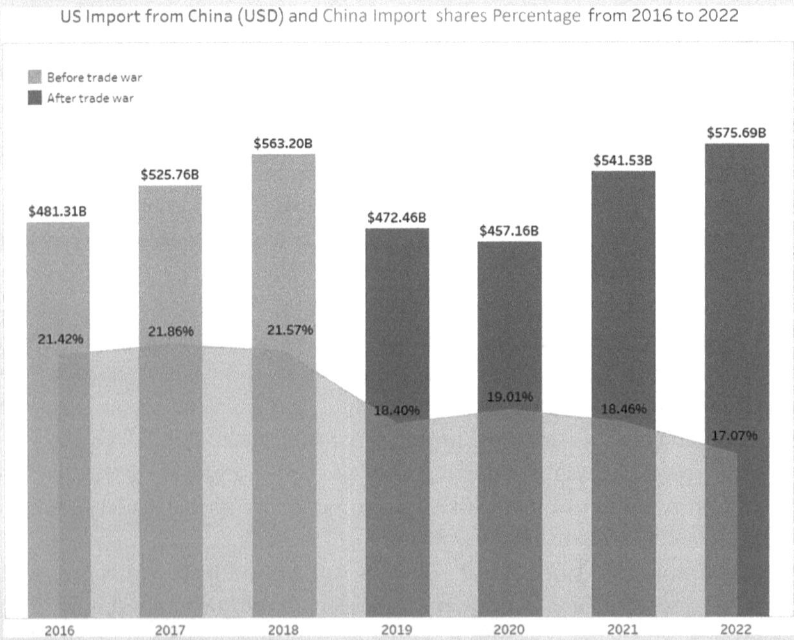

FIGURE 3.5 US import value from China and China's import shares per total import of US from 2016 to 2022

steel products (Fajgelbaum et al., 2020). These protectionist policies aim to address claims about China's subsidies for Chinese industries. In response to the US tariff increase, China imposed a 25% tariff on agricultural products, machinery equipment, and automobile imports from the US (Casas-Klett & Li, 2021). Moreover, the trade war had broader implications for the global economy, raising concerns about decoupling between the US and Chinese economies and a fragmented global economy.

Figure 3.5 exhibits the US import value from China and the percentage of US imports from China between 2016 and 2022. The data shows that the 2018 first-round tariff caused a 16.1% decline in the US import value from China in 2019. Despite the escalating trade war between these two countries, US imports from China gradually recovered in the following years. However, the percentage of imports from China declined from 2018 to 2022. This indicates that the two countries impose strategic decoupling strategies by maintaining the interdependence of several industries and limiting trade relations in particular critical industries (Cui et al., 2023).

Shifting Balance of Power

The global business landscape has experienced a significant transformation over the past few decades, represented by a shift in the balance of power from developed economies to emerging markets. Following the classification by International Monetary Fund (2018), developed countries consist of 35 countries, such as Australia, Belgium, Canada, Germany, Japan, the US, and the UK. Emerging markets encompass 21 countries, such as Brazil, China, Chile, India, Indonesia, and Russia. This shift of power is manifested in the economic and political dimensions of the global economy. From an economic perspective, emerging markets have undergone unprecedented rates of economic growth and have increasingly contributed to global economic growth in recent decades. Emerging markets grew almost twice as fast as developed countries in the period before the COVID-19 pandemic (International Monetary Fund, 2023). For example, during the period from 2015 to 2019, developed countries recorded an average of 2.1% GDP growth while emerging markets accounted for an average of 4.4% GDP growth.

Figure 3.6 exhibits the share of GDP from developed and emerging markets to world GDP over the past five decades. The growing contribution of emerging markets is indicated in the increasing share of these countries in the world economy, from around 27.2% in 1990 to 46.3% in 2023. In contrast, the share of developed countries has declined from 57.2% in 1990 to 38.9% in 2023. The shifting of economic power has accelerated in the last few years, with the

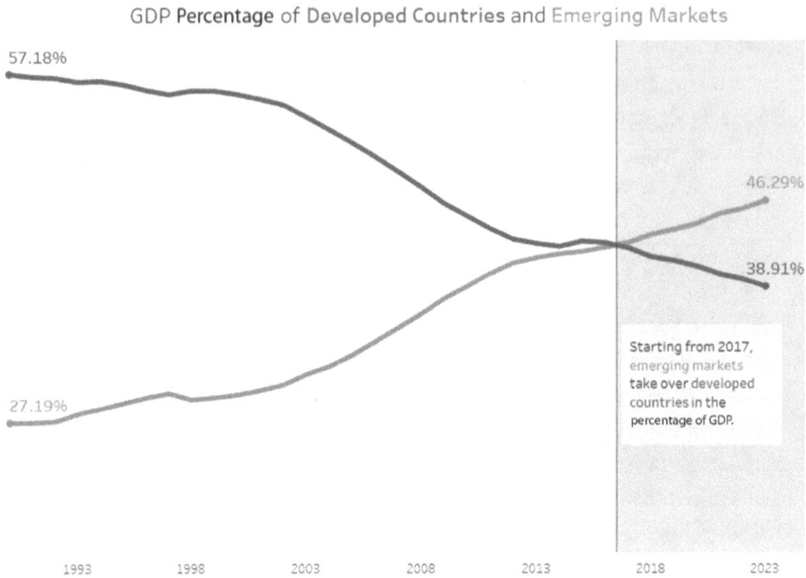

FIGURE 3.6 GDP (based on purchasing power parity) share of developed countries and emerging markets to world GDP, 1990–2023

GDP shares of emerging markets exceeding developed countries in 2017. Projections from the IMF suggest that emerging markets will continue to grow at a faster pace than developed countries in the future. As a result, emerging markets are expected to contribute around 60% of the world economy in 2029, compared to around 38% of developed countries in the same year.

Population demographics also play a crucial role in shifting the balance of economic power. Emerging markets possess a significant share of the world's population. Data from the World Bank indicates that the three largest emerging markets, China, India, and Indonesia, accounted for 3.1 billion people in 2023 (around 40% of the world population). Their population has increased substantially in the past few decades, from 2.6 billion in 2003 to 3.1 billion in 2023. Although the population growth rate in some of these emerging markets, such as China, has begun to slow in recent years, the growing income levels and corresponding consumer demand make these markets the largest consumer base in the world. This further exacerbates the economic shift from developed countries to emerging markets.

These demographic factors of emerging markets offer significant advantages for accelerating economic growth. The increase in the working-age population indicates a surge in labor supply, which provides key drivers of economic growth. On the other hand, a growing population reflects a larger domestic demand for goods and services. As domestic demand surges, businesses are prompted to expand their operations, generate jobs, and invest in new technologies.

Emerging markets have also experienced rapid industrialization in recent decades. This is indicated by the transformation of the economic structure from agriculture to manufacturing and services. Firms in emerging markets utilize their competitive advantages, such as lower labor costs and abundant resources, to compete in the domestic and global markets. Companies from emerging markets aim to strengthen their position in the domestic market while also seeking global expansion opportunities through international trade and investment. For example, Vale, the largest mining company in Brazil, has grown to become one of the largest iron ore producers in the world, supplying raw materials for multiple industries in various countries.

Figure 3.7 depicts the percentage of exports of goods and services from developed and emerging markets. The data depicts a general downtrend in developed countries' export shares and an increasing trend of exports from emerging markets in the past five decades. Furthermore, there has been a significant shift in emerging markets from exporting raw materials and consumer goods to capital goods. For example, data from the World Bank (2024) shows that China's export shares of raw materials to total exports have declined from 12.7% in 1990 to 1.4% in 2022, while the export shares of capital goods have

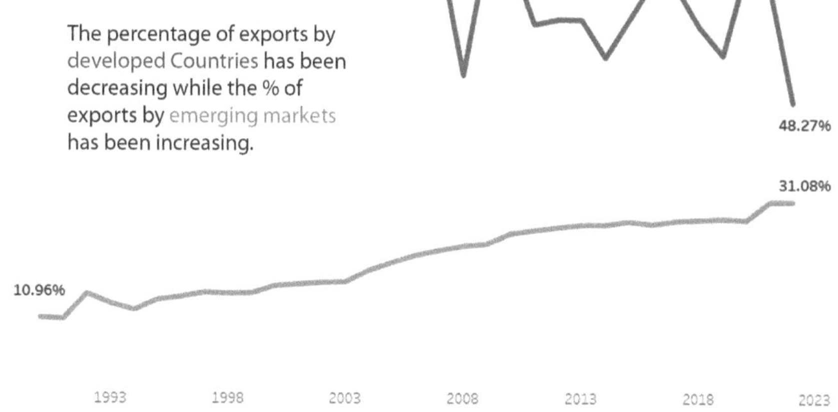

FIGURE 3.7 The export share of developed and emerging countries to world export, 1990–2023

surged from 10% to 43.6% during the same period. This trend indicates the changes in global trade dynamics, with emerging markets increasingly promoting global trade and economic integration.

The rise of emerging markets not only reshaped the global economy but also had significant implications for the international political landscape. As their contribution to the global economy grew, emerging markets have become more proactive in advocating their political agenda. Emerging market countries, such as China and India, are increasingly engaged in international cooperation through their geopolitical strategies. For example, China has launched the Belt and Road Initiative (BRI), a massive development project that aims to enhance economic and political relationships between Asia, Europe, and Africa. BRI and the implementation of various trade and investment policies have supported Chinese businesses to expand their operations by investing in several countries. Another example is India's Act East Policy, which aims to strengthen engagement in regional trade and investment partnerships with Southeast Asian countries. It has enabled Indian businesses to expand their international operations in Southeast Asia through cross-border trade, joint infrastructure projects, and strategic investments in various industries. These initiatives aim to enhance their political influence and challenge developed countries' dominance in political power.

On the other hand, developed countries, such as the US and European countries, seek to maintain their political influence in global cooperation. These countries have historically been positioned as the leaders of international institutions such as the IMF, WTO, and United Nations, shaping the rule of the institutions to achieve their economic and political interests. As emerging economies' power grows, they demand changes in the trade rules that incorporate their economic and political interests. However, developed countries often resist changes that could undermine their dominance in international cooperation.

The growing political competition between developed and emerging markets is one of the driving factors of geopolitical turmoil. This competition can exacerbate tensions, as conflicting interests and priorities between countries may hinder the ability to reach a consensus in international agreements. It, then, will fundamentally disrupt international cooperation, causing a shift from trade liberalization to a protectionist paradigm in the global order.

Case Study 3. The Growth of Emerging Market Multinationals and Geopolitical Turmoil

There has been a rapid global expansion of emerging market multinationals (EMNEs) in recent decades that reshaped the global business landscape. While maintaining their leading position in the domestic market, EMNEs have expanded their operations to developed countries. For example, firms from China (e.g., Alibaba Group Holding Limited, Huawei, and Lenovo) and India (e.g., Tata Group) have diversified their business portfolio in Europe and North America.

The growing contribution to global business is depicted by the presence of EMNEs in the Fortune Global 500 firms. As of 2023, 173 companies in the Fortune Global 500 firms are from emerging markets. EMNEs have locational competitive advantages, such as lower labor costs and access to resources. Additionally, by learning from developed MNEs, EMNEs have improved their technological and innovation capabilities, marketing capabilities, and international experience. These competitive advantages have enabled EMNEs to increase their business size and compete with developed countries' MNEs.

However, the rise of geopolitical turmoil has challenged the rapid growth of EMNEs in the global market. A prominent example is TikTok, a social media platform developed by Chinese company ByteDance that has been globally expanded in the last few years. TikTok has been under criticism from governments of the US and European countries on how they handle data privacy and whether the company adequately protects it from access by the Chinese state. As a result, the company deals with several restrictions and bans from various jurisdictions that hamper international expansion and business growth (Gray, 2021).

In response to the increasingly turbulent environment, TikTok has implemented several operational strategies and improved its governance as well as public relations. One of the key operational strategies was to localize its data storage and processing management. In this context, TikTok declared that they migrated US users' data to Oracle servers located in the US Furthermore, the company also engaged in extensive public relations campaigns and enhanced its transparency efforts to increase legitimacy within the social and political environment.

Geopolitical Turmoil and Resilience of GVCs

The Evolution of GVCs

Over the past decades, changes in the global trade and investment environment coupled with advancements in information technologies have altered how MNEs operate and compete in the global market. In this context, GVCs have become increasingly important for MNEs in facilitating business growth, promoting specialization, and connecting strategic alliances between firms from different countries. According to Antràs (2020), GVC is a series of stages involved in producing a product or service, with at least two stages of value-added activities being produced in different countries.

GVCs support the optimal allocation of resources across countries and industries along the value chain by allowing firms from a particular country to specialize in the production stages where they have comparative advantages. For example, firms from countries with low-labor cost advantages may specialize in labor-intensive stages such as assembly and manufacturing. In contrast, firms with advanced technological capabilities focus on research and development. By doing so, GVCs allow firms to access cheaper inputs and increase the optimization of capital usage. Thereby, it promotes cost efficiency and operational productivity along the GVCs.

Figure 3.8 presents the GVC's participation rates in global trade, measured using the World Input-Output Database. Forward GVC participation indicates how the export of inputs to trading partners contributes to production in their countries. On the other hand, backward GVC participation reflects how an economy relies on foreign inputs in the production of goods and services for export. Figure 3.8 shows a trend of rising GVC participation from 1995 to 2008. During this period, forward GVC participation grew from 16.9% to 19.7%, and backward GVC participation increased from 16.4% to 19.6%.

However, the rise of geopolitical turmoil has reshaped the configuration of GVCs. As the world becomes increasingly interconnected, disruption caused

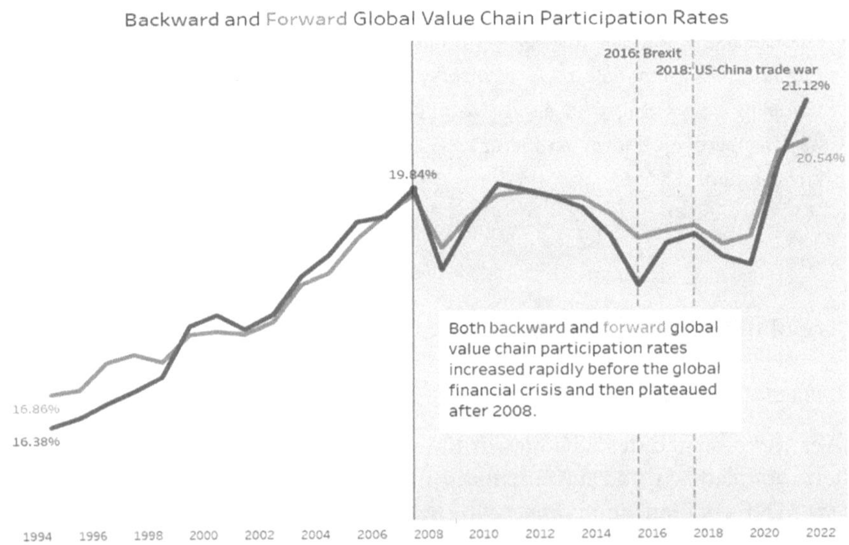

FIGURE 3.8 Backward and forward GVC participation rates, 1995–2022

by geopolitical turmoil can adversely impact businesses and the global economy. In recent years, these disruptive events, such as wars, conflicts, and tensions between nations, have become more frequent. These disruptive events may cause significant supply chain disruptions, leading to delays in production, shortages of raw materials, and increased costs of operations.

The impact of geopolitical turmoil on GVCs is indicated in the fluctuation of GVC participation rates by WTO in the last decades. As visualized in Figure 3.8 in 2009, there was a significant drop in GVC participation following the global financial crisis in 2008. Despite the slow recovery in 2010, the forward and backward GVC participation has gradually declined from 19.7% and 19.9% in 2011, respectively, to 19.1% and 18.7% in 2020. This decline is attributed to several disruptive events, such as Brexit in 2016 and the US–China trade wars in 2018 that hampered business operations and disrupted the supply chain in several countries. This was followed by the COVID-19 pandemic that disrupted the movement across borders from 2019 to 2020. Furthermore, data shows a strong rebound in GVC participation in 2021 and reached the highest point in 2022.

The trend highlights the impact of geopolitical turmoil and disruptive events between 2011 and 2020 on the progression of GVC. Events such as Brexit in 2016 and the US–China trade war in 2018 have led to a contraction of GVCs. Geopolitical turmoil causes uncertainty, increases production costs, and heightens risks for international operations. Correspondingly, firms opt to minimize risk under this uncertainty by restructuring their operations and supply chains.

Geopolitical Turmoils and GVCs Resilience

The rise of geopolitical turmoil has also challenged the resilience of GVCs. Resilience refers to the ability of an entity or system to recover from a disruption or shock (Martin, 2011). In the context of GVCs, firms continuously improve their resilience in the supply chain by leveraging their capabilities to withstand and adapt to geopolitical risk.

The resilience of GVCs varies based on the industry and complexity of the supply chain. Firms operating in industries that rely on a globally distributed supply network and that are highly dependent on foreign subunits or suppliers, such as consumer electronics, are more vulnerable to the impact of geopolitical turmoil. Globalization has prompted firms to improve the efficiency of operations by shifting from traditional supply chain systems to just-in-time and lean production systems. These systems aim to minimize inventory levels by synchronizing production with demand. However, this shift leads the firm to become vulnerable to geopolitical risk because they are increasingly embedded into GVCs.

As geopolitical turmoil becomes increasingly frequent and severe, businesses need to be more proactive in deploying strategies to ensure supply chain resiliency. In response to the rise of geopolitical turmoil, many companies are now adjusting their supply chain strategy by increasing their inventory. Lund et al. (2020) highlight that several industries, such as automobile, energy, and semiconductor equipment, have increased their level of inventory between 2012 and 2019, to minimize supply chain risk caused by geopolitical turmoil during this period.

Firms also increasingly opt to relocate their operations and production facilities to countries with lower geopolitical risks through strategies such as reshoring, nearshoring, and friend-shoring. By moving production and operations back to their home countries or those of politically allied countries, firms minimize the impact of disruption from trade barriers and restrictive regulations caused by geopolitical turmoil. For example, many US companies have adopted a China Plus One strategy, for example, moving their international operations and supply chain networks away from China to reduce dependency on the Chinese market (Khorana et al., 2022). After the trade war, many MNEs have moved their operations toward countries with closer political interests with the US, such as India and Vietnam, to serve the Southeast Asia market.

Another way in which firms can limit their risk exposure to geopolitical turmoil is through diversifying their supply chain network to countries or regions with less risky political environments. When firms over-concentrate their supply chain networks, they have a higher exposure to geopolitical risk. For example, the semiconductor industry is highly concentrated in a few countries and regions, such as China, Taiwan, the US, South Korea, and Singapore, which makes the industry vulnerable to disruptions caused by geopolitical tensions between the US and China. This disruption also affects semiconductor manufacturers from Taiwan and South Korea by limiting their expansion to the Chinese market, as they are heavily embedded in US advanced technologies industries. By diversifying the supply chain, firms create backup plans to maintain their global operations and mitigate the negative impact of disruptions.

In addition, firms seek to minimize the impact of geopolitical turmoil through a vertical integration strategy of their supply chain network. Vertical integration through the acquisition of suppliers allows the firm to gain control over different stages of the supply chain. Firms secure the continuity of their crucial inputs and have better control of their internal processes when facing uncertainty caused by geopolitical turmoil. Moreover, it provides firms with greater flexibility and autonomy in managing supply chain strategies in response to changes in trade and investment regulation under geopolitical turmoil.

Case Study 4. The US-China Technological Rivalry and Implications CHIPS and Science Act on Nvidia

Semiconductor manufacturing is one of the most important components in the value chain of the technology and communication industries. US-based companies such as Intel, Nvidia, and AMD have maintained their position as global leaders for a long time. However, in recent decades, this dominance has faced increasing challenges from other countries. Data shows that between 1990 and 2021, the US global manufacturing capacity shares decreased from 40% to less than 15% (Luo & Van Assche, 2023). To address this decline and bolster its domestic semiconductor industry, the US enacted the CHIPS and Science Act. The legislation allocates over $52 billion to boost domestic semiconductor manufacturing, research, and development. The primary goals are to strengthen the US semiconductor supply chain, reduce dependency on foreign producers, and enhance national security.

While the Act offers benefits, it also poses several negative impacts on companies like Nvidia, particularly regarding export restrictions to China. Nvidia has been a key player in the industry, with significant shares of 80% of the global graphics processing unit (GPU) semiconductor market in 2023. Based on the recent Nvidia Corporation (2024) report, international revenue (other than the US) accounts for 69% of its total revenue in 2023. China is one of Nvidia's largest markets, especially for high-performance GPUs used in artificial intelligence (AI), data cent, and supercomputing. Corresponding to the Act, the US government has imposed restrictions on advanced computing chips by setting thresholds on the performance level of chips that can be exported to China. In response to this restriction, Nvidia introduced modified versions of its performance GPUs for the Chinese market. For instance, the company developed the A800 GPU, a variant of the A100 GPU, designed specifically to comply with the thresholds on export control regulations to serve Chinese customers.

In addition to adjusting product lines for Chinese customers, Nvidia has also increased its investment in the US and strategically relocated operations back to the US. This reshoring strategy helped the company to capitalize on the CHIPS Act's funding for innovation and workforce development. On the other hand, the company was forced to relocate specific operations, including testing, validation, supply, and distribution, out of China and Hong Kong. This relocation has resulted in significant expenses and delays, requiring substantial investments in new factories, infrastructure, and human capital.

Furthermore, the CHIPS and Science Act have broader implications for the global semiconductor market. It inspires other countries to promote similar policies with the objective of prioritizing their domestic semiconductor industries. As a response to the Act, in September 2024, the Chinese government put pressure on local firms to use local chips instead of Nvidia's AI chips as part of a broader strategy to grow the country's semiconductor sector and respond to US sanctions. This condition leads to a more fragmented global semiconductor market that presents a threat to Nvidia as one of the prominent global players in the industry.

Conclusion

Globalization has changed in response to ongoing geopolitical turmoil. Traditional paradigms of open markets and seamless international cooperation are being reevaluated as nations are under internal and external pressures. The rise of protectionism, shifting power between countries, and regional conflicts have introduced complexities that challenge the very essence of globalization. The rapid economic growth in emerging markets and the desire to seek more political power fuelled the political competition between emerging markets and developed countries, which further gave rise to protectionism that hindered the trend of globalization. Looking ahead, the future of globalization is likely to be characterized by a more fragmented world.

To cope with the challenges associated with an increasingly fragmented world, MNEs have to include geopolitical risks in their risk management portfolio and adjust their global penetrations. From the demand end, firms need to diversify their customer base and invest in regional partnerships to mitigate risks associated with overreliance on any single nation or region. From the supply end, firms can adopt a combination of reshoring, friend-shoring, and nearshoring strategies to achieve supply chain resilience. By using case studies, this chapter illustrates the dynamic future ahead of firms in managing these trends.

References

Antràs, P. (2020). Conceptual aspects of global value chains. *The World Bank Economic Review*, *34*(3), 551–574. https://doi.org/10.1093/wber/lhaa006

Caldara, D., & Iacoviello, M. (2022). Measuring geopolitical risk. *American Economic Review*, *112*(4), 1194–1225. https://doi.org/10.1257/aer.20191823

Casas-Klett, T., & Li, J. (2021). Assessing the belt and road initiative as a narrative: Implications for institutional change and international firm strategy. *Asia Pacific Journal of Management*, *39*(3), 857–873. https://doi.org/10.1007/s10490-021-09757-x

Corporation, N. (2024). *NVIDIA corporation annual review*. https://s201.q4cdn.com/141608511/files/doc_financials/2024/ar/NVIDIA-2024-Annual-Report.pdf

Cui, V., Vertinsky, I., Wang, Y., & Zhou, D. (2023). Decoupling in international business: The 'new' vulnerability of globalization and MNEs' response strategies.

Journal of International Business Studies, 1–15. https://doi.org/10.1057/s41267-023-00602-5
Evenett, S. J. (2019). Protectionism, state discrimination, and international business since the onset of the global financial crisis. *Journal of International Business Policy*, *2*(1), 9–36. https://doi.org/10.1057/s42214-019-00021-0
Evenett, S. J., & Fritz, J. (2021). *Subsidies and market access: Towards an inventory of corporate subsidies by China, the European Union and the United States (The 28th global trade alert report issue)*. CEPR Press.
Fajgelbaum, P. D., Khandelwal, A. K., Kennedy, P. J., & Goldberg, P. K. (2020). The return to protectionism*. *The Quarterly Journal of Economics*, *135*(1), 1–55. https://doi.org/10.1093/qje/qjz036
Fischer, S. (2003). Globalization and its challenges. *American Economic Review*, *93*(2), 1–30. http://www.jstor.com/stable/3132195
Fund, I. M. (2018). *World economic outlook: Challenges to steady growth (World economic outlook issue)*. D. I. M. F. (Original work published 1980).
Fund, I. M. (2023). *World economic outlook: A rocky recovery (World economic outlook issue)*. D. I. M. F.
Godsell, D., Lel, U., & Miller, D. (2023). U.S. national security and de-globalization. *Journal of International Business Studies*, *54*(8), 1471–1494. https://doi.org/10.1057/s41267-023-00621-2
Gray, J. E. (2021). The geopolitics of 'platforms': The TikTok challenge. *Internet Policy Review*, *10*(2). https://doi.org/10.14763/2021.2.1557
Guenette, J. D., Kenworthy, P. G., & Wheeler, C. M. (2022). *Implications of the war in Ukraine for the global economy* (Policy Notes No. 3 Issue). Equitable Growth, Finance and Institutions.
Khorana, S., Escaith, H., Ali, S., Kumari, S., & Do, Q. (2022). The changing contours of global value chains post-COVID: Evidence from the commonwealth. *Journal Business Research*, *153*, 75–86. https://doi.org/10.1016/j.jbusres.2022.07.044
Lund, S., Manyika, J., Woetzel, J., & Barriball, E. (2020). *Risk, resilience, and rebalancing in global value chains*. Mckinsey Global Institute.
Luo, Y., & Van Assche, A. (2023). The rise of techno-geopolitical uncertainty: Implications of the United States CHIPS and science act. *Journal of International Business Studies*, 1–18. https://doi.org/10.1057/s41267-023-00620-3
Martin, R. (2011). Regional economic resilience, hysteresis and recessionary shocks. *Journal of Economic Geography*, *12*(1), 1–32. https://doi.org/10.1093/jeg/lbr019
World Bank. (2024). World bank development indicators. *The World Bank Group*.
World Trade Organization. (2023). The evolution of market access over 16 years of "world tariff profiles". *World Trade Organization*.
World Trade Organization. (2024). Trade concerns database. *World Trade Organization*. Retrieved October 2024, from https://tradeconcerns.wto.org/en

4

THE IMPACT OF GLOBAL VALUE CHAINS ON LABOUR MARKETS AND EMPLOYMENT

Ahmad Arslan

Introduction

Global value chains (GVCs) have emerged as a central tenet of the global economy, as they represent a network where different stages of design, production, and distribution of industrial goods are spread across countries (e.g., Taglioni & Winkler, 2016). These chains are governed by lead firms (mostly MNEs, i.e., multinational enterprises), which coordinate the flow of goods, services, and capital across borders. Labour markets, in this context, represent the workforce at different points along the value chain, varying in terms of wages, skills, and working conditions based on their position within the GVC (e.g., Nathan et al., 2016). The integration of labour markets into GVCs has resulted in both opportunities for economic growth (for both individuals and countries) as well as concerns about issues such as exploitation, standards degradation and precarious work conditions (e.g., Soundararajan et al., 2025).

These GVCs have consequently made labour (both blue-collar and white collar) not only distributed globally but also have caused a significant variance in the standards and conditions under which this labour operates. Hence, understanding the influences of GVCs on global labour markets has been of interest to not only academics but also practitioners and policymakers due to significant socio-economic aspects linked with this phenomenon in both developed and emerging/developing economies. On one hand, GVCs have been credited with employment growth by bringing mostly low-tech production to developing and emerging economies, as well as by integrating local industries into global production networks. It has been observed that countries with comparative advantages such as cheap labour, vast resources or strategic location became key suppliers of both goods and services in global production

DOI: 10.4324/9781003468899-4

networks in different industries and sectors. Along with manufacturing, GVCs have helped in employment creation in associated sectors such as agriculture, mining, and services (including financial and technology services). Hence, on one hand, workers in developing and emerging economies, for instance, have gained access to employment through GVC participation but often face challenges such as low wages, informal (third-party contractor) employment, and poor working conditions.

On the other hand, GVCs have received criticism from politicians as well as low-skilled workers, mostly in developed (western) economies for shift of the jobs from these locations, and resulting unemployment. The Rust Belt in the USA and deindustrialized areas in other developed economies, like Europe, are examples of how GVCs have had a big negative effect on employment in developed economies as jobs have moved to developing and emerging economies. At the same time, new highly skilled and innovation (research and development [R&D]) focused jobs have appeared in the same developed (mostly) western economies linked to GVC activities (e.g., Hauge, 2023). Hence, a major influence of GVCs on labour markets can be referred to as "labour market polarization", as explained in the next section.

Labour Market Polarization

GVCs have contributed to labour market polarization at a global level, where low-skilled jobs moved from developed to emerging and developing economies while new dynamics emerged concerning middle-skill and high-skill jobs. A common observation in this concern is that MNEs in developed (mostly western economies) often outsource labour-intensive, routine tasks to developing and emerging economies, leaving high-skilled positions related to design, innovation, and management in those advanced economies. Workers in high-skill jobs benefit from better wages and working conditions, while low-skill workers tend to face job insecurity, low wages, and limited opportunities for upward mobility. This labour market polarization is further exposed in developing and emerging economies, resulting in a more fragmented and layered labour market. Workers operating in GVCs linked to export-oriented industries (such as textiles or electronics assembly) may have access to relatively stable jobs, though often with significantly lower pay than compatriots in developed economies and weak labour protections. However, those workers who work in firms outside GVCs—particularly in informal sectors—become even more marginalized and face greater economic uncertainty and risks. This is even though some of those firms may be indirectly linked to GVCs in the form of contractors or suppliers at some level. At the same time, GVCs have also contributed to the upgrading of labour standards in certain developing economies, particularly when lead MNEs enforce strict labour standards in their supply chains. Due to an increased awareness as well as media attention, along with reputational risks, many MNEs are increasingly strict about these aspects. Moreover, within developing and emerging market economies, jobs can move on from those countries that have reached a certain level of development (e.g., China) to other countries that are still lower on the development scale (e.g., Laos or Pakistan), due to lower labour costs drive.

Labour market polarization also manifests itself in other ways in GVCs. For example, concentration of low-skill, labour-intensive activities in certain regions (mostly Asia, Africa, and Latin America) often leads to job growth in manufacturing or assembly lines in developing economies. This type of employment growth can be precarious, contingent on external demand, and heavily influenced by international trade policies. Hence, in current times, when anti-globalization sentiment is high in the USA and other western economies, such risks increase further. Additionally, such low-skilled jobs are also vulnerable to automation and shifts in GVC configurations, as MNEs can relocate their production based on cost, regulation, or technological advancement. Hence, in the case of reshoring (shifting of manufacturing activities back to the home base in a developed economy), which is another visible trend of the current times (e.g., De Luca, 2023), labour market polarization can also become more visible in developed (western) economies. This is because even though some jobs are reshored, cost and competitiveness concerns may force lead firms (MNEs) to use a multilayered hiring model consisting of their own employees, third-party contract workers, and gig workers.

After presenting an overview of labour market polarization, the discussion on wage structure and dynamics in GVCs is presented as follows.

Wage Structures and Dynamics

The integration of local firms into GVCs has significantly influenced wage structures in both developed and emerging economies (e.g., Milberg & Winkler, 2013). Wages in GVC-linked sectors often reflect the relative position of a country or firm within the whole chain. Workers in countries specializing in high-value-added segments, such as R&D or high-tech manufacturing, tend to receive relatively better wages than those focusing on labour-intensive production or raw material extraction. This segmentation reinforces global wage disparities, with workers in low-cost production hubs, particularly in emerging and developing economies, receiving significantly lower compensation than their counterparts in developed economies.

GVCs are characterized by a hierarchical structure, where different tiers represent the position and importance of the players involved. Lead firms (MNEs), typically from developed countries, occupy the top tier, overseeing design, R&D, innovation, and marketing. The middle tier includes suppliers who manufacture components, while the lower tiers are often responsible for low-value-added assembly production and, in some cases, raw material extraction. The dynamics of skills and wages vary substantially across these tiers, as briefly explained below.

Lead Firms and High-Skilled Labour: At the top of the value chain, lead firms (MNEs require high-skilled labour for research, development, and management. Workers in this tier typically enjoy high wages, job security, and favourable working conditions. For example, MNEs like Apple, Toyota, and H&M employ knowledge workers, designers, and executives at the upper tier, where wages are significantly higher than in other parts of the value chain (e.g., producers of parts/components of their products in developing/emerging economies). The high-skill requirements and the focus on innovation also push these MNEs to maintain competitive salaries and benefits to attract (and retain) talent. Hence, wage gains are visible for this specific segment in GVCs.

Suppliers and Semi-Skilled Labour: In the middle tier, suppliers engage in the production of intermediate goods or components, often requiring semi-skilled labour. These firms, while more skilled than lower-tier suppliers, face cost pressures from the lead MNEs to maintain competitive pricing, leading to wage suppression. Countries such as Mexico in the automotive sector or Taiwan and Malaysia in electronics manufacturing have developed semi-skilled labour forces to meet the needs of this tier. However, workers in these firms earn significantly lower wages than those in lead firms, despite possessing a certain level of technical skills.

Assembly and Low-Skilled Labour: At the bottom tier, assembly and raw material production rely heavily on low-skilled labour, typically in developing countries. Wages are the lowest in this tier, with workers often engaged in monotonous tasks and exposed to poor working conditions. For instance, garment assembly factories in countries like Cambodia, Pakistan, or Bangladesh employ low-skilled labour at minimum wage levels, with limited opportunities for skill upgrading or wage growth. Similarly, in the agricultural sector, workers in coffee or cocoa production in countries such as the Ivory Coast or Guatemala often receive wages far below living standards, even though the raw material produced by them is used even in elite retail outlets, restaurants, and brands.

After presenting an overview of the impacts of GVCs on labour markets and employment, the next section presents a brief practical example to show the current trends in GVCs in relation to labour markets and employment.

Practical Example: Electronics GVCs in China and Southeast Asia

The electronics manufacturing industry has been a cornerstone of China's economic ascent, placing the country at the centre of electronics GVCs (e.g., Yeung, 2022). Over the past few decades, China benefitted from its extensive labour force, robust infrastructure, and government policies in this concern.

However, a noticeable shift in electronics manufacturing towards other Southeast Asian countries, particularly Vietnam, Thailand, and Indonesia, is reshaping electronics GVCs, especially in low-tech and labour-intensive electronic manufacturing. It should be noted that Taiwan (Chinese Taipei) is already a large player in electronics manufacturing and GVCs. This shift away from China is driven by factors such as rising labour costs in China, trade tensions (particularly with the USA), and the diversification strategy of electronics MNEs. Southeast Asian nations are increasingly integrated into GVCs, benefitting from favourable trade agreements, government incentives, and a growing workforce. For instance, Vietnam has attracted significant investments from major electronics manufacturers like Samsung and Intel, transforming it into a regional production hub (e.g., Nakamura & Marukawa, 2024). This diversification reduces the overreliance on a single country, making GVCs more resilient to disruptions such as geopolitical tensions or pandemics. However, the relocation of manufacturing does not imply a complete disconnection from China (e.g., Wong et al., 2024) as most Southeast Asian nations remain dependent on China for components and raw materials (of which the majority are mined in China, especially rare earth materials), indicating regional interdependence, with China maintaining its role as a key supplier within the broader Asian electronics manufacturing ecosystem.

The shift in electronics manufacturing has significant implications for labour markets across Southeast Asia. Countries like Vietnam and Indonesia offer a relatively younger, skilled, and cost-competitive workforce compared to China. Hence, a number of new jobs are being created due to the relocation of some electronics manufacturing to these countries. However, the benefits are not evenly distributed. Skilled workers are increasingly benefitting from improved wages and employment conditions. At the same time, the emphasis on low-cost labour may mean that even though low-skilled jobs are created, the conditions may not be ideal for those workers.

In China, the electronics GVC focus has shifted towards moving up the value chain, promoting automation, artificial intelligence, and innovation-driven industries. While this transition has reduced the reliance on labour-intensive manufacturing, it has also necessitated a structural shift in employment patterns. Skilled workers and managerial staff have mostly gained from this shift in the Chinese context. Hence, this GVCs relocation requires China to develop policies for upskilling and reskilling workers who were earlier working in cost-effective, labour-intensive manufacturing to mitigate the negative influences of this shift. Finally, along with its criticality for raw material and component supply, China can further leverage its advanced manufacturing capabilities to remain integral to electronics GVCs, even as low-cost production migrates elsewhere. This is expected to result in positive outcomes for both employment patterns and wages for low- to semi-skilled workers in China.

Conclusion

GVCs are a critical element of the modern economy and will remain so despite the current anti-globalization backlash and political changes. As a result, it is anticipated that GVCs will continue to have an impact on labour markets in both developed and emerging economies in some capacity in the near future. To ensure decent work possibilities and fair wages for high-skilled, medium-skilled, and low-skilled workers, policymakers need to continue to engage with lead firms in GVCs as well as their supplier firms at the second and third tiers. Finally, as GVCs are readjusting and restructuring (e.g., in the form of reshoring and regionalization) currently due to geopolitical changes, this engagement becomes even more vital to ensure (re)skilling of those workers who lose jobs in this process.

References

De Luca, A. (2023). *Reshoring strategies in the wake of globalization and pandemics: Trends, drivers, and implications* [Doctoral dissertation, Politecnico di Torino]. https://webthesis.biblio.polito.it/28432/

Hauge, J. (2023). *The future of the factory: How megatrends are changing industrialization*. Oxford University Press.

Milberg, W., & Winkler, D. (2013). *Outsourcing economics: Global value chains in capitalist development*. Cambridge University Press.

Nakamura, H., & Marukawa, T. (2024). How can the value added of Vietnam's export industries be increased? *The Japanese Political Economy*, *50*(2), 120–140.

Nathan, D., Tewari, M., & Sarkar, S. (Eds.). (2016). *Labour in global value chains in Asia*. Cambridge University Press.

Soundararajan, V., Wilhelm, M., Crane, A., Agarwal, P., & Shetty, H. (2025). Towards a systemic approach for improving working conditions in global supply chains: An integrative review and research agenda. *Academy of Management Annals*, *19*(1), 230–264.

Taglioni, D., & Winkler, D. (2016). *Making global value chains work for development*. World Bank Publications. https://documents1.worldbank.org/curated/en/450521467989506537/pdf/106305-PUB-ADD-ISBN-DOI-AUTHORS-SERIES-ABSTRACT-OUO-9.pdf

Wong, C. Y., Yeung, H. W. C., Huang, S., Song, J., & Lee, K. (2024). Geopolitics and the changing landscape of global value chains and competition in the global semiconductor industry: Rivalry and catch-up in chip manufacturing in East Asia. *Technological Forecasting and Social Change*, *209*, 123749.

Yeung, H. W. C. (2022). *Interconnected worlds: Global electronics and production networks in East Asia*. Stanford University Press.

5

THE EVOLUTION OF PRODUCTION NETWORKS AND BUSINESS MODEL INNOVATION IN GLOBAL VALUE CHAINS

Towfique Rahman and Sanjoy Kumar Paul

Introduction

Production networks have undergone significant transformations over the past century, becoming a central component of global value chains (GVCs). Businesses and policymakers need to understand their evolution and the factors driving these changes. This chapter attempts to provide a comprehensive overview of the historical evolution of production networks, their changing nature in GVCs, the impact of regional integration dynamics, and the role of technological advancements. By incorporating contemporary case studies, the chapter offers practical insights into production network dynamics and innovative business models within GVCs (Choksy et al., 2022).

Production networks refer to the intricate web of relationships and processes involved in creating and distributing goods and services. These networks have evolved from simple, localized systems to complex, globally dispersed structures. Initially, production networks were limited to small geographical areas, often within a single country. The Industrial Revolution made a huge turning point, introducing dynamic mechanization and mass production systems that expanded the scope of production networks (Peters et al., 2023).

As global trade barriers diminished in the latter half of the 20th century, production networks extended across borders, giving rise to GVCs. These chains link various stages of production, from raw material extraction to final product assembly, across multiple countries. The significance of GVCs lies in their ability to optimize production efficiency and reduce costs by leveraging the comparative advantages of different regions. This interconnectedness has profound implications for global economic growth, employment, and development (Choksy et al., 2022).

DOI: 10.4324/9781003468899-5

This chapter offers an in-depth examination of production networks and business model innovation within GVCs. It seeks to enhance our understanding of the evolving landscape of global production and trade amid technological and economic shifts. The findings from this research can guide business strategies, influence policymaking, and support academic studies in the field of GVCs.

Historical Evolution of Production Networks

This section elaborates on the historical evolution of production networks, such as early production networks, the Industrial Revolution, and the rise of GVCs in businesses.

Early Production Networks

Early production networks were characterized by their simplicity and localization. In the preindustrial era, most production activities were confined to small, local communities. The concept of a production network was rudimentary, typically involving a linear chain of production stages from raw material extraction to the final product. Artisans and small workshops were the main producers, relying on manual labor and basic tools (Mizgier et al., 2012).

During this period, production was primarily driven by local demand and limited by the technological capabilities of the time. Trade routes, although established, were relatively slow and perilous, restricting the flow of goods and materials. The division of labor was minimal, with most production processes handled by individuals or small groups working together (Wang et al., 2012).

Despite these limitations, early production networks laid the groundwork for more complex systems. Establishing trade guilds and developing early marketplaces facilitated the exchange of goods and ideas, leading to incremental improvements in production techniques. The use of simple machines, such as looms and water mills, began to enhance productivity, although on a modest scale (Priya Datta et al., 2007).

The early production networks were also heavily influenced by geographical and cultural factors. Regions with abundant natural resources or favorable climatic conditions often became hubs of specific types of production. For example, the textile industry thrived in areas with access to high-quality wool or flax, while metalworking flourished in regions with rich mineral deposits. Though limited in scope, these early networks set the stage for the more expansive and intricate production systems that would follow (Demirel et al., 2018).

The Industrial Revolution and Its Impacts

The Industrial Revolution, which took place from the late 18th to the early 19th century, was a crucial period in the development of production networks.

Technological advancements during this period fundamentally transformed production processes and organizational structures. The introduction of mechanization, particularly in the textile industry, revolutionized how goods were produced (Glöser-Chahoud et al., 2021).

Key innovations such as the spinning jenny, the power loom, and the steam engine significantly increased production capacity and efficiency. Factories replaced small workshops, centralizing production and enabling economies of scale. The division of labor became more pronounced, with tasks subdivided into simpler, repetitive actions that unskilled workers could perform. This shift boosted productivity and reduced production costs (Tseng et al., 2022).

The Industrial Revolution also saw the rise of new industries, such as steel manufacturing and chemical production, which further diversified the production networks. Transportation infrastructure development, including railways and steamships, facilitated the movement of raw materials and finished goods over greater distances. This expansion of transport networks integrated regional markets and laid the groundwork for global trade (Nagy et al., 2016).

Moreover, the Industrial Revolution fostered significant social and economic changes. Urbanization accelerated as people moved from rural areas to cities, searching for factory jobs. This migration created dense labor markets and stimulated demand for various goods and services. The rise of capitalist economies and the growth of consumer markets further propelled the expansion of production networks (Ghosh & Shah, 2015).

The impact of the Industrial Revolution extended beyond the economic realm, influencing societal structures and cultural norms. The shift toward industrial production altered work patterns, family dynamics, and social hierarchies. The emphasis on efficiency and productivity also spurred innovation in management practices and organizational behavior, setting the stage for modern industrial enterprises (Rapaccini et al., 2020).

The Rise of GVCs

The late 20th century witnessed the emergence of GVCs, marking a new phase in the evolution of production networks. Several factors contributed to this development, including advancements in transportation and communication technologies, trade liberalization, and the globalization of markets (Choksy et al., 2022).

GVCs represent a significant departure from traditional production networks. Instead of concentrating all production stages within a single country or region, GVCs distribute different stages of production across multiple countries. This geographic dispersion allows firms to capitalize on the comparative advantages of different regions, optimizing production efficiency and cost-effectiveness (Aouad et al., 2019).

A critical driver of GVCs is the modularization of production processes. By breaking down production into discrete modules that can be outsourced to specialized suppliers, firms can achieve better flexibility and scalability. This approach reduces production costs and enables companies to respond more rapidly to changes in market demand and technological advancements (Argyres & Bigelow, 2010).

Trade liberalization policies and the establishment of regional trade agreements (RTAs) have also played a crucial role in the rise of GVCs. Reductions in tariffs and nontariff barriers have facilitated cross-border trade, making it easier for firms to source materials and components worldwide. Economic partnerships and regional integration initiatives have further enhanced the efficiency and competitiveness of GVCs (Xu & Choi, 2021).

Technological advancements, particularly in information and communication technologies (ICTs), have been instrumental in the proliferation of GVCs. The advent of the internet, digital communication tools, and advanced logistics systems has enabled seamless coordination and management of dispersed production activities. These technologies have also improved transparency and traceability within GVCs, enhancing quality control and risk management (Chesbrough, 2007).

The rise of GVCs has had profound implications for global trade and economic development. Developing countries, in particular, have benefited from integrating into GVCs, gaining access to international markets and technologies. By participating in GVCs, these countries can specialize in specific production stages, leveraging their labor and resource advantages to attract foreign investment and stimulate economic growth (Arora et al., 2010).

However, the expansion of GVCs has also raised several challenges and concerns. The reliance on dispersed production networks increases vulnerability to disruptions, such as natural disasters, geopolitical conflicts, and supply chain bottlenecks. Additionally, the unequal distribution of value-added activities within GVCs can exacerbate economic disparities between countries and regions (Mostert et al., 2021).

Therefore, the historical evolution of production networks from localized systems to complex GVCs reflects the dynamic interplay of technological, economic, and social factors. Each phase of this evolution has brought about significant changes in production processes, organizational structures, and global trade patterns. Understanding this historical context is essential for comprehending the current landscape of production networks and anticipating future developments in the global economy.

Changing Nature of Production Networks in GVCs

The contemporary landscape of production networks has evolved significantly, reflecting the dynamic and interconnected nature of the global economy. This section explores the transformation of production networks in GVCs by examining contemporary production networks, innovative production models, and distribution models (Demirel et al., 2018).

Contemporary Production Networks

Contemporary production networks are characterized by their complexity, geographical dispersion, and reliance on advanced technologies. Unlike traditional production systems that were often confined within national borders, contemporary production networks span multiple countries and continents. This global reach allows firms to leverage the comparative advantages of different regions, optimizing costs and enhancing production efficiency (Fernández-Miguel et al., 2022).

One of the defining features of contemporary production networks is their high degree of interconnectivity. Companies collaborate with numerous suppliers, manufacturers, and distributors across the globe, forming intricate webs of relationships. These networks are facilitated by advancements in communication and transportation technologies, which enable real-time coordination and efficient logistics (Zhen et al., 2016).

Flexibility and Agility in Production: In modern production networks, flexibility and agility are crucial. Companies must quickly respond to changing market conditions, consumer demands, and technological progress. To achieve this, many businesses have adopted flexible manufacturing systems that can be easily reconfigured to produce different products or modify production volumes (Wang & Webster, 2021).

For example, Toyota's production system, known for its "Just-In-Time (JIT)" manufacturing approach, emphasizes minimizing inventory and producing goods in response to demand. This system allows Toyota to reduce waste, lower costs, and respond swiftly to market fluctuations. Similarly, in the electronics industry, companies like Foxconn employ flexible production techniques to meet the diverse and rapidly changing demands of their clients, such as Apple and Samsung (Moktadir et al., 2020).

Role of ICTs: The incorporation of ICTs has played a crucial role in revolutionizing modern production networks. ICT facilitates smooth communication, data sharing, and collaboration among the participants in these networks. For instance, enterprise resource planning (ERP) systems provide companies with comprehensive tools to manage and optimize their supply chains, production processes, and logistics (Chen et al., 2019).

Additionally, digital platforms and marketplaces facilitate global sourcing and procurement. Companies can connect with suppliers worldwide, compare offerings, and make informed decisions based on real-time data. This level of connectivity and transparency enhances the efficiency and resilience of production networks, allowing firms to mitigate risks and capitalize on opportunities (Cavalcante et al., 2019).

Innovative Production Models

Lean Production: Lean production is a forward-thinking approach designed to reduce waste and enhance value. Developed from Toyota's production system, lean principles have been embraced by numerous industries. This model focuses on ongoing improvement, mapping value streams, and removing activities that do not add value (Ivanov, 2021).

For example, companies like Nike have implemented lean manufacturing techniques to streamline their production processes and improve efficiency. By adopting lean principles, Nike has reduced lead times, minimized waste, and enhanced product quality. This approach lowers costs and allows the company to respond to consumer demand and market trends effectively (Yılmaz et al., 2023).

Mass Customization: Mass customization is another innovative production model that combines the benefits of mass production and customization. It allows companies to produce goods at scale while catering to individual customer preferences. Advances in manufacturing technologies, such as 3D printing and flexible manufacturing systems, have made mass customization feasible (Kumar et al., 2016).

One notable example is Dell, which pioneered the mass customization model in the computer industry. Dell's build-to-order approach enables customers to configure their computers based on their specific requirements. This model reduces inventory costs, shortens delivery times, and enhances customer satisfaction by offering personalized products (Rahman et al., 2022).

Circular Economy and Sustainable Production: The circular economy is a new production model that prioritizes sustainability and efficient use of resources. Unlike the conventional linear model of "take-make-dispose," the aims of circular economy are to close the loop by recycling, reusing, and regenerating products and materials. This method reduces waste, conserves resources, and lessens environmental impact (Aurisano et al., 2021).

Philips and Unilever are adopting circular economy principles to enhance their sustainable production methods. Philips, for example, provides lighting as a service, enabling customers to pay for light usage instead of purchasing the equipment. This strategy motivates Philips to develop durable, energy-efficient products that are simple to maintain and upgrade. Similarly, Unilever is committed to producing all its plastic packaging reusable, biodegradable, recyclable, or compostable by 2025, aligning with its sustainability goals (Moktadir et al., 2018).

Distribution Models in GVCs

Traditional Distribution Models: Traditional distribution models in GVCs typically involve multiple intermediaries, including wholesalers, distributors, and retailers, before products reach the end consumer. This multitiered approach can add complexity and costs to the supply chain. However, it also provides extensive market reach and distribution capabilities (Das & Hanaoka, 2014).

For example, in the consumer goods industry, companies like Procter & Gamble (P&G) utilize extensive distribution networks to ensure their products are available in diverse markets. P&G's distribution strategy involves collaborating with regional distributors and retailers to penetrate local markets effectively. This approach allows P&G to leverage the expertise and infrastructure of local partners while maintaining control over its global supply chain (Peng et al., 2021).

Direct-to-Consumer (DTC) Models: The increasing use of e-commerce and digital platforms has facilitated the expansion of DTC distribution models. DTC enables companies to eliminate traditional middlemen and sell products straight to customers. This approach provides numerous benefits, such as higher profit margins, enhanced control over the customer experience, and the opportunity to collect valuable customer data (Abdolazimi et al., 2023).

Warby Parker, a DTC eyewear brand, showcases the effectiveness of this model. By selling directly to customers via its website and retail stores, Warby Parker has revolutionized the traditional eyewear market. The company provides high-quality, affordable glasses and uses customer data to improve its products and marketing strategies. The DTC approach has also allowed Warby Parker to cultivate strong customer relationships and enhance brand loyalty (Hohenstein et al., 2015).

Omnichannel Distribution: Omnichannel distribution merges various sales channels to deliver a smooth and unified customer experience. This strategy integrates online and offline channels, allowing customers to interact with the brand through various touchpoints, including e-commerce websites, mobile apps, physical stores, and social media (Zhang et al., 2021).

Retailers such as Walmart and Target have effectively adopted omnichannel strategies to improve their distribution capabilities. Walmart's omnichannel approach includes services like "buy online, pick up in-store" (BOPIS) and same-day delivery, providing customers with flexible shopping options. Target's digital and physical channels integration ensures a cohesive shopping experience, enabling customers to browse, purchase, and return products through their preferred channels (Hamzaoui-Essoussi et al., 2013).

Collaborative Distribution Networks: Collaborative distribution networks entail partnerships and alliances among companies to enhance distribution and logistics. By pooling resources, information, and infrastructure, companies can boost efficiency, lower costs, and elevate service levels (Abdolazimi et al., 2023).

For instance, in the pharmaceutical industry, companies often collaborate with third-party logistics providers (3PLs) to manage the distribution of their products. These partnerships allow pharmaceutical companies to leverage the expertise and infrastructure of 3PLs, ensuring timely and secure delivery of medications. Collaborative distribution networks also enhance visibility and traceability, enabling better inventory management and demand forecasting (Hohenstein et al., 2015).

Technological Innovations in Distribution

Technological innovations have revolutionized distribution models in GVCs. Automation, robotics, and artificial intelligence (AI) have transformed warehousing and logistics operations, improving efficiency and accuracy. For instance, Amazon's fulfillment centers utilize sophisticated robotics and automated systems to optimize the picking, packing, and shipping operations (Perotti et al., 2012).

Moreover, digital platforms and data analytics facilitate real-time shipment tracking and monitoring, boosting transparency and shortening lead times. Blockchain technology is also being investigated for its ability to enhance traceability and security in supply chains. By offering a decentralized and unchangeable ledger, blockchain can increase trust and minimize fraud risk in distribution networks (Fosso Wamba et al., 2020; Paul & Chowdhury, 2020).

The changing nature of production networks in GVCs reflects the dynamic interplay of technological, economic, and strategic factors. Contemporary production networks are characterized by their complexity, flexibility, and reliance on advanced technologies. Innovative production models, such as lean production, mass customization, and the circular economy, have transformed how goods are produced and delivered. Distribution models have also evolved, with DTC, omnichannel, and collaborative networks reshaping how products reach customers (Durach et al., 2017).

As GVCs continue to evolve, companies must adapt to these changes by leveraging technological advancements, optimizing their production and distribution strategies, and embracing innovative business models. By doing so, they can enhance their competitiveness, improve operational efficiency, and meet the ever-changing demands of the global market.

Impacts of Regional Integration Dynamics

Regional integration dynamics play a crucial role in shaping the configuration and efficiency of production networks within GVCs. This section examines the influence of RTAs, economic partnerships, and value-added distribution on the evolution of production networks and business model innovation. RTAs are treaties among several countries in a specific region aimed at boosting trade and investment by reducing or removing tariffs, quotas, and other trade barriers. These agreements foster economic integration and cooperation among the member nations, thereby improving their collective economic growth and competitiveness (APEC, 2023).

RTAs come in various forms, including free trade agreements (FTAs), customs unions, common markets, and economic unions. FTAs, such as the North American Free Trade Agreement (NAFTA), remove tariffs and trade barriers among member countries while allowing each nation to maintain its own trade policies with nonmembers. Customs unions, like the Southern Common Market (MERCOSUR), eliminate internal tariffs and establish a common external tariff for nonmember countries. Common markets, such as the European Union (EU), further integrate member economies by enabling the free movement of goods, services, capital, and labor. Economic unions, exemplified by the EU's economic and monetary union, involve even deeper economic integration, including harmonized economic policies and a shared currency (Singh, 2018).

RTAs significantly impact production networks by creating larger and more integrated markets, facilitating economies of scale, and enhancing the efficiency of production and distribution processes. By reducing trade barriers, RTAs enable companies to source raw materials and components from member countries at lower costs, optimizing their production networks.

NAFTA, which includes the United States, Canada, and Mexico, has transformed the automotive industry by integrating production processes across the three countries. Automakers can source parts and components from suppliers in different member countries, leveraging cost advantages and enhancing efficiency. This integration has created highly interconnected production networks, with parts crossing borders multiple times before final assembly (Singh, 2018).

RTAs encourage foreign direct investment (FDI) by establishing a stable and predictable trade environment. Companies are more likely to invest in production facilities within RTA member nations, confident in their preferential access to regional markets. This investment boosts local economies, creates jobs, and enhances technological capabilities.

Challenges and Opportunities: RTAs offer numerous benefits but also present challenges. The harmonization of standards and regulations can be complex and time-consuming, requiring significant coordination among member countries. Additionally, the benefits of RTAs are not always evenly distributed, with some regions or industries gaining more than others. This disparity can lead to political and economic tensions (APEC, 2023).

However, RTAs also present opportunities for innovation and collaboration. By fostering closer economic ties, member countries can collaborate on research and development (R&D) initiatives, sharing knowledge and resources to drive technological advancements. This collaboration can lead to the development of innovative business models and production techniques that enhance the competitiveness of regional industries.

Economic Partnerships

Economic partnerships extend beyond traditional trade agreements by encompassing broader aspects of economic cooperation, including investment, services, intellectual property, and regulatory alignment. These partnerships aim to create a comprehensive framework for economic integration, addressing a wide range of issues that affect cross-border trade and investment (Singh, 2018).

A prominent example of an economic partnership is the Comprehensive and Progressive Agreement for Trans-Pacific Partnership (CPTPP). This pact includes 11 Asia-Pacific countries and covers a variety of economic activities, including trade in products and services, investment, intellectual property, and environmental standards. The CPTPP aims to reduce trade barriers, enhance regulatory cooperation, and promote sustainable development among its members (Minister for Trade and Tourism Special Minister of State, 2023).

Another example is the Regional Comprehensive Economic Partnership (RCEP), which brings together 15 Asia-Pacific countries, including China, Japan, South Korea, Australia, and the ASEAN nations. RCEP aims to establish a broad economic partnership by aligning trade and investment rules, lowering tariffs, and boosting collaboration in areas such as e-commerce, intellectual property, and competition policy (ADB, 2020).

Economic partnerships enhance the integration of production networks by providing a stable and predictable framework for cross-border trade and investment. By reducing tariffs and harmonizing regulations, these partnerships facilitate the seamless flow of goods, services, and capital across member countries. This integration helps companies optimize production processes, reduce costs, and improve efficiency (ADB, 2020; Minister for Trade and Tourism Special Minister of State, 2023).

The CPTPP has enabled companies in member countries to access new markets and diversify their production networks. By reducing tariffs and nontariff barriers, the agreement has created new opportunities for businesses to source raw materials and components from a wider range of suppliers, enhancing flexibility and resilience. Additionally, the CPTPP's provisions on intellectual property and investment protection have encouraged companies to invest in R&D, driving innovation and technological advancements (Minister for Trade and Tourism Special Minister of State, 2023; Singh, 2018).

Economic partnerships also promote regulatory alignment and cooperation, reducing the complexity and cost of compliance for businesses operating in multiple countries. For instance, RCEP aims to harmonize standards and regulations across member countries, making it easier for companies to navigate different regulatory environments and streamline their operations (ADB, 2020).

Economic partnerships face several challenges, including the complexity of negotiations, the need for regulatory harmonization, and the potential for unequal distribution of benefits. Negotiating comprehensive agreements that address a wide range of economic activities requires significant coordination and compromise among member countries. Additionally, maintaining regulations, laws, and standards can be a lengthy and complex process, requiring substantial resources and cooperation (APEC, 2023; Singh, 2018).

However, economic partnerships also present significant opportunities. By fostering closer economic ties, these partnerships can enhance regional stability and promote sustainable development. They can also drive innovation and technological advancements by facilitating collaboration and knowledge sharing among member countries. For example, the CPTPP's environmental standards and sustainable development provisions encourage member countries to work together to face climate change and promote green technologies (Minister for Trade and Tourism Special Minister of State, 2023).

Value-Added Distribution

Value-added distribution refers to the process of enhancing the value of a product at various stages of the production network. This enhancement can occur through manufacturing, assembly, packaging, branding, and logistics. The distribution of value-added activities across different countries and regions is a crucial feature of GVCs, reflecting the comparative advantages of various locations (Abdolazimi et al., 2023).

The distribution of value-added activities within GVCs is influenced by many factors, including the availability of skilled labor, access to raw materials, technological capabilities, and regulatory environments. Companies strategically allocate value-added activities to different locations to optimize costs, improve efficiency, and enhance competitiveness (Hohenstein et al., 2015).

In the electronics industry, companies often source components from countries with advanced technological capabilities, such as Japan and South Korea, and assemble final products in countries that offer lower labor costs, such as China and Vietnam. This distribution of value-added activities allows companies to leverage the strengths of different regions, optimizing their production networks and reducing costs (Chunsheng et al., 2019).

Value-added distribution also has significant implications for economic development. Countries that participate in higher value-added activities, such as R&D, design, and branding, tend to capture a larger share of the economic benefits generated by GVCs. In contrast, countries focusing on lower value-added activities, such as raw material extraction and basic manufacturing, may experience slower economic growth and development.

Distributing value-added activities within GVCs presents challenges and opportunities. One challenge is the potential for economic disparities between regions specializing in high-value-added activities and those focusing on lower-value-added tasks. This disparity exacerbates income inequality and creates social and political tensions (Son & Orchard, 2013).

However, the distribution of value-added activities also presents opportunities for economic development and innovation. Countries that invest in education, infrastructure, and technological capabilities can enhance their participation in higher value-added activities, driving economic growth and development. For example, South Korea has transformed its economy by investing in education and technology, becoming a global leader in the electronics, automotive, and biotechnology industries.

Policymakers are vital in influencing the distribution of value-added activities within GVCs. By enacting policies that support education, innovation, and infrastructure development, governments can boost their countries' involvement in higher value-added activities. Furthermore, trade and investment policies that ensure the smooth flow of goods, services, and capital can enhance the efficiency and competitiveness of production networks (Paul & Chowdhury, 2020).

The EU's regional development and cohesion policies aim to reduce economic disparities among member states by promoting investment in education, infrastructure, and innovation. These policies have helped enhance the participation of less-developed regions in higher value-added activities, driving economic growth and reducing inequality. Regional integration dynamics, RTAs, economic partnerships, and value-added distribution profoundly impact the configuration and efficiency of production networks within GVCs. By reducing trade barriers, promoting regulatory alignment, and facilitating the seamless flow of goods, services, and capital, these integration efforts enhance the competitiveness and resilience of production networks (ADB, 2020).

However, the advantages of regional integration are not always equally shared, posing challenges for policymakers and businesses. To fully capitalize on regional integration, it is crucial to address economic disparities and promote inclusive growth and development. By investing in education, innovation, and infrastructure, countries can improve their involvement in higher value-added activities and secure a larger portion of the economic benefits generated by GVCs (ADB, 2020; Peng et al., 2021). As regional integration progresses, it is essential for businesses and policymakers to adapt by utilizing technological advancements, refining their production and distribution strategies, and adopting innovative business models. This approach will help them boost competitiveness, enhance operational efficiency, and meet the evolving demands of the global market.

Technological Advancements as Drivers of Change

This section describes the technological advancements as drivers of change, such as digitization, automation, modularization, outsourcing and other advanced manufacturing techniques.

Digitalization and Automation

Digitalization and automation play a pivotal role in the context of the evolution of production networks and business model innovation in GVCs. Digitalization refers to the adoption of digital technologies and processes, transforming traditional production methods into more efficient, scalable, and interconnected systems. Conversely, automation involves using technology to perform tasks with minimal human intervention, increasing productivity, and reducing errors (Upadhyay et al., 2021).

Digitalization has revolutionized production networks by enabling real-time data sharing, seamless communication, and enhanced coordination among different nodes in the network. For instance, implementing Internet of Things (IoT) devices allows for the remote monitoring and management of production processes. This connectivity ensures the synchronization of all network parts, improving efficiency and reducing downtime (Njomane & Telukdarie, 2022).

Automation further enhances production networks by streamlining repetitive tasks and optimizing workflows. RPA and AI can perform complex operations with high precision, reducing the likelihood of human error and increasing production speed. For example, in the automotive industry, companies like Tesla use automated assembly lines that integrate robots and AI to produce vehicles faster than traditional methods (Furstenau et al., 2022).

The integration of digitalization and automation into production networks has also led to significant business model innovations. Companies can now offer personalized products at scale through mass customization, responding to individual customer preferences without compromising efficiency. This capability is particularly evident in the electronics industry, where firms like Dell and HP allow customers to configure their products online before production (Ambrogio et al., 2022).

Additionally, digital platforms have facilitated the emergence of new business models like subscription services and pay-per-use. For instance, companies such as Siemens and General Electric provide machinery and equipment as a service, allowing customers to pay based on usage instead of purchasing the equipment outright. This model lowers upfront costs for customers and guarantees ongoing revenue for the providers (Xu & Dang, 2020).

Modularization and Outsourcing

Modularization and outsourcing are critical components of the evolution of production networks, significantly impacting GVCs by promoting flexibility and cost efficiency. Modularization involves breaking down production processes into distinct modules that can be independently developed and assembled. Outsourcing, meanwhile, refers to contracting out certain production activities to external suppliers (Kamalahmadi et al., 2021).

Modularization allows for greater adaptability in production networks. By standardizing components and processes, firms can quickly adjust to dynamic changes in demand or integrate new technologies without overhauling the entire system. For example, the smartphone industry heavily relies on modularization, with companies like Apple and Samsung using standardized components that can be easily sourced and assembled (Rahman et al., 2022).

Outsourcing complements modularization by enabling firms to leverage the expertise and cost advantages of external suppliers. This approach allows companies to focus on core competencies while relying on specialized partners for other aspects of production. The apparel industry is a prime example, where brands like Nike and Adidas design and market their products but outsource manufacturing to countries with lower labor costs (Sayed et al., 2020).

The combination of modularization and outsourcing has led to the rise of platform-based business models. Companies like Amazon and Alibaba operate vast e-commerce platforms connecting millions of buyers and sellers, facilitating transactions without owning the inventory. This model relies on a modular approach to logistics and distribution, where various service providers handle different stages of the process (Martínez-Noya & García-Canal, 2018).

Furthermore, the gig economy, exemplified by companies like Uber and Airbnb, leverages outsourcing by utilizing independent contractors to provide services. This model reduces operational costs and increases scalability, allowing companies to expand rapidly without significant capital investment (Rahman et al., 2022; Xu & Choi, 2021).

Advanced Manufacturing Techniques

Advanced manufacturing mechanisms, including additive manufacturing such as 3D printing, advanced materials, and nanotechnology transform production networks and foster business model innovation in GVCs. These technologies enable more precise, efficient, and sustainable production processes (Abedian et al., 2022). Additive manufacturing allows for the creation of complex, customized products with minimal waste. This technique is particularly beneficial in industries such as aerospace and healthcare, where precision and customization are crucial. Companies like Boeing and General Electric use 3D printing to produce lightweight, high-strength components that enhance performance and reduce costs (Bastas & Garza-Reyes, 2022).

Advanced materials, such as composites and smart materials, provide superior properties compared to traditional materials, enabling the production of lighter, stronger, and more durable products. Nanotechnology further enhances manufacturing by allowing manipulation at the molecular level, leading to innovations in electronics, medicine, and energy storage (Babaei et al., 2023). The adoption of advanced manufacturing techniques has led to the development of decentralized production models. With 3D printing, companies can establish localized production hubs closer to their customers, reducing shipping costs and lead times. This approach is evident in the footwear industry, where brands like Adidas have set up "Speedfactories" that use 3D printing to produce shoes on demand (Jain et al., 2017; Rahman et al., 2022).

Moreover, advanced materials and nanotechnology have created entirely new product categories. For instance, smart textiles embedded with sensors can monitor health metrics, opening up opportunities for companies in the healthcare and fitness industries to offer innovative products and services (Adobor & McMullen, 2018).

Technological advancements in digitalization, automation, modularization, outsourcing, and advanced manufacturing techniques are driving significant changes in production networks and business models within GVCs. These technologies enhance efficiency, flexibility, and scalability, enabling companies to innovate and adapt to the dynamic global market. As firms continue to integrate these advancements, they will unlock new opportunities for growth and competitive advantage in the evolving global trade landscape (Sayed et al., 2020).

Innovative Business Models in GVCs

This section discusses the emergence of new business models and business value creation. The evolution of production networks and advanced technologies has catalyzed the emergence of new business models within GVCs. These innovative models transform how companies operate, compete, and create value in an increasingly interconnected and dynamic global market.

One of the most significant developments in GVCs is the rise of digital platforms and ecosystems. Companies like Amazon, Alibaba, and Google have leveraged digital technologies to create platforms that connect multiple stakeholders, including producers, consumers, and service providers. These platforms facilitate seamless transactions and interactions, enabling businesses to reach a global audience with minimal barriers (Rahman et al., 2022).

Digital platforms operate on network effects, where the value of the platform increases as more users join. This model allows companies to scale rapidly and create robust ecosystems that encompass a wide range of products and services. For instance, Amazon started as an online bookstore but has evolved into a comprehensive digital ecosystem offering e-commerce, cloud computing, and streaming services (Michel-Villarreal et al., 2021).

Servitization: Another emerging business model in GVCs is servitization, which involves shifting from selling products to offering integrated products and services. This model focuses on delivering value through service-based solutions rather than traditional product sales. Companies like Rolls-Royce and General Electric have successfully implemented servitization by offering "power by the hour" and "outcome-based" services, where customers pay for the performance and reliability of equipment rather than owning it (Rahman et al., 2022).

Servitization enables companies to build long-term relationships with customers, generate recurring revenue, and differentiate themselves from competitors. It also encourages continuous innovation and improvement, as companies must ensure their services consistently meet customer needs and expectations (Liu et al., 2018).

Circular Economy: The circular economy model focuses on sustainability and resource efficiency by encouraging the reuse, recycling, and regeneration of materials. Unlike the traditional linear economy of "take-make-dispose," the circular economy seeks to close the loop, reducing waste and minimizing environmental impact (Aurisano et al., 2021).

Companies such as Philips and IKEA are at the forefront of embracing circular economy principles. Philips provides lighting as a service, allowing customers to pay for light usage instead of buying the equipment. This approach motivates Philips to create durable, energy-efficient products that are easy to maintain and upgrade. Similarly, IKEA has introduced programs to encourage customers to return used furniture for refurbishment and resale, thereby reducing waste and promoting sustainability (Khan et al., 2021).

Value Creation and Competitive Advantage

Innovative business models within GVCs are reshaping how companies create value and achieve competitive advantage. These models leverage technological advancements, strategic partnerships, and customer-centric approaches to enhance value creation and strengthen market positioning.

Enhanced Customer Experience: One of the main drivers of value generation in innovative business models is the focus on enhancing customer experience. Companies leverage digital technologies and data analytics to understand customer preferences, personalize offerings, and provide seamless interactions across multiple channels. For instance, Starbucks uses its mobile app to offer personalized rewards and promotions, enhancing customer loyalty and driving repeat business (Mitręga & Choi, 2021).

Operational Efficiency: Innovative business models drive value creation through improved operational efficiency. Companies can streamline production processes, reduce costs, and increase productivity by adopting advanced manufacturing techniques, automation, and digital tools. For example, Toyota's lean manufacturing approach minimizes waste and optimizes resource utilization, allowing the company to deliver high-quality products at competitive prices (Moktadir et al., 2020).

Strategic Partnerships: Strategic partnerships and collaborations are crucial for creating value and gaining a competitive edge in GVCs. Companies increasingly form alliances with suppliers, technology providers, and other stakeholders to leverage complementary capabilities and access new markets. For instance, Apple collaborates with various suppliers worldwide to source high-quality components and ensure efficient production and assembly of its products (Vecchi et al., 2020).

Innovation, Research and Development: Investing in innovation, R&D is another critical factor in value creation and competitive advantage. Companies prioritizing innovation can develop cutting-edge products and services, differentiate themselves from competitors, and capture new market opportunities. Tesla, for example, invests in R&D to accelerate electric vehicle (EV) technology and expand its product portfolio, maintaining its leadership in the automotive industry (Martínez-Noya & García-Canal, 2018; Parast, 2020). Several companies have successfully implemented innovative business models within GVCs, demonstrating the potential for value creation and competitive advantage. The following are some examples of innovation initiated by several world-renowned companies.

Tesla's business model innovation revolves around its integrated approach to EVs. Unlike traditional automakers, Tesla controls the entire value chain, from designing and manufacturing to sales and service. This vertical integration allows Tesla to maintain high-quality standards, streamline operations, and quickly respond to market changes. Tesla's model of DTC sales also bypasses traditional dealerships, providing a seamless purchasing experience and fostering strong customer relationships (Macri, 2018).

Spotify has revolutionized the music industry with its subscription-based streaming model. By offering unlimited access to a vast library of music for a monthly fee, Spotify has attracted millions of subscribers worldwide. This model provides consistent revenue and valuable data on user preferences, enabling Spotify to personalize suggestions and increase user experience. Additionally, Spotify's freemium model enables users to enjoy basic services at no cost, with the option to upgrade to premium features. This approach effectively drives user acquisition and retention (Fund, 2019).

Uber's innovation in its business model lies in its platform-based approach to ride-hailing. Uber has created a scalable and flexible transportation solution by connecting drivers and passengers through a mobile app. The company's use of dynamic pricing, real-time data, and advanced algorithms ensures efficient matching of supply and demand, optimizing resource utilization. Uber's model has disrupted traditional taxi services and expanded into various segments, including food delivery and freight transportation (Usher, 2022).

Unilever's adoption of the circular economy model exemplifies successful business model innovation. The company has committed to making all its plastic packaging reusable, recyclable, or compostable by 2025. By integrating sustainability into its operations, Unilever reduces environmental impact and meets the growing consumer demand for eco-friendly products. This commitment to sustainability enhances Unilever's brand reputation and positions it as a leader in corporate responsibility (Engel, 2019).

Additionally, the other recent case studies also demonstrate how companies have effectively adapted to the changing dynamics of GVCs. For example, Apple Inc. has revolutionized its production networks through modularization and strategic outsourcing, while its integrated ecosystem of hardware, software, and services has driven business model innovation (APPLE, 2024). Toyota Motor Corporation has leveraged lean manufacturing principles and strategic partnerships to enhance operational efficiency and sustainability (Shih, 2022).

The emergence of innovative business models within GVCs is transforming how companies operate, compete, and create value. Digital platforms, servitization, and the circular economy are reshaping traditional business practices and driving significant changes in production networks. These models enhance customer experience, improve operational efficiency, and foster strategic partnerships, enabling companies to achieve competitive advantage in a dynamic global market. Successful examples, such as Tesla, Spotify, Uber, Apple Inc., Toyota, and Unilever, illustrate the potential of these innovative business models to drive growth and sustainability. As GVCs continue to evolve, companies must embrace these models, invest in innovation, and adapt to dynamic, changing market dynamics to thrive in the competitive landscape of global trade.

Conclusion

The evolution of production networks and business model innovation within GVCs has been a dynamic process driven by technological advancements, economic integration, and strategic business decisions. This chapter has provided a comprehensive overview of how production networks have transformed over time, highlighting key milestones, the impact of regional integration dynamics, and the role of technological advancements. By examining contemporary case studies, we have illustrated the practical implications of these insights and the emergence of innovative business models within GVCs.

Historically, production networks were simple and localized, often confined to small geographical areas. The Industrial Revolution marked a significant turning point by introducing mechanization and mass production techniques, which expanded the scope of production networks beyond national borders. This era saw the rise of factories, centralized production, and economies of scale, laying the groundwork for the complex, globally dispersed production networks that characterize GVCs today.

As global trade barriers diminished in the latter half of the 20th century, production networks extended across borders, giving rise to GVCs. These chains link various stages of production, from raw material extraction to final product assembly, across multiple countries. The significance of GVCs lies in their ability to optimize production efficiency and reduce costs by leveraging the comparative advantages of different regions. This interconnectedness has profound implications for global economic growth, employment, and development.

Technological advancements have significantly transformed production networks. Digitalization and automation have revolutionized production by enabling real-time data sharing, seamless communication, and improved coordination. Technologies like the IoT, robotic process automation (RPA), and AI have streamlined operations, boosted productivity, and minimized errors. These innovations have also led to new business models, such as mass customization and digital platforms, allowing companies to offer personalized products at scale and engage with global consumers.

Modularization and outsourcing have further enhanced the flexibility and scalability of production networks. By breaking down production into discrete modules that can be outsourced to specialized suppliers, firms can achieve greater efficiency and responsiveness to market changes. This approach has led to the rise of platform-based business models, exemplified by companies like Amazon and Alibaba, which operate vast e-commerce platforms, connecting millions of buyers and sellers.

The impact of regional integration dynamics on production networks has been significant. RTAs and economic partnerships have facilitated the seamless flow of products, services, and capital across member countries, enhancing the efficiency and competitiveness of GVCs. For example, the NAFTA integrated production processes across the United States, Canada, and Mexico, transforming industries such as automotive manufacturing. However, regional integration also presents challenges, including the need for regulatory harmonization and the potential for economic disparities between regions.

Therefore, the evolution of production networks and business model innovation in GVCs reflects the dynamic interplay of technological, economic, and social factors. Understanding this historical context is essential for comprehending the current landscape of production networks and anticipating future developments in the global economy. By embracing technological advancements, optimizing production and distribution strategies, and adopting innovative business models, companies can enhance their competitiveness, improve operational efficiency, and meet the ever-changing demands of the global market. As GVCs continue to evolve, businesses and policymakers must collaborate to address challenges, promote inclusive growth, and ensure the sustainable development of global production networks.

References

Abdolazimi, O., Salehi Esfandarani, M., Salehi, M., Shishebori, D., & Shakhsi-Niaei, M. (2023). Development of sustainable and resilient healthcare and non-cold pharmaceutical distribution supply chain for COVID-19 pandemic: A case study.

International Journal of Logistics Management, *34*(2), 363–389. https://doi.org/10.1108/IJLM-04-2021-0232

Abedian, M., Saghafinia, A., & Hejazi, M. (2022). A fuzzy analysis approach to green-resilient supplier selection in electronic manufacturing systems. *Cybernetics and Systems*, *54*(5), 577–603. https://doi.org/10.1080/01969722.2022.2067633

ADB. (2020). *Regional comprehensive economic partnership: Overview and economic impact.* https://www.adb.org/publications/regional-comprehensive-economic-partnership-impact

Adobor, H., & McMullen, R. S. (2018). Supply chain resilience: A dynamic and multidimensional approach. *International Journal of Logistics Management.* https://doi.org/10.1108/IJLM-04-2017-0093

Ambrogio, G., Filice, L., Longo, F., & Padovano, A. (2022). Workforce and supply chain disruption as a digital and technological innovation opportunity for resilient manufacturing systems in the COVID-19 pandemic. *Computers and Industrial Engineering*, *169*, 108158. https://doi.org/10.1016/j.cie.2022.108158

Aouad, A., Levi, R., & Segev, D. (2019). Approximation algorithms for dynamic assortment optimization models. *Mathematics of Operations Research.* https://doi.org/10.1287/moor.2018.0933

APEC. (2023). *Free trade agreements and regional trading agreements.* https://www.apec.org/groups/other-groups/fta_rta

APPLE. (2024). *Supply chain innovation.* https://www.apple.com/au/supply-chain/

Argyres, N., & Bigelow, L. (2010). Innovation, modularity, and vertical deintegration: Evidence from the early U.S. auto industry. *Organization Science.* https://doi.org/10.1287/orsc.1090.0493

Arora, H., Raghu, T. S., & Vinze, A. (2010). Resource allocation for demand surge mitigation during disaster response. *Decision Support Systems.* https://doi.org/10.1016/j.dss.2010.08.032

Aurisano, N., Weber, R., & Fantke, P. (2021). Enabling a circular economy for chemicals in plastics. *Current Opinion in Green and Sustainable Chemistry*, *31*, 100513. https://doi.org/10.1016/j.cogsc.2021.100513

Babaei, A., Khedmati, M., & Akbari Jokar, M. R. (2023). A new branch and efficiency algorithm for an optimal design of the supply chain network in view of resilience, inequity and traffic congestion. *Annals of Operations Research*, *321*(1–2), 49–78. https://doi.org/10.1007/s10479-022-05080-w

Bastas, A., & Garza-Reyes, J. A. (2022). Impact of the COVID-19 pandemic on manufacturing operations and supply chain resilience: Effects and response strategies. *Journal of Manufacturing Technology Management*, *33*(5), 962–985. https://doi.org/10.1108/JMTM-09-2021-0357

Cavalcante, I. M., Frazzon, E. M., Forcellini, F. A., & Ivanov, D. (2019). A supervised machine learning approach to data-driven simulation of resilient supplier selection in digital manufacturing. *International Journal of Information Management*, *49*, 86–97. https://doi.org/10.1016/j.ijinfomgt.2019.03.004

Chen, H. Y., Das, A., & Ivanov, D. (2019). Building resilience and managing post-disruption supply chain recovery: Lessons from the information and communication technology industry. *International Journal of Information Management.* https://doi.org/10.1016/j.ijinfomgt.2019.06.002

Chesbrough, H. (2007). Business model innovation: It's not just about technology anymore. *Strategy and Leadership.* https://doi.org/10.1108/10878570710833714

Choksy, U. S., Ayaz, M., Al-Tabbaa, O., & Parast, M. (2022). Supplier resilience under the COVID-19 crisis in apparel global value chain (GVC): The role of GVC governance and supplier's upgrading. *Journal of Business Research*, *150*, 249–267. https://doi.org/10.1016/j.jbusres.2022.05.068

Chunsheng, L., Wong, C. W. Y., Yang, C. C., Shang, K. C., & Lirn, T. C. (2019). Value of supply chain resilience: Roles of culture, flexibility, and integration.

International Journal of Physical Distribution and Logistics Management. https://doi.org/10.1108/IJPDLM-02-2019-0041

Das, R., & Hanaoka, S. (2014). An agent-based model for resource allocation during relief distribution. *Journal of Humanitarian Logistics and Supply Chain Management*. https://doi.org/10.1108/JHLSCM-07-2013-0023

Demirel, S., Kapuscinski, R., & Yu, M. (2018). Strategic behavior of suppliers in the face of production disruptions. *Management Science*, *64*(2), 533–551. https://doi.org/10.1287/mnsc.2016.2626

Durach, C. F., Glasen, P. C., & Straube, F. (2017). Disruption causes and disruption management in supply chains with Chinese suppliers: Managing cultural differences. *International Journal of Physical Distribution and Logistics Management*. https://doi.org/10.1108/IJPDLM-07-2017-0228

Engel, M. (2019). *Supply chain transformation: Towards a purpose led future fit supply ecosystem*. https://www.unilever.com/files/origin/aa2b7261b82d3493319d4f46176e4e245a45c051.pdf/Investor-Event-2019-Marc-Engel-Supply-Chain.pdf

Fernández-Miguel, A., Riccardi, M. P., Veglio, V., García-Muiña, F. E., Fernández del Hoyo, A. P., & Settembre-Blundo, D. (2022). Disruption in resource-intensive supply chains: Reshoring and nearshoring as strategies to enable them to become more resilient and sustainable. *Sustainability (Switzerland)*, *14*(17). https://doi.org/10.3390/su141710909

Fosso Wamba, S., Queiroz, M. M., & Trinchera, L. (2020). Dynamics between blockchain adoption determinants and supply chain performance: An empirical investigation. *International Journal of Production Economics*. https://doi.org/10.1016/j.ijpe.2020.107791

Fund, E. D. (2019). *What the world needs now? Spotify for sustainable supply chains*. https://www.forbes.com/sites/edfenergyexchange/2019/02/27/what-the-world-needs-now-spotify-for-sustainable-supply-chains/

Furstenau, L. B., Zani, C., Terra, S. X., Sott, M. K., Choo, K. K. R., & Saurin, T. A. (2022). Resilience capabilities of healthcare supply chain and supportive digital technologies. *Technology in Society*, *71*, 102095. https://doi.org/10.1016/j.techsoc.2022.102095

Ghosh, D., & Shah, J. (2015). Supply chain analysis under green sensitive consumer demand and cost sharing contract. *International Journal of Production Economics*, *164*, 319–329. https://doi.org/10.1016/j.ijpe.2014.11.005

Glöser-Chahoud, S., Huster, S., Rosenberg, S., Baazouzi, S., Kiemel, S., Singh, S., Schneider, C., Weeber, M., Miehe, R., & Schultmann, F. (2021). Industrial disassembling as a key enabler of circular economy solutions for obsolete electric vehicle battery systems. *Resources, Conservation and Recycling*, *174*, 105735. https://doi.org/10.1016/j.resconrec.2021.105735

Hamzaoui-Essoussi, L., Sirieix, L., & Zahaf, M. (2013). Trust orientations in the organic food distribution channels: A comparative study of the Canadian and French markets. *Journal of Retailing and Consumer Services*. https://doi.org/10.1016/j.jretconser.2013.02.002

Hohenstein, N. O., Feise, E., Hartmann, E., & Giunipero, L. (2015). Research on the phenomenon of supply chain resilience: A systematic review and paths for further investigation. *International Journal of Physical Distribution and Logistics Management*. https://doi.org/10.1108/IJPDLM-05-2013-0128

Ivanov, D. (2021, February). Lean resilience: AURA (active usage of resilience assets) framework for post-COVID-19 supply chain management. *International Journal of Logistics Management*. https://doi.org/10.1108/IJLM-11-2020-0448

Jain, V., Kumar, S., Soni, U., & Chandra, C. (2017). Supply chain resilience: Model development and empirical analysis. *International Journal of Production Research*. https://doi.org/10.1080/00207543.2017.1349947

Kamalahmadi, M., Shekarian, M., & Mellat Parast, M. (2021). The impact of flexibility and redundancy on improving supply chain resilience to disruptions. *International Journal of Production Research*, 1–29. https://doi.org/10.1080/00207543.2021.1883759

Khan, S. A. R., Ponce, P., Tanveer, M., Aguirre-Padilla, N., Mahmood, H., & Shah, S. A. A. (2021). Technological innovation and circular economy practices: Business strategies to mitigate the effects of COVID-19. *Sustainability (Switzerland)*, *13*(15), 1–17. https://doi.org/10.3390/su13158479

Kumar, S., Luthra, S., Govindan, K., Kumar, N., & Haleem, A. (2016). Barriers in green lean six sigma product development process: An ISM approach. *Production Planning and Control*. https://doi.org/10.1080/09537287.2016.1165307

Liu, C. L., Shang, K. C., Lirn, T. C., Lai, K. H., & Lun, Y. H. V. (2018). Supply chain resilience, firm performance, and management policies in the liner shipping industry. *Transportation Research Part A: Policy and Practice*. https://doi.org/10.1016/j.tra.2017.02.004

Macri, K. P. (2018). *Case study: How Tesla changed the auto industry*. https://www.supplychaindive.com/news/case-study-how-tesla-changed-the-auto-industry/517251/

Martínez-Noya, A., & García-Canal, E. (2018). Location, shared suppliers and the innovation performance of R&D outsourcing agreements. *Industry and Innovation*. https://doi.org/10.1080/13662716.2017.1329085

Michel-Villarreal, R., Vilalta-Perdomo, E. L., Canavari, M., & Hingley, M. (2021). Resilience and digitalization in short food supply chains: A case study approach. *Sustainability (Switzerland)*, *13*(11), 1–23. https://doi.org/10.3390/su13115913

Minister for Trade and Tourism Special Minister of State. (2023). *Comprehensive and progressive agreement for trans-pacific partnership (CPTPP) joint ministerial statement*. https://www.trademinister.gov.au/minister/don-farrell/statements/comprehensive-and-progressive-agreement-trans-pacific-partnership-cptpp-joint-ministerial-statement

Mitręga, M., & Choi, T. M. (2021). How small-and-medium transportation companies handle asymmetric customer relationships under COVID-19 pandemic: A multi-method study. *Transportation Research Part E: Logistics and Transportation Review*, *148*. https://doi.org/10.1016/j.tre.2021.102249

Mizgier, K. J., Wagner, S. M., & Holyst, J. A. (2012). Modeling defaults of companies in multi-stage supply chain networks. *International Journal of Production Economics*. https://doi.org/10.1016/j.ijpe.2010.09.022

Moktadir, M. A., Dwivedi, A., Rahman, A., Chiappetta Jabbour, C. J., Paul, S. K., Sultana, R., & Madaan, J. (2020). An investigation of key performance indicators for operational excellence towards sustainability in the leather products industry. *Business Strategy and the Environment*, *29*(8), 3331–3351. https://doi.org/10.1002/bse.2575

Moktadir, M. A., Rahman, T., Rahman, M. H., Ali, S. M., & Paul, S. K. (2018). Drivers to sustainable manufacturing practices and circular economy: A perspective of leather industries in Bangladesh. *Journal of Cleaner Production*. https://doi.org/10.1016/j.jclepro.2017.11.063

Mostert, C., Sameer, H., Glanz, D., & Bringezu, S. (2021). Climate and resource footprint assessment and visualization of recycled concrete for circular economy. *Resources, Conservation and Recycling*, *174*, 105767. https://doi.org/10.1016/j.resconrec.2021.105767

Nagy, D., Schuessler, J., & Dubinsky, A. (2016). Defining and identifying disruptive innovations. *Industrial Marketing Management*. https://doi.org/10.1016/j.indmarman.2015.11.017

Njomane, L., & Telukdarie, A. (2022). Impact of COVID-19 food supply chain: Comparing the use of IoT in three South African supermarkets. *Technology in Society*, *71*, 102051. https://doi.org/10.1016/j.techsoc.2022.102051

Parast, M. M. (2020). The impact of R&D investment on mitigating supply chain disruptions: Empirical evidence from U.S. firms. *International Journal of Production Economics*. https://doi.org/10.1016/j.ijpe.2020.107671

Paul, S. K., & Chowdhury, P. (2020). A production recovery plan in manufacturing supply chains for a high-demand item during COVID-19. *International Journal of Physical Distribution and Logistics Management*. https://doi.org/10.1108/IJPDLM-04-2020-0127

Peng, X., Ji, S., Thompson, R. G., & Zhang, L. (2021). Resilience planning for Physical Internet enabled hyperconnected production-inventory-distribution systems. *Computers and Industrial Engineering*, *158*, 107413. https://doi.org/10.1016/j.cie.2021.107413

Perotti, S., Zorzini, M., Cagno, E., & Micheli, G. J. L. (2012). Green supply chain practices and company performance: The case of 3PLs in Italy. *International Journal of Physical Distribution & Logistics Management*, *42*(7), 640–672. https://doi.org/10.1108/09600031211258138

Peters, E., Knight, L., Boersma, K., & Uenk, N. (2023). Organizing for supply chain resilience: A high reliability network perspective. *International Journal of Operations and Production Management*, *43*(1), 48–69. https://doi.org/10.1108/IJOPM-03-2022-0167

Priya Datta, P., Christopher, M., & Allen, P. (2007). Agent-based modelling of complex production/distribution systems to improve resilience. *International Journal of Logistics Research and Applications*. https://doi.org/10.1080/13675560701467144

Rahman, T., Paul, S. K., Shukla, N., Agarwal, R., & Taghikhah, F. (2022). Supply chain resilience initiatives and strategies: A systematic review. *Computers and Industrial Engineering*, *170*, 108317. https://doi.org/10.1016/j.cie.2022.108317

Rapaccini, M., Saccani, N., Kowalkowski, C., Paiola, M., & Adrodegari, F. (2020). Navigating disruptive crises through service-led growth: The impact of COVID-19 on Italian manufacturing firms. *Industrial Marketing Management*. https://doi.org/10.1016/j.indmarman.2020.05.017

Sayed, M., Hendry, L. C., & Zorzini Bell, M. (2020). Sustainable procurement: Comparing in-house and outsourcing implementation modes. *Production Planning and Control*. https://doi.org/10.1080/09537287.2020.1717661

Shih, W. C. (2022). What really makes Toyota's production system resilient. *Harvard Business Review*. https://hbr.org/2022/11/what-really-makes-toyotas-production-system-resilient

Singh, G. C. M. P. J. (2018). Regional trade agreements and their impact on export firms. *Australasian Journal of Regional Studies*. https://www.anzrsai.org/assets/Uploads/PublicationChapter/AJRS–24.2-pages-237-to–255.pdf

Son, J. Y., & Orchard, R. K. (2013). Effectiveness of policies for mitigating supply disruptions. *International Journal of Physical Distribution and Logistics Management*. https://doi.org/10.1108/IJPDLM-04-2012-0109

Tseng, M. L., Bui, T. D., Lim, M. K., Fujii, M., & Mishra, U. (2022). Assessing data-driven sustainable supply chain management indicators for the textile industry under industrial disruption and ambidexterity. *International Journal of Production Economics*, *245*, 108401. https://doi.org/10.1016/j.ijpe.2021.108401

Upadhyay, A., Mukhuty, S., Kumar, V., & Kazancoglu, Y. (2021). Blockchain technology and the circular economy: Implications for sustainability and social responsibility. *Journal of Cleaner Production*, *293*, 126130. https://doi.org/10.1016/j.jclepro.2021.126130

Usher, I. (2022). *Uber case study | success story, and SWOT analysis*. https://idea-usher.medium.com/uber-case-study-success-story-and-swot-analysis-5a323a918fd

Vecchi, V., Cusumano, N., & Boyer, E. J. (2020). Medical supply acquisition in Italy and the United States in the era of COVID-19: The case for strategic procurement

and public–private partnerships. *American Review of Public Administration*, *50*(6–7), 642–649. https://doi.org/10.1177/0275074020942061
Wang, X., Chan, H. K., Yee, R. W. Y., & Diaz-Rainey, I. (2012). A two-stage fuzzy-AHP model for risk assessment of implementing green initiatives in the fashion supply chain. *International Journal of Production Economics*, *135*(2), 595–606. https://doi.org/10.1016/j.ijpe.2011.03.021
Wang, Y., & Webster, S. (2021). Product flexibility strategy under supply and demand risk. *Manufacturing & Service Operations Management*. https://doi.org/10.1287/msom.2021.1037
Xu, X., & Choi, T. M. (2021). Supply chain operations with online platforms under the cap-and-trade regulation: Impacts of using blockchain technology. *Transportation Research Part E: Logistics and Transportation Review*, *155*, 102491. https://doi.org/10.1016/j.tre.2021.102491
Xu, Z., & Dang, Y. (2020). Automated digital cause-and-effect diagrams to assist causal analysis in problem-solving: A data-driven approach. *International Journal of Production Research*, *58*(17), 5359–5379. https://doi.org/10.1080/00207543.2020.1727043
Yılmaz, Ö. F., Yeni, F. B., Gürsoy Yılmaz, B., & Özçelik, G. (2023). An optimization-based methodology equipped with lean tools to strengthen medical supply chain resilience during a pandemic: A case study from Turkey. *Transportation Research Part E: Logistics and Transportation Review*, *173*, 103089. https://doi.org/10.1016/j.tre.2023.103089
Zhang, L., Wu, L., Huang, L., & Zhang, Y. (2021). Wield the power of omni-channel retailing strategy: A capability and supply chain resilience perspective. *Journal of Strategic Marketing*, 1–25. https://doi.org/10.1080/0965254X.2021.1972440
Zhen, X., Li, Y., Cai, G. G., & Shi, D. (2016). Transportation disruption risk management: Business interruption insurance and backup transportation. *Transportation Research Part E: Logistics and Transportation Review*, *90*, 51–68. https://doi.org/10.1016/j.tre.2016.01.005

6

THE ROLE OF TECHNOLOGY IN TRANSFORMING GLOBAL VALUE CHAINS

Dolly Gaur, Abhinav Pal, Kanishka Gupta, Rashida Salmani and Abhishek Behl

Introduction

Global value chains (GVCs) describe the entire value chain that industries and companies undertake through the production process, from idea development to customer usage worldwide. These chains consist of various forms of linked up companies across many countries within different continents—suppliers, manufacturers, logistics, etc. Today, outsourcing has grown to be among the most critical features of the globalization process, allowing companies to manage production processes in the best way possible, given the geographic division of work and world resources. Advancements in technological requirements for GVCs are now a critical factor that amplifies efficiency and sustainability. Blockchain technologies offer significant advantages in that they are impervious to modification, which allows them to maintain systematic records of transaction processes in supply chain management (SCM). Additionally, data analytics technologies, such as big data analytics, significantly mitigate risks associated with supply chain disruptions and enhance the decision-making process (Kuang & Luo, 2023). The application of the Internet of Things (IoT) and artificial intelligence (AI) through Industry 4.0 fine-tunes operations and enhances resource utilization and adaptability to market fluctuations (Rodchenko & Prus, 2023).

Furthermore, the digitalization of GVCs is a need for moving towards sustainability as it will create a clear path of accountability and transparency to regulatory standards and consumers' demands (Zhang, 2023). Incorporation of such technologies offers organizations more robust end-to-end operations while paving the way for a more sustainable global supply chain environment (Zelbst et al., 2023). IBM and Maersk developed blockchain-based products

DOI: 10.4324/9781003468899-6

like TradeLens cooperatively, thereby providing end-to-end supply chain visibility and improving shipping productivity. General Electric has used big data analytics through its Predix platform to optimize machinery preventive maintenance schedules in the area of energy and aviation operations. Using real-time data of IoT-enabled devices, the platform at GE does away with breakdown and maintenance to machines. It enables and enhances productivity in the productive aspect along with the production resilience in GVCs. Amazon uses AI while standardizing its inventory coupled with logistics. Utilizing the predictive analytics system provides an optimum degree of inventories along with avoiding the stock-outs against the demands of the clients, resulting in minimizing any unwanted inventories coupled with the wastage of inventory in the warehouses.

GVCs' evolution with the help of technology goes beyond mere efficiency: technology is driving a change in production models to more sustainable and responsible ones. The growth in green technologies and newer smart manufacturing methods is forcing organizations to minimize or eliminate their waste emissions and to embrace circular economy practices. Technology will be at the forefront of shaping and implementing sustainable solutions across the world's industries as the global population busily addresses climate change. This book chapter addresses the concerns of how new technologies are reshaping GVCs will be discussed with examples of these technologies and their implications for production, trade, and sustainable growth. The objectives of the chapter are as follows:

1. Analyze the role of emerging technologies for efficiency, sustainability, and transparency in GVCs.
2. Identify and discuss the key technological enablers—for example, AI, IoT, blockchain—in transforming production and trade across global networks.
3. Analyze the risks and challenges of technology integration in GVCs—including cybersecurity concerns, workforce displacement, and economic disparities.

The chapter will highlight that these technological shifts have their advantages and disadvantages and identify the directions for GVCs of further development in the context of modern advanced technology.

Technology as an Enabler for GVCs

The last few decades have seen how economies have opened their doors to the world, and the emerging globalization has transformed the way businesses operate. The changing patterns of international trade have made the firms outsource the activities that were earlier being taken care of internally to their global partners while focusing on their core competencies. As explained by Gereffi et al. (2001) regarding GVCs, with the increasing popularity of business operations conducted at geographically scattered places, GVCs got traction. As suggested by Kano et al. (2020), with the integration of digital technologies, the design and managing process of GVCs got revolutionized. These technologies also drive the sustainability goals for SCM (Birkel & Müller, 2021). For instance, the application of big data analytics, smart robots, and the IoT can help collect real-time data for optimizing the processes of production, logistics, and distribution. Supporting this view, Hennelly et al. (2020) propounded that manufacturers are enjoying the benefits of technologies in the form of reduced time for the production cycle, timely order fulfillment for customers, more efficient operations, and improved supply chain agility. The statistics of 'United Nations Conference on Trade and Development (UNCTD)' provide evidence in support of a tremendous increase in technology-enabled GVCs. The period from 2005 to 2020 saw the contribution of global digital services in total exports expand from 44.73 percent to 63.55 percent (Gao et al., 2023). Showing huge potential, India reached the fourth position worldwide in making digitally delivered services available globally (Global Trade Outlook and Statistics report, World Trade Organization). India's export of digital services saw a jump of 17 percent in 2023 as compared to the previous year, making the country put a mark for itself on the globe.

Against this backdrop, this section will discuss in detail the adoption of technology for GVCs and various aspects of it.

Economics of Technology Enabled GVC

With the infusion of advanced technology, GVCs have undergone substantial remodeling, creating new economic paradigms. Technology empowers firms through cost cuts, increased productivity, and access to the market to optimize operations towards improving economic growth (Siaw & Okorie, 2022). However, with a scenario this transformative, organizations have to meet its challenges to harness the fullest possibilities of technology in GVCs. The integration of advanced technologies is an unfolding future; it will continue to reshape the GVCs' structure and dynamics, thereby shaping the way companies innovate, collaborate, and create value (Awan et al., 2022). Hence, the adoption of such transformation will be significant for companies facing challenges to survive in a more interconnected world.

The impact of technology integration into GVCs reaches labour markets in fundamental ways. Even though automation and AI may replace a few low-skilled jobs, they are expected to increase the demand for high-skilled workers who can manage and maintain the use of these technologies (Szymczak & Wolszczak-Derlacz, 2022). This shift requires workforce development and upskilling as workers learn to adapt to new job requirements. Furthermore, as companies optimize their operations through technology, they can invest in their workforce, offering training programs that enhance employee capabilities. This investment can lead to higher productivity and job satisfaction, ultimately benefitting the overall economy.

Technology adoption in GVCs can spur economic growth by harnessing efficiency and innovation. With more efficiency, firms manufacture cost-effective goods, thus reducing prices for consumers, which in turn can then spur demand and contribute to the growth of the economy. Moreover, technology-enabled GVCs improve the competitive positioning of nations in terms of attracting investment (Siaw & Okorie, 2022). Any country that makes investments in and promotes digital infrastructure and technological innovation will become an attractive destination for MNCs with operations expansion objectives. Such investment may increase the number of jobs, boost local economies, and enhance the standard of living.

Architecture of Technology as an Enabler for GVC

The technology infuses life into GVCs by providing the much-needed infrastructure, frameworks, and systems for effective and efficient communications across different geographies. The architecture of these technologies focuses on combining hardware, software, networks, and protocols to create an ecosystem that allows businesses to innovate, collaborate, and optimize processes. Understanding of this framework is pivotal for the firms aiming to reap the benefits of such technology to effectively enhance their GVCs (Szalavetz, 2019).

- *Infrastructure Layer:* The infrastructure layer of the technology architecture includes the tangible and virtual resources that act as facilitators for the business operations. Encompassing components like cloud computing and networking, the infrastructure layer proves to be substantial for the success of GVCs (Lechowski & Krzywdzinski, 2022). Cloud platforms enable businesses to access on-demand computing power and storage space, thereby reducing investment in capital-intensive physical infrastructure. Through providers such as Amazon Web Services (AWS), Microsoft Azure, and Google Cloud, it is possible to obtain solutions that can be scaled according to the specific needs of organizations. High-speed internet and strong network capabilities are what help to allow real-time communications and data exchange. Technology integration, such as 5G connectivity, increases the speed of data transmission while supporting the demand of increasingly installed IoT devices within GVCs.
- *Data Management and Analytical Layer:* The transformation of raw data into actionable insights is facilitated by the data management and analytical layer. Data warehousing enables the collection and storage of large volumes

of data coming from different sources, such as transactions, customer interactions, or operational metrics, which can be later retrieved efficiently for analysis using solutions like Snowflake or Google BigQuery. Leveraging machine learning and AI, data patterns can be analyzed to predict the trends and optimize decision-making (Akbari & Hopkins, 2022). Predictive analytics helps firms forecast market demands so that they can calibrate production and inventory accordingly.

- *Application Layer:* This includes software solutions that provide specific functionalities to enhance GVC operations (Chen, 2019). Integrating core business processes, enterprise resource planning (ERP) provides a unified view of operations and thus enables overall management of diverse activities. The SCM applications optimize the flow of goods and services through the value chain. They facilitate planning, execution, and monitoring, ensuring that products are delivered efficiently and on time. Tools like Microsoft Teams, Slack, and Trello enable groups to communicate and collaborate across global borders, fostering teamwork and innovation.
- *Integration Layer:* It ensures that several different components of the technology architecture work harmoniously together. For instance, Application Programming Interfaces (APIs) are used to interface several software applications together and share data or functionalities (Akbari & Hopkins, 2022). For example, using an API to connect a customer relationship management (CRM) system with an SCM application is handy because customer demand information helps drive inventory decisions. Middleware facilitates communication and data exchange between heterogeneous systems, making it possible for an organization to use existing systems while adopting new technologies.
- *Security Layer:* With increased dependence on technology in organizations, security must be robust to safeguard sensitive information and trust. Encrypting the data in transit and at rest protects sensitive information and maintains confidentiality. Technologies like encryption prevent unauthorized access and data breaches (Lechowski & Krzywdzinski, 2022). A very strong authentication and authorization protocol is to be used to limit access to certain systems and data by only authorized users. This is imperative, especially for GVCs, where several stakeholders interact and access different types of systems. Up-to-date security measures in the form of firewalls and intrusion detection protect the technology architecture integrity.

Design of Technology as an Enabler for GVC

Technology design enables GVCs to design systems not only to be functional but also to align with the strategic goals of organizations. A well-designed technological ecosystem supports collaboration, efficiency, and in-real-time data exchange for various stakeholders (Kano et al., 2020). As business engages in global markets, there is an increasing dependency on technology, and thus, understanding technology design principles to optimize GVC operations becomes imperative. A user-centric design philosophy is about putting the needs and experiences of the end users, whether they are an employee, supplier, or customer, at the forefront of product design and use. It should be intuitive and easy to use, driving adoption and engagement. A modular design approach makes it possible to develop and integrate disparate technology components that are part of the overall architecture; in the case of GVCs, requirements might come about based on market demands or business strategies. This is a measure where heterogeneous systems and technologies share information and cooperate seamlessly. In a GVC, smooth operations for stakeholders' diverse systems require interoperability. In an integrated GVC, security issues about technology increase with the centrality of technology in this process. Security in the design of technology requires proactive measures to protect sensitive data and create trust among stakeholders.

Diffusion and Adoption of Technologies in GVC

The fusion of technology has further revamped the GVCs, gradually changing the business scenarios. Some of the factors that have come into play in transforming the integration process include globalization, competition, and improvements in digital infrastructure. In the outset, improved communication tools like emails, teleconferencing, and, in due course, the arrival of instant messaging platforms led the way in unifying technology with GVCs (Sanguineti et al., 2023). These tools were able to better connect business people from remote locations, providing the platform for joint venture business deals and ultimately paving the way for more advanced systems. This, in turn, facilitated collaborations among global partners, enabling rationalized negotiations and coordination. The other major stride was the introduction of information systems, including ERP and SCM software. In this context, organizations are now enabled to account for data in one place, automate processes, and enhance visibility along their supply chain (Fedyunina et al., 2024). Cloud computing was another shift in the management of business operations. Because data and applications can now be hosted from a remote location, organizations have the liberty and flexibility to scale (Birkel & Müller, 2021). As organizations have started gathering such massive amounts of data, analytics has become a new need. With advanced analytics and big data tools, companies started gathering insights from this humongous data, thus leading to decision-making with higher degrees of intelligence. Technological change in robotics and AI is driving automation in the processes, which minimizes human error and reduces manual labour within GVCs (Hennelly et al., 2020). The IoT enables physical devices to communicate with each other and gather data in real time. This integration provided untested visibility into logistics and production processes. Blockchain technology emerged as a game changer in enhancing the transparency and security of GVCs. It allows for the secure tracking of transactions and origins through a decentralized and immutable ledger.

Sustainability and Technology in GVCs

Sustainability and technology are very important elements in transforming GVCs into more effective, transparent, and robust GVCs. For instance, with IoT, one can monitor and manage the usage of resources optimally, reduce wastage, increase the transparency of supply chains through blockchain technology, and make responsible investment decisions with the application of AI. This technological integration not only brings about benefits to the environment but also social responsibility through proper labour practices and fair trade. It also will promote better governance through enhanced data analytics, which enables organizations to navigate the depths of the complexity of regulation and manage risks properly. As sustainability would increasingly become crucial for companies, the use of technology is necessary to design resilient and responsible GVCs aligned with global sustainability goals. In the recent past, Unilever has applied blockchain in sourcing tea from smallholder farmers in Malawi to track them as a clarification of transparency that enhances sustainable and ethical practices. This measure supports SDG 12, "Responsible Consumption and Production", as it promotes support for farmers through incentives that rely on sustainable methods (Lei Win, 2017).

Similarly, collaboration between IBM and companies like Nestlé and Tyson Foods in their blockchain does make their chains stronger in terms of traceability. Better traceability of products, especially food items, enhances their safety in terms of sustainability compliance that helps in achieving the goals concerning sustainability, which includes SDG 8, "Decent Work and Economic Growth" (High, 2020). This section looks at these dynamics, with a particular focus on three critical dimensions: the role of technology in achieving environmental stability, social stability, and governance stability within GVCs that technology has enabled.

Environmental Stability in Technology-Enabled GVC

Environmental stability forms part of sustainable practices in technology-enabled GVCs. Technologies such as IoT and blockchain are emerging as strategic means that minimize ecological footprints. The resource use can be monitored and optimized in real time through the IoT-based approach, which makes it possible for a company to track the amount of energy consumed and emissions in terms of sensor results. Thus, informed decisions can lead to better efficiency (Qin et al., 2024). Tumula et al. (2024) add that IoT applications have a significant impact on energy efficiency and lead to a high percentage of waste reduction. Blockchain technology further adds environmental sustainability, which in itself can be read as opening up immutable records of the product's movement along the supply chain. This brings greater transparency so that companies can check for and address themselves to proper sourcing conducts. Carrefour uses blockchain to trace the origin of fresh produce, such as chickens and eggs, along its chain. No individual will tamper with the information. This can help reduce food waste, reflecting SDG 12 (Carrefour Press Release, 2019). Unilever utilizes blockchain to trace the origins of palm oil bought for use in the business. This limits deforestation. Through this, there is a reduction in wasting natural resources. This reflects SDG 12 and SDG 13 (McDermott, 2017).

In essence, Kouhizadeh and Sarkis (2018) demonstrate that blockchain reduces the risks of greenwashing by allowing stakeholders access to credible information regarding the origin and production method of products. This integration of technology concurs with circular economy thinking as a mode through which lifecycle management can be applied to reduce waste (Zhang, 2023). Tracking a product from inception to disposal can help organizations implement effective recycling and reusing policies. Home Depot is leveraging the blockchain to monitor the source of the timber acquired by them within their supply chain, therefore ensuring that there is responsible forestry and that it helps in the reduction of illegal logging to contribute to attaining environmental standards under SDG 15 (The Home Depot, Sustainable Forestry Report, 2024). Similarly, Anheuser-Busch InBev applies blockchain and IoT in tracking water usage and agricultural practices across its supply chain, hence improving resource efficiency in line with SDG 6 and SDG 13. It is undoubtedly that tracking product circulation from birth to death will help an organization to formulate the correct policy for recycling and reusing (Anheuser-Busch InBev, 2020). The World Economic Forum (2020) contended that the integration of technology in GVCs not only reduced the environmental footprint but also facilitated innovation and improved competitiveness. As a whole, IoT and blockchain must be embraced in pursuit of environmental stability and adjustments of operations with the elaborations of worldwide sustainability.

Social Stability in Technology-Enabled GVC

Social stability as a means to ensure fair labour practices and benefit to the community is of increasing importance within the modern era of technology-enabled GVCs. Some of these technologies, such as IoT and blockchain, can be so powerful towards improving the transparency of accountability in terms of how the workers are disposed of. For instance, IoT devices can monitor working conditions in real time to the point where organizations can respond to issues like unsafe working conditions or overtime instantly (Zhou et al., 2019; Egwuonwu et al., 2022). Such monitoring leads to the observance of labour standards, hence enhancing worker satisfaction. Blockchain expands this functionality further by allowing tracing along the chains of supply and, therefore, proper labour practices as well as ethical sourcing. An example is Coca-Cola, Cola who has invested in blockchain with its own supply chain with the safeguarding of the rights of all workers. Consequently, it serves as a pioneer in corporate transparency by eliminating the hazards associated with forced labour in a supply chain (Liebkind, 2019).

Similar examples include how the RSBN has employed blockchain technologies in tracing responsible sourcing based on the mineral supply chain, which highlights ethics with fair labour practices related to mining activities (Dickinson, 2020). Blockchain technology ensures to verify fair labour practices and eliminates any risk of human trafficking by having unalterable records of supply chains, as discovered by Kim and Laskowski (2018). This level of openness allows consumers to make the right purchasing decisions with the consideration of ethical aspects. For example, technology can be developed for creating opportunities regarding the training and upskilling of workers to enhance the employability and economic resilience of the latter one. Beyond checking and compliance, technology aids social stability through training or upskilling of people, enhancing employability, and overall economic resilience. As Lwesya (2022) mentions, integration of technology in the GVCs may lead to improved working conditions and empowerment of the community that can result in social stability and ultimately support a sustainable world economy.

Governance Stability in Technology-Enabled GVC

Governance stability in technology-enabled GVCs serves as a critical means of ensuring compliance, accountability, and risk control. Therefore, as organizations increasingly rely on digital tools and platforms, blockchain and AI-based technologies have emerged as very important factors for improving governance frameworks. The basic blockchain technology principle entails an immutable record that allows stakeholders to trace transactions and monitor compliance in real time. Such capability further enhances accountability and reduces fraud risk significantly to near-negligible amounts (Zhan, 2021). For example, De Beers applies blockchain technology to its diamond supply chain using the *Tracr* platform to ensure stakeholders can verify the origin and ethical sourcing of diamonds. This, in turn, builds trust and transparency in an industry otherwise opaque (Ledger Insights, 2022). Walmart's Food Trust blockchain platform traces food products from farm to shelf, thereby boosting consumer confidence and ensuring regulatory compliance through transparent records (Pixelplex, 2021).

In addition, AI-based predictive analytics will further the risk management capabilities of GVCs. Hong and Zahid (2023) stated in their study that using AI in predictive analytics might be a very effective tool for enhancing risk management so that companies will have an anticipatory approach to weaknesses within their GVCs. Moreover, technology helps in proper communication and collaboration among the stakeholders involved, which is the essence of good governance. Reports can be streamlined, and pieces of information will become available or accessible to enhance greater transparency; thus, regulatory compliance becomes easier for an organization to achieve. According to Sun et al. (2020), it is through the integration of technology that GVC governance will reduce the compliance risks while ensuring that stakeholders have trust in the end towards a more stable and robust global supply chain.

Obstacles and Risks in Technology-Driven GVCs

The integration of technology into GVCs leads to various advantages, like significant improvements in efficiency, transparency, and flexibility; it also presents a range of obstacles and risks that companies must address. These challenges are multidimensional, involving cybersecurity risks, technological disparities, and regulatory issues. Understanding and addressing these risks is crucial for companies aiming to utilize the full potential of technology while minimizing potential threats. Technology-driven GVCs face numerous obstacles and risks that can significantly impact their efficiency and sustainability. One major risk is the vulnerability of information technology systems, which can disrupt supply chain activities and lead to substantial operational setbacks (Özkan-Özen et al., 2022). Additionally, the complexity of GVCs, exacerbated by globalization and technological advancements, increases exposure to various risks, including cybersecurity threats and data management challenges (Ngo et al., 2023). Moreover, the reliance on digital technologies such as blockchain and AI introduces both opportunities and risks. While these technologies can enhance transparency and efficiency, they also require substantial investment and pose integration challenges across different regions and sectors (Hongjiang et al., 2024). Furthermore, geopolitical tensions, particularly between major economies like the United States and China, can lead to disruptions in supply chains, affecting the stability and predictability of GVC operations.

In many ways, technology is improving GVCs, but it is also potentially making inequalities worse. One persistent challenge for the effective and equitable implementation of technologies is the so-called digital divide, distinguishing between developed and developing countries. Most developing nations have not benefitted from complex technologies such as AI, robotics, and blockchain and the rest due to inadequate infrastructure, skills, and resources. These causes result in a competitive disadvantage for firms located in such regions, owing to the fact that their technological capabilities remain far behind those nations. Consequently, such organizations may be locked out of accessing higher value segments of GVCs that could help them innovate, diversify, and generate employment. Technological disparity is also observed at interfirm levels and often arises because numerous small firms are often unable to expand the necessary capital which is required for the implementation of such superior technologies. The global 1,000 giants are in the position to implement the newest innovations to their supply chains, whereas the thousands of first-tier suppliers may be unable to invest in related technologies, lack the required knowledge, or employ a qualified workforce. Such an imbalance could lead to a 'dual-track' value chain, where only firms that are technologically 'smart' enough digitize their supply chain to accrue the benefits.

The obstacles are categorized as follows: sociopolitical, organizational, and technological factors to bring out a structured view of challenges:

Sociopolitical Obstacles:

- Political Tensions: The uncertainty of trade wars between countries, such as the United States and China, and political conflicts create uncertainties for GVCs.
- Regulatory Variability: Different countries possess unique regulations, which sometimes become compliance challenges.
- Data Sovereignty: Data localization regulations prevent the free flow of data across borders, and therefore, transparency is limited.

Organizational Challenges:

- Difficulty in Changing: There would be cultural resistance against it, and hence it wouldn't be easy to have a change in technology among organizations.
- Talent Gaps: Finding talent that would be skilled in the application of emerging technologies like AI and blockchain would continue to be a major pain point for organizations.
- Investment Challenges: Highly capitalized technology adoption acts as a barrier to participation from small and medium enterprises (SMEs) in GVCs.

Technological Obstacles:

- Poor Interoperability Issues: The systems used at supply chain levels may not interlink well, leading to problems in data flow as well as decision-making.
- Digital Divide: This divide in the infrastructural aspect of technology usage between developed and developing countries further limits the GVC's inclusiveness.

- Technical Complexity: In most implementations, using the latest available technologies is usually associated with high training and infrastructural change levels.

In summary, while technology offers transformative potential for GVCs, it also brings significant risks that necessitate robust risk management strategies to ensure resilience and sustainability. By comprehending and tackling these obstacles and risks, companies can ensure to thrive in an increasingly digital world while minimizing risks to their GVCs.

Projected Developments

The research across the world on GVCs has been restricted to only a few parameters like trade policies and tariffs, supply chain diversification, e-commerce, and digital sales channels, whereas little emphasis has been laid on the technological aspect. As GVCs is an emerging concept, there is a dearth of literature in this context. While this study bridges that gap, there remain a lot of areas wherein interventions can be made as it is vast and multifaceted. Additional study is required to acknowledge and apprehend the impending digital transformation and automation. The impact of AI and machine learning on GVCs can also form a basis for future studies, alongside their interaction with green technologies and circular value chains (CVCs).

An analysis of how technology is reshaping globalization trends should also be made to ascertain the difference between localization and globalization under the implementation of GVC practices. Researchers may also examine how big data analytics is applied to evaluate and reduce potential dangers in GVCs. With a plethora of research, technology has proven to foster collaboration among firms across different geographies and industries; collaboration and innovation networks can, therefore, be studied concerning GVCs. We can consider the example of Toyota in this regard. Toyota has adapted GVCs by housing its designing and research and development (R&D) team in Japan, their parts production happens in multiple countries. They develop their engines in the United States and electronics in Europe, and their vehicles are assembled and sold all across the world. Without the integration of technology in their GVC, this couldn't have been possible. Not just in the automobile sector but across all industries, technology integration in GVCs has proven to be highly successful. Pfizer, the pharmaceutical giant, has its R&D being conducted primarily in the United States and Europe while its manufacturing happens in India, Ireland, and China and they depend on the global supply chain for their distribution. Through the exploration of these domains, researchers may enhance their understanding of how technology is transforming GVCs and pinpoint optimal approaches for capitalizing on these transformations to propel creativity, durability, and adaptability.

Policy Recommendation

In this chapter, the authors have come up with certain policy recommendations to provide evidence-based guidance to policymakers, helping them make informed decisions that can positively impact economic and social outcomes in the realm of GVCs by creating structured frameworks that can be easily understood and implemented by various stakeholders.

Strengthening Digital Infrastructure

Investment in connectivity should be increased to enhance broadband and mobile internet access, especially in rural and semi-urban areas, to facilitate seamless participation in GVCs. Smart logistics setup can also be developed to promote smart transportation and logistics systems using IoT and AI to improve supply chain efficiency.

Promoting Industry 4.0 Adoption

Incentives for automation could be provided in the form of tax incentives or subsidies for industries that adopt automation and smart manufacturing technologies. There has been a surge in skill development programs, especially in the Indian context. Under this program, the government, along with public and private intervention, can establish training initiatives to upskill the workforce in advanced technologies, like AI, machine learning, and robotics.

Fostering Innovation and R&D

Support for startups focused on developing innovative solutions for GVCs can help them in availing funding and mentorship. Public-private partnerships must be encouraged to increase collaboration between the government and private sector for R&D in technologies relevant to GVCs.

Enhancing Regulatory Frameworks

To boost confidence in digital transactions, explicit guidelines on cybersecurity and data protection ought to be developed and regularly put into practice. The policymakers must strive towards the simplification and streamlining of compliance and procedures to enable simpler operations for the participating businesses. In view of the issues around data security and privacy, additional focus is needed.

Support for SMEs

India is currently witnessing a boom in entrepreneurship, with SMEs being the biggest contributors to the entrepreneurial setup. Access to technology should therefore, be promoted so that SMEs can benefit from advanced technologies and digital tools. Mentorship and networking must also be provided to facilitate networking platforms for SMEs where they can network with larger firms and access global markets.

India can position itself well to harness technology, improve participation in GVCs, and eventually drive economic growth if these recommendations are implemented.

Conclusion

This chapter has emphasized how technology is changing GVCs and shown how technology interaction offers GVCs depth and complexity. As new digital technologies appear, they not only transform established procedures but also improve productivity and encourage cross-border cooperation. AI, blockchain, and IoT are examples of technologies that help organizations increase supply chain transparency, streamline processes, and react swiftly to changes in the market. By cutting waste and improving resource management, these innovations also support sustainability in addition to stimulating economic growth. But there are difficulties accompanying this transition. Organizations need to make sure that everyone can profit from these technology improvements by navigating concerns like cybersecurity, data privacy, and the digital divide. To fully utilize technology in GVCs moving forward, adopting a balanced strategy that emphasizes both innovation and accountability will be essential. Companies worldwide need to follow the footsteps of Apple, Zara, Coca-Cola, Nike, Boeing, Samsung, and Nestlé, among others, which are a testament to the fact that GVCs are the future in making a successful business, and there is something for everyone when we consider technological integration in GVCs. In the end, the future will depend on how well companies use these resources to build inclusive, flexible, and resilient value networks that can survive in a world that is becoming progressively more interconnected.

References

Akbari, M., & Hopkins, J. L. (2022). Digital technologies as enablers of supply chain sustainability in an emerging economy. *Operations Management Research*, *15*(3), 689–710.

Anheuser-Busch InBev. (2020). *From barley to bar: AB InBev trials blockchain with farmers to bring supply chain transparency all the way to beer drinkers.* https://ab-inbev.eu/news/from-barley-to-bar-ab-inbev-trials-blockchain-with-farmers-to-bring-supply-chain-transparency-all-the-way-to-beer-drinkers/

Awan, U., Gölgeci, I., Makhmadshoev, D., & Mishra, N. (2022). Industry 4.0 and circular economy in an era of global value chains: What have we learned and what is still to be explored? *Journal of Cleaner Production*, *371*, 133621.

Birkel, H., & Müller, J. M. (2021). Potentials of industry 4.0 for supply chain management within the triple bottom line of sustainability–a systematic literature review. *Journal of Cleaner Production*, *289*, 125612.

Carrefour Press Release. (2019). *Carrefour—Nestlé Blockchain: Technology for food transparency with Mousline!* https://www.carrefour.com/en/news/carrefour-nestle-blockchain-technology-food-transparency-mousline
Chen, C. L. (2019). Value creation by SMEs participating in global value chains under industry 4.0 trend: Case study of textile industry in Taiwan. *Journal of Global Information Technology Management*, *22*(2), 120–145.
Dickinson, A. (2020). Blockchain and sustainability through responsible sourcing. *IBM Insights*. https://www.ibm.com/think/insights/blockchain-and-sustainability-through-responsible-sourcing
Egwuonwu, A., Mordi, C., Egwuonwu, A., & Uadiale, O. (2022). The influence of blockchains and internet of things on global value chain. *Strategic Change*, *31*(1), 45–55.
Fedyunina, A. A., Gorodnyi, N. A., & Simachev, Y. V. (2024). How the adoption of industry 4.0 technologies is related to participation in global and domestic value chains: Evidence from Russia. *International Journal of Innovation Studies*, *8*(2), 93–108.
Gao, Y., Li, M., Yu, A., & Pan, H. (2023). Digital global value chains: An analysis from the perspective of a value-added decomposition. *Journal of Digital Economy*, *2*, 162–174.
Gereffi, G., Humphrey, J., Kaplinsky, R., & Sturgeon, T. J. (2001). *Introduction: Globalisation, value chains and development*. Institute of Development Studies.
Hennelly, P. A., Srai, J. S., Graham, G., & Fosso Wamba, S. (2020). Rethinking supply chains in the age of digitalization. *Production Planning & Control*, *31*(2–3), 93–95.
High, M. (2020). Supply chain insight: Inside IBM's food trust blockchain system. *Supply Chain Digital*. https://supplychaindigital.com/technology/supply-chain-insight-inside-ibms-food-trust-blockchain-system
Home Depot. (2024). *Sustainable forestry report*. https://corporate.homedepot.com/sites/default/files/2024–01/THD%20Sustainable%20Forestry%20Report%20-%20January%202024.pdf
Hong, Z., & Zahid, R. A. (2023). The security of global value chains (GVC): Recent trends, challenges, and future risk management. In *Emerging trends in sustainable supply chain management and green logistics* (pp. 194–228). IGI Global.
Hongjiang, Z., Adu-Damoah, M., & Boakye, E. A. (2024). *Predicting financial capital availability through blockchain technology-driven supply chain financing: An innovation capability-based moderation role*. https://doi.org/10.21203/rs.3.rs-4118575/v1
Kano, L., Tsang, E. W., & Yeung, H. W. C. (2020). Global value chains: A review of the multi-disciplinary literature. *Journal of International Business Studies*, *51*(4), 577–622.
Kim, H. M., & Laskowski, M. (2018). Toward an ethics of blockchain technology. *Communications of the ACM*, *61*(4), 26–28.
Kouhizadeh, M., & Sarkis, J. (2018). Blockchain practices, potentials, and perspectives in greening supply chains. *Sustainability*, *10*(10), 3831.
Kuang, Y., & Luo, G. (2023). Research on application strategy of big data analysis in logistics supply chain technology innovation. In *Advances in social science, education and humanities research* (pp. 1197–1206). https://doi.org/10.2991/978-2-38476-126-5_133
Lechowski, G., & Krzywdzinski, M. (2022). Emerging positions of German firms in the industrial internet of things: A global technological ecosystem perspective. *Global Networks*, *22*(4), 666–683.
Ledger Insights. (2022). *De Beers' diamond provenance blockchain Tracr launched at scale*. https://www.ledgerinsights.com/digital-asset-custody-firm-metaco-partners-with-brinks-to-protect-keys/

Lei Win, T. (2017). Can blockchain ensure Unilever's tea farmers produce a fairer brew? *Eco Business*. https://www.eco-business.com/news/can-blockchain-ensure-unilevers-tea-farmers-produce-a-fairer-brew/

Liebkind, J. (2019). *Coca-Cola and US state dept use blockchain to combat forced labor*. https://www.investopedia.com/news/cocacola-and-us-state-dept-fight-forced-labor/

Lwesya, F. (2022). Integration into regional or global value chains and economic upgrading prospects: An analysis of the East African Community (EAC) bloc. *Future Business Journal*, *8*(1), 33.

McDermott, B. (2017). Improving confidence in food safety with IBM Blockchain. *IBM Blockchain*. https://newsroom.ibm.com/IBM-blockchain?item=30284

Ngo, V. M., Quang, H. T., Hoang, T. G., & Duong, A. T. B. (2023). Sustainability-related supply chain risks and supply chain performances: The moderating effects of dynamic supply chain management practices. *Business Strategy and the Environment*, *33*(2), 839–857. https://doi.org/10.1002/bse.3512

Özkan-Özen, Y. D., Sezer, M. D., Özbiltekin-Pala, M., & Kazançoğlu, Y. (2022). Risks of data-driven technologies in sustainable supply chain management. *Management of Environmental Quality: An International Journal*, *34*(4), 926–942. https://doi.org/10.1108/meq-03-2022-0051

PixelPlex. (2021). How Walmart strives for food safety using blockchain technology solutions. *PixelPlex*. https://pixelplex.io/blog/walmart-strives-for-food-safety-using-blockchain/

Qin, L., Xie, W., & Jia, P. (2024). Value chain digitalization, global value chain embeddedness, and distributed innovation in value chains. *Sustainability*, *16*(7), 2845.

Rodchenko, V., & Prus, Y. (2023). Digital technologies in logistics and supply chain management. *Facta Universitatis, Series: Economics and Organization*, 191. https://doi.org/10.22190/fueo230517012r

Sanguineti, F., Magnani, G., & Zucchella, A. (2023). Technology adoption, global value chains and sustainability: The case of additive manufacturing. *Journal of Cleaner Production*, *408*, 137095.

Siaw, C. A., & Okorie, C. (2022). Value co-creation on technology-enabled platforms for business model responsiveness and position enhancement in global value chains. *Strategic Change*, *31*(1), 9–18.

Sun, Y., Bi, K., & Yin, S. (2020). Measuring and integrating risk management into green innovation practices for green manufacturing under the global value chain. *Sustainability*, *12*(2), 545.

Szalavetz, A. (2019). Digitalisation, automation and upgrading in global value chains–factory economy actors versus lead companies. *Post-Communist Economies*, *31*(5), 646–670.

Szymczak, S., & Wolszczak-Derlacz, J. (2022). Global value chains and labour markets–simultaneous analysis of wages and employment. *Economic Systems Research*, *34*(1), 69–96.

Tumula, S., Ramadevi, Y., Padmalatha, E., Kiran Kumar, G., Venu Gopalachari, M., Abualigah, L., Chithaluru, P., & Kumar, M. (2024). An opportunistic energy-efficient dynamic self-configuration clustering algorithm in WSN-based IoT networks. *International Journal of Communication Systems*, *37*(1), e5633.

World Economic Forum. (2020). *Global technology governance: A multistakeholder approach*. World Economic Forum.

Zelbst, P. J., Yang, L., Green, K. W., & Sower, V. E. (2023). Linkages between technologies and supply chain performance: Benefits, power and risk reduction. *Supply Chain Management: An International Journal*, *29*(1), 207–218. https://doi.org/10.1108/scm-03-2023-0131

Zhan, J. X. (2021). GVC transformation and a new investment landscape in the 2020s: Driving forces, directions, and a forward-looking research and policy agenda. *Journal of International Business Policy*, *4*(2), 206–220.

Zhang, D. (2023). Can digital finance empowerment reduce extreme ESG hypocrisy resistance to improve green innovation? *Energy Economics*, *125*, 106756.

Zhou, H., Zhang, C., & Yang, Y. (2019). The role of IoT in promoting worker welfare in the manufacturing industry. *Journal of Cleaner Production*, *234*, 145–156.

7

THE ROLE OF GOVERNMENTS IN SHAPING GLOBAL VALUE CHAINS AMID GEOPOLITICAL TUMULT

Waqas Khan and Qasim Ali Nisar

Introduction

Global value chains (GVCs) have restructured the economy by allowing firms to harness efficiency gains, streamline production, and exploit location advantages for cheaper factors and input through international economic integration. Firms now have enough power to get inputs/labor from anywhere in the world, and this has given rise to massive wealth and capacity on the industrial side due to globalization. That said, global geopolitics—and the volatility inherent in it—are not great allies of interconnected networks like these, either. Trade wars, economic nationalism, and geopolitical blocs are causing governments to have a strong hand in determining GVCs (Barbieri, 2024). In addition, governments are hardly passive and use policy interventions, trade regulations, fiscal incentives, and potential strategic alliances to impose dynamic and ever-changing concerts on GVCs. Businesses need to tread carefully through this landscape to retain their position.

Government involvement in GVCs takes place through several channels, from free trade agreements (FTAs) and all the way to tariff regimes, but also in terms of foreign direct investment (FDI) and incentives for the development of industry. National economic interests, security doctrines, and political aspirations often make these interventions possible. In addition, trade policies (tariffs, export restrictions, etc.) can directly affect the flow of goods and services across borders and drive changes in sourcing and production strategies. Similarly, investment regimes that invite the localization of industry by providing tax and subsidy incentives affect the global calculus of production to the degree that firms may choose to locate in these states. Last but not least, labor standards, environmental standards, and intellectual property rights (IPR) protection

DOI: 10.4324/9781003468899-7

constitute a regulatory environment conditioning the functioning and sustainability of GVCs (Huang et al., 2023). Accordingly, these entities that operate across jurisdictions need to remain on their toes to be aware of changing policies and regulatory frameworks that impact their supply chains and market access.

As geopolitical turmoil intensifies, firms must come up with robust adaptive strategies to minimize risk and seize emerging opportunities. An instance would be the sweeping structural shifts hinted at because of the ongoing U.S.–China trade war—compelling corporations to rearrange their offer chains, diversifying their manufacturing bases, and lowering reliance on the person markets. Similarly, the geopolitical fallout from Brexit forced companies performing business within the European Union (EU) and the UK to face trade deals and adjustments to rules and regulations (Leal-Arcas et al., 2024). Against this background, the Russia-Ukraine conflict has merely underscored the urgency of the crisis in energy supply chains despite major governments accelerating investments in renewable energy while diversifying supply sources. Together, these illustrations emphasize direct and indirect impacts that government policy can have on GVCs, reinforcing our assertion that businesses need to be developing responsive policies because shifts in the GVC landscape can derail operations or create opportunities to enhance capabilities to operate.

The stability of GVCs is, however, more than a by-product of domestic government action; it also needs international cooperation and multilateral institutions. Trade—as embodied by the World Trade Organization (WTO), regional blocs like the EU, or multilateral instruments like the Comprehensive and Progressive Agreement for Trans-Pacific Partnership (CPTPP)—operates under specific factors. By mediating disagreements, harmonizing regulations, and stimulating economic integration, they contribute to a more certain business environment and strengthen economic activity by alleviating trade costs. Yet the ability of these institutions to perform their roles has frequently been undermined by geopolitical dynamics that have led to changes in political priorities, the rise of trade disputes, and the forces of economic protectionism (Leal-Arcas et al., 2024). Consequently, firms are required not only to comply with national policies but also to interact with various global governance structures influencing the ground rules of international trade and commerce.

In times of geopolitical uncertainties, the role of the governments in creating GVCs is further analyzed in this chapter. It surveys new paths that the next generation of trade and investment policy might take and gives a taxonomy of the major policies and regulations affecting global trade and investment and when and how to adapt to them. Another point highlighted in the chapter is the importance of working closely with, not just the cooperation of, governments, companies, and systems to help deliver more resilient, sustainable, and safe supply chains. Based on updated case studies, this chapter provides practical implications of the consequences of government interventions on GVCs to provide firms with the information necessary to develop the appropriate strategic decisions. Firms may identify challenges and opportunities that arise from the unique and complex interaction between government policies and global trade networks and position themselves favorably in response.

Government Policies and Regulations Impacting GVCs

Many policies and regulations set the conditions for trade and investment flows, labor, and environment standards, and others that affect GVCs. Such policies are instruments to promote or curb the conduct of multinational corporations (MNCs), influencing the structure of supply chains and the risk and opportunity landscapes of businesses. In an international environment characterized by heightened geopolitical uncertainty, GVCs can no longer rely on the assumption of an ever-integrating global economy; an increasing connection between government practices and GVCs means that companies must have a profound understanding of the relevant regulatory environments to remain resilient and competitive. The next section considers major interest and/or relevant policy areas, including trade agreements, protectionist policies, policies on investment, labor, and the environment, and the enablers and in-biters of global trade and economic growth.

Trade Policies and Agreements

Whereas GVCs rely on cross-border flows of goods and services, trade policies are similarly essential in GVCs (Bondi et al., 2025). Trade refers to the exchange of goods and services between countries governed by trade agreements, tariffs, and regulatory frameworks that allow governments to encourage economic integration or protect domestic industries. The formulation and domain of trade policies decide how well the businesses WADE through to foreign markets, splurge minimal production costs, and expedite their footprint on a global scale.

Free Trade Agreements

FTAs are critical tools that enable smooth cross-border trade by lowering or removing tariffs, quotas, and regulatory barriers (Ajewumi et al., 2024). Agreements like the USA-Mexico-Canada Agreement (USMCA), the EU Single Market, and the CPTPP have very much increased the efficiency of trade through increasingly harmonized regulatory standards and by furthering economic integration. They provide clear and consistent expectations for trade, thereby enabling firms to plan for long-run investment and supply chain decisions. On the other hand, FTAs have their challenges, such as rules of origin and detailed provisions at the sector level, which may complicate effective access for the benefit of the firms.

Protectionism and Tariffs

Even though trade liberalization has its benefits, a lot of governments employ protectionist methods of shielding domestic industries from international competition. They utilize tariffs, import quotas, and trade restrictions to diminish access to foreign markets and virtually always trigger retaliation that ends with a trade war (Chaisse & Su, 2025). The most glaring example would be the U.S.–China trade war tariffication of hundreds of billions of dollars' worth of goods and disrupting the dynamics of global supply chains. With the increase in geopolitical tensions, these protectionist prerogatives are adding cost to production, making supply chains inefficient, creating price instability in the market, and placing an onus on firms to reassess. Their sourcing decisions are to balance their supplier bases through diversification as a means to mitigate this political risk.

Export Controls and Sanctions

Export controls and economic sanctions are perhaps the best-known tools governments can use to reduce the access of potential adversaries to critical goods, technologies, and raw materials (Bown, 2024). These are often broad measures of national security or even geopolitical conflict and diplomatic character. A clear example here is semiconductors, where the limitation of exports of advanced chip technologies to China has changed the structure of global supply chains. In addition to that, there are more and more sanctions implementations on particular countries, as with Russia since the Ukraine War, making every aspect of trade unnecessary. However, it is a must for companies to comply to be on the right side of the rapidly changing regulatory landscape to avoid litigation and financial penalties.

Industrial and Investment Policies

This is not just through trade regulations; industrial and investment policies governments adapt to help their economies, attract foreign capital, and strengthen domestic industries. Such policies may consist of subsidies, tax incentives, and FDI policies affecting the resource allocation and business strategies in the GVCs.

Subsidies and Incentives

The government provides certain subsidies and incentives that are necessary for all government projects to enhance the competitiveness of the domestic industry through financial assistance for research and development (R&D), infrastructure development, and technology adoption. That's exemplified by

China's "Made in China 2025" program that provides massive state support for "strategic" industries, from artificial intelligence to robotics to clean energy, as part of a plan that, it hopes, will propel the nation to the global technological forefront. Likewise, the EU Green Deal funds sustainable industrial development and solidifies the shift toward greener supply chains (Bharti, 2025). According to earlier studies, while subsidies can stimulate innovation and economic growth, they can also be a source of tension in international trade, especially when they are perceived as exacerbating competition distortions.

FDI Regulations

FDI regulations, on the other hand, give clarity and control as to which sectors a foreign company can invest in on a country's industrial and/or infrastructure level (Kim et al., 2025). Most countries, especially in the areas of defense, telecommunications, and critical infrastructure, have one or another form of investment screening mechanism to protect strategically important sectors from foreign control. To avoid foreign threats to national security, foreign acquisitions are closely scrutinized by the Committee on Foreign Investment in the United States (CFIUS). The EU has also recently begun introducing a foreign investment screening framework for protecting strategic industries. However, these regulatory measures pose challenges for MNCs looking to expand operations and require careful consideration of the investment environments and compliance requirements.

Labor and Environmental Standards

We thus do not stop at trade and investment policies as mentioned labor and environmental regulations are also crucial for the driving of GVCs. Governments create laws to protect the rights of workers, hold firms accountable for their production processes, and enforce corporate social responsibility (CSR) practices. Such regulations have implications on sourcing practices, production costs and brand image in international markets.

Labor Rights and Regulations

Such policies include laws on wages, safety, and health standards at work and protection of labor rights, and they affect how businesses operate in GVCs (Walters et al., 2024). Global institutions like the International Labour Organization (ILO) push for decent wages, rights to bargaining, and scrapping of exploitative work practices, thereby forcing national governments to legislate tougher labor laws. This forces businesses to comply with labor standards to maintain social legitimacy and prevent stopping work caused by labor disputes. Examples like the Rana Plaza disaster in Bangladesh reinforce the danger present when labor regulations are lax, making the need for tough oversight in areas of the world where products are made essential.

Environmental Regulations

Governments around the world have begun to enforce more environmental regulations to address climate change and/or sustainable business practices. Carbon pricing, emissions regulations, and sustainable sourcing requirements drive a reshaping of GVCs, pushing businesses to adopt greener technologies and to decarbonize (Blasinsky, 2025). For example, the EU's Carbon Border Adjustment Mechanism (CBAM) levies duties on carbon-intensive imports, pushing firms toward low-carbon modes of production. Sustainability programs are now valued by consumers and investors alike, and compliance with environmental regulations is becoming a competitive edge.

Collaboration between Governments and Stakeholders

Due to the complexity of GVCs, solutions will need to be delivered through collaborative endeavors by governments, businesses, multilateral institutions, and regional economic bodies. Since these issues often concern several countries in a region and due to the global character of supply chains, government actors cannot act alone in adapting to disruptions of GVC, regulatory challenges or crises caused by pandemics or economic downturns. In contrast, multi-stakeholder collaboration leads to supply chains that are more robust, flexible, and sustainable. It discusses the importance of public-private partnerships (PPPs), multilateral institutions, and regional economic integration when it comes to interaction and a sustainable trade environment.

Public-Private Partnerships

PPPs are a key solution-oriented mechanism for joint action between governments and businesses with a view of overcoming the GVC challenges (Oyenuga & Jeresa, 2025). Such partnerships play to the strengths of each sector: governmental authority and regulatory oversight, matched with private sector efficiency and innovation. PPPs are more effective in infrastructure development, technology advancement, and crisis response.

Cases of PPPs

An important example of the promise of PPP is the coordination of supply chains for COVID-19 vaccines. The COVID-19 pandemic revealed the fragility of the global healthcare supply chain that demanded an unprecedented level of collaboration between government, pharmaceutical companies, logistics firms, and global organizations. An example of multilateral PPPs that enabled equitable vaccine distribution is the COVAX initiative curated by the World Health Organization (WHO), Gavi, and Coalition for Epidemic Preparedness Innovations (CEPI). Regulatory approvals and funding came from governments, while production, distribution, and logistics were served by the private sector. In addition to speeding up the deployment of vaccines, these partnerships reinforced the need for coordination when tackling future global disasters.

Apart from healthcare, PPPs are imperative for infrastructure development that is required for effective GVC functioning. Linking the global supply chain, the government often works with private firms to develop and maintain infrastructure—transport networks, ports, and increasingly digital infrastructure—that encourages connectivity. China's Belt and Road Initiative (BRI) shows the scale of infrastructure PPPs to deepen trade connections from Asia to Africa to Europe. These types of initiatives do spur economic growth; however, they can also create concerns around debt sustainability, geopolitical influence, and regulatory alignment. So, while PPPs can generate great economic benefits, balancing benefits with transparency and sustainability is necessary for their soundness within GVCs.

Multilateral Institutions and Trade Governance

An open rules-based trading system is key to maintaining GVCs, and multilateral institutions are at the center of managing these structures. Organizations like the WTO, International Monetary Fund (IMF), and World Bank play a crucial role in trade by promoting trade governance, international trade dispute resolution, and economic stabilization, which together create a stable and predictable trade environment.

Industrial Examples of Multilateral Institutions and Trade Governance

Cooperation on other multilateral issues multilateral cooperation, as seen in the WTO's trade dispute settlement system, WTO, by having rules to adjudicate trade disputes, decreases uncertainty, and helps avoid tit-for-tat trade wars that can disrupt GVCs. For example, we can turn to the cases of major economies that the WTO's Dispute Settlement Body (DSB) has dealt with, namely the trade wars over IPR and tariffs between the United States and China. Although political tensions in recent years have called the WTO's credibility into question by blunting its appeal against competing geopolitical priorities and allowing bilateral trade agreements to proliferate, the WTO still has an important role in trade governance, guaranteeing equal conditions among firms involved in GVCs.

Besides the provision of financial, technical, and policy assistance toward easing the access of developing economies into GVCs, there are also multilateral institutions that are in place to undertake dispute settlement functions (Gnangnon, 2025). The IMF and World Bank have been promoting trade facilitation programs that enhance the expansion of the supply chain in developing countries. Such initiatives will help smaller economies to achieve better integration into global trade networks by addressing the shortfalls in infrastructure, the inefficiencies in regulation, and the limitations in finance. This answer is their persistent institutional effectiveness, which is dependent on ongoing commitment by member states, a reality that augments pressures for reform and transformation to better reflect changing global trade.

Regional Economic Integration

Regional economic integration has played a central role in facilitating trade and enabling more efficient globalization. Regional Trade Agreements reduce trade barriers, stimulate market access, and increase business competitive advantages through the cooperation of neighboring nations in the same region. One such weapon of regionalization is through integration with the African Continental Free Trade Area (AfCFTA).

Real Side Cases of Regional Economic Integration

The AfCFTA came into force in 2021 and aims to establish a single market across 54 African states with tariffs removed on 90% of goods, alongside mechanisms for addressing nontariff barriers (Ajibo, 2024). The agreement enhances the resilience of regional supply chains through intra-African trade and reduces dependence on foreign nations while promoting investments in local industries. With the youth population booming, natural resources, and a burgeoning market for consumer goods, Africa can attract foreign investment and industry through the AfCFTA, thereby connecting African firms to GVCs. Yet, to unlock the rewards of regional integration, the continent must first overcome infrastructure deficits, regulatory fragmentation, and political instability.

It shows how regional trade networks can be strengthened in cooperation between countries through other regional processes, such as the EU's Single Market, the ASEAN Economic Community, or the USMCA. They encourage trade between nations, encourage policy coordination, and provide economies of scale for some companies working in GVCs. That said, real deep integration goes well beyond economic disparities. It involves (i) regulatory convergence and (ii) meaningful political harmonization among members.

Case Studies: The Real-World Impact of Government Policies on GVCs

The examination of practical case studies gives a clearer view of how global policy directives influence the anatomy of GVCs. Each case study highlights the impact of trade disputes, environmental regulation, and geopolitical conflict on global supply chains with implications for business, government, and academia. This section will delve into three main case studies: the impact of the U.S.–China trade war on semiconductor supply chains, the contribution of the European Green Deal toward sustainable supply chains, and the disruption of energy supply chains during the Russia-Ukraine War.

Case Study 1: U.S.–China Trade War and Semiconductor Supply Chains

The U.S.–China trade war that began in 2018 sent seismic waves through the global semiconductor supply chains. Amid wider geopolitical and economic tensions, the U.S. government has also been imposing tariffs on Chinese products and placing tariffs on Chinese technology firms for reasons of national security and free market economy upholders under the banner of a war on terror. Such policies especially hit home for the semiconductor industry, which serves as a critical backbone of global technology supply chains.

But the biggest move was placing restrictions on the export of semiconductors from the U.S. to Chinese firms, such as Huawei. Huawei was put on the entity list by the U.S. Department of Commerce, which barred American firms from selling it advanced semiconductors and other strategic components. As such, this policy has forced Huawei and other Chinese tech companies to seek alternative sources and reshape global semiconductor supply chains. In response, China accelerated its domestic industrial push to build homegrown semiconductor production capacity, pouring tens of billions of dollars into state-owned enterprises, including Semiconductor Manufacturing International.

The trade war was not only bilateral between the two suspect nations but also had global repercussions for the semiconductor industry. Those companies needed to shift from a trade environment where they enjoyed free trade with China to one where U.S. trade restrictions were now determining the flow of semiconductors through their supply chains. For this, Taiwan, South Korea, and Japan were critical to semiconductor production. As recently as last year, the U.S. government proposed the CHIPS and Science Act to provide billions of dollars in subsidies to enhance domestic production of semiconductors and reduce dependency on foreign countries (Peters, 2023). It is emblematic of how government interference with trade policies has caused broken supply chains, increased production costs, and a huge restructuring of global industries.

Case Study 2: European Green Deal and Sustainable Supply Chains

The European Green Deal is a comprehensive strategic framework aimed at, among other things, achieving carbon neutrality by 2050 for EU member states, which was finalized in 2019. The top-line ramifications for global supply chains are huge and revolve directly around auto manufacturers, energy providers, and consumers. Strict environmental regulations and carbon pricing mechanisms of the European Green Deal could also stimulate sustainable supply chains through its various sustainability standards.

At the heart of the Green Deal is the CBAM, a form of carbon tax on the carbon in the product and the energy that was used to make it when imported. Preventing carbon leakages, which is basically where companies relocate their production to countries with low environmental standards to escape their compliance costs, is one of the main objectives of this policy. As a result, non-EU manufacturers whose exports go to Europe must now either meet the higher environmental standard or pay a price penalty. Due to this regulation, companies all over the world are investing in pollution-free technology, renewable energy, and sustainable production methods just to keep their door to the European market open.

A clear illustration of the Green Deal's impact on supply chains is the automotive sector. European automakers are moving faster with the shift to electric vehicles (EVs), and targets have become more stringent. This change has affected international providers of batteries, raw elements, and digital elements, with rising demand for lithium, cobalt, and nickel. As a result, actors throughout the supply chain in regions like Latin America and Africa, where these inputs are extracted, have been pushed to advance sustainable mining and labor practices. The same applies to the European Green Deal, which is an example of systemic change in GVCs, guiding firms toward sustainable production processes while fundamentally altering global trade patterns. Nonetheless, things like regulatory compliance costs, supply chain disruptions, and technological adaptation need to be overcome for sustainable production to take off smoothly.

Case Study 3: Russia-Ukraine War and Energy Supply Chains

The conflict between Russia and Ukraine, which started in 2022, has massively disrupted energy supply chains around the world and has shown us how dangerous our reliance on fossil fuel imports is. Extensive economic sanctions enacted against Russia, one of the largest exporters of oil and natural gas, have resulted in a reshaping of global fossil fuel trade routes and pricing structures.

And, of course, the EU itself, which had depended on Russian gas for at least 40% of its energy needs, was forced to find new supply sources on an urgent basis. In response, liquefied natural gas (LNG) imports from the United States, Qatar, and Norway surged, along with investments in renewable energy that would eventually lessen reliance on fossil fuels (Wood, 2024). The crisis also served as a wake-up call about energy security in a strategic sense, leading many governments to reconsider their energy policy and infrastructure choices over the medium term.

The war has plunged many companies operating in energy-intensive sectors into the chaos of exorbitant energy prices, headaches with production standstills, and supply chain clogs. The cost competitiveness of European manufacturers was put into question as governments rolled out expensive subsidies and energy relief packages for struggling sectors. This coincided with new geopolitical realignments, with Russia rapidly searching for more markets for its energy exports and deepening its economic relationship with China and India. This case study reflects the interlocking nature of geopolitics and GVCs, highlighting how wars in one corner of the world can lead to Ricardian vibrations in far-off regions. The experience from the Russia-Ukraine conflict underlines the importance of diversification, resilience, and a long-term perspective in energy supply chain management.

Implications for Businesses in GVCs

Government policies and geopolitics (GVC on them, they on GVCs) businesses should turn risk into upside by treating their compliance as an area for competitive differentiation and focusing on operational agility by diversifying their supply chains, embedding sustainability into their value proposition, and actively lobbying governments to keep the economy open during adverse times. This section discusses these basic dimensions and their importance for firms operating on the paradigm of international trade.

Policy Awareness and Compliance

A still better understanding of the evolving nature of government policy—the government, after all, is a primary actor influencing trade flows and the investment and operational choices of GVC firms. Compliance with trade agreements, environmental regulations, and labor standards remains vital for obtaining market access and continuing operations. Fines, tariffs, or exclusion from key markets for companies that do not comply with such regulations.

A big example of the need for policy awareness is the EU's CBAM, which imposes carbon tariffs on imports based on their carbon footprint. And those exporting into the EU will need to have their value chains conform to carbon mitigation goals or face increased costs. There are export control laws for technology firms (e.g., U.S. export controls on semiconductor exports to China). By keeping tabs on trade agreements, customs regulations, and industry-specific policies, companies can reduce their risks and remain competitive on the global stage.

Supply Chain Diversification

Geopolitical disruptions, trade restrictions, and supply chain bottlenecks are happening with increasing frequency and forcing businesses to diversify their supply chains. Dependency on one supplier or region for vital inputs significantly increases the risk to firms through production disruptions, cost increases, and shortages of supply. To overcome volatility, resilience should be built through alternative sourcing, nearshoring, and multiregional production networks.

For example, the semiconductor industry and the U.S.-China trade tensions. Apple and Intel, among others, have tried to diversify their supply chains by building more factories in Vietnam, India, and the United States. Likewise, the wounds caused by the COVID-19 pandemic brought to the surface the weaknesses of medical supply chains—pharmaceuticals began to move away from reliance on China and India for active pharmaceutical ingredients (APIs) by creating production hubs closer to home in Europe and North America. However, it also cements a growing practice of supply chain diversification, allowing businesses to alleviate their geopolitical exposure by diverse geography and keep their engines running.

Sustainability Integration

Increased legislative oversight, consumer expectations, and investor demands on ethical practices have made sustainability a key focus for companies in GVCs. All over the world, governments are rolling out stricter environmental and labor standards, forcing corporations to adopt major areas of sustainability into their core activities. Otherwise, it can lead to reputation damage, lost access to markets, and fines.

For instance, MNCs in the fashion industry are under growing pressure to adopt sustainable sourcing from the Corporate Sustainability Due Diligence

Directive (CSDDD) of the EU. The legislation can require companies to carry out human rights and environmental due diligence concerning their supply chains. Similarly, in the automotive sector, phasing out toward EVs is being aligned with the carbon neutrality targets encapsulated in the European Green Deal. While companies that take the lead in embracing sustainable supply chain practices through innovative solutions to drive down carbon footprints, ensure a circular economy, and ensure responsible labor enjoy competitive advantages, they also fulfill their responsibilities as global citizens.

Engagement in Policy Advocacy

Creating a corporate strategy to deliver added social and environmental value in a sustainable way, American businesses are increasingly recognizing that government—both at the global level through multilateral and national governments—shapes their business activities, and advocacy for local and global policy is turning into a top priority for firms that engage in GVCs. By engaging in industry associations, trade councils, and PPPs, businesses can contribute to policy debates, influence regulatory frameworks, and ensure their interests are represented in the government decision-making process.

A clear example of winning policy advocacy can be found in the tech industry around data privacy law. Over the last few years, companies such as Google, Microsoft, and Meta have attempted to shape the writing of data privacy laws like the EU General Data Protection Regulation (GDPR) and the U.S. CLOUD Act, forcing policymakers into a reactionary position. Likewise, unrivaled automotive makers have proceeded to lobby the administration for impetuses and tax reductions to lead the world in natural vehicles and green energies. It allows businesses to sidestep regulatory roadblocks more easily, secure superior trading terms, and assist in shaping policies that will drive their industries in the right direction by cultivating an ongoing conversation with their policymakers.

Conclusion

Although a novel version of GVCs was observed by the end of the last decade, since the outbreak of the current geopolitical crisis, the prominence of the vendors has been elevated worldwide by how it reflected on trade, industrial, and regulatory policies, which reshaped the way of functioning of world business. Under global pressures of geopolitical angst, rising economic nationalism, and sustainability imperatives, government interventions are redesigning the systems and shape of GVCs, and firms must adapt their restructuring strategies to ensure both resilience and competitiveness. Governments wield a set of tools (FTAs, tariffs, and export controls) to regulate trade across their borders, which ultimately modifies market access and cost structures for businesses.

Liberalization of trade agreements enhances economic integration and efficiency, but trade protection and economic sanctions change everything, bringing uncertainty and requiring firms to reimagine their supply chains.

At the same time, FDI policies reveal a fine-tuned compromise between economic opening and national security concerns, affecting not only the flows of capital and transfer of technology but also the geography of production locations. As seen in the recent national industrial and innovation policy releases, the strategic role of governments in developing technological competitiveness and economic self-sufficiency is even more apparent, with a range of state-led initiatives such as subsidies, tax incentives, and R&D grants increasingly determining industry pathways and national competitive advantages.

At the same time, labor and environmental regulations are progressively characterizing the sustainability aspects of more GVCs and pressing firms to fall into line with ethical labor standards, carbon reduction programs, and wider environmental, social, and governance (ESG) platforms just to remain in access within the markets and are accepted as a good corporate citizen. This interaction between public policy in terms of implementing regulations and private sector reaction in achieving compliance demands more collaborative governance with PPPs, multilateral trade institutions, and regional economic integration mechanisms as the key instruments for finding the right trade-off between ensuring compliance with regulation while not hampering the business. Recent case studies of the U.S.–China trade war, European Green Deal, and Russia-Ukraine conflict show how government policies have a material impact on global supply chains, highlighting the need for businesses to remain proactive in policy monitoring, diversify supply chain networks, mainstream sustainability into business models, and engage in policy advocacy for good policy outcomes. As a global economic landscape slowly creeps toward one of geopolitical instability, firms that can read between the simplistic black-and-white lines of governmental interventions will endure and thrive in the long term through foresight, agility in compliance strategy, and proactivity through engagement.

References

Ajewumi, O. E., Afolabi, J. A., & Joe-Akunne, I. (2024). Regional trade agreements and economic integration in Africa: Assessing the impact of the African continental free trade area (AFCFTA). *World Journal of Advanced Research and Reviews*, *23*(3), 2783–2801.

Ajibo, C. C. (2024). *The African continental free trade area agreement: Legal and policy frameworks*. Taylor & Francis.

Barbieri, K. (2024). Geopolitics and international trade. In *The Palgrave handbook of contemporary geopolitics* (pp. 957–979). Springer.

Bharti, M. S. (2025). The EU's green economy policy and its sustainable development goals: Prospects and challenges. In *Global economic interconnectedness: International trade and finance* (pp. 269–294). IGI Global.

Blasinsky, K. J. (2025). *Greening the supply chain: Financial tools to catalyze decarbonization by small businesses.* http://dx.doi.org/10.2139/ssrn.5128369

Bondi, A., Baccini, L., Fiorini, M., Hoekman, B., Altomonte, C., & Colantone, I. (2025). Global value chains and the design of trade agreements. *The Review of International Organizations*, 1–33.

Bown, C. P. (2024). *Trade policy, industrial policy, and the economic security of the European Union* (Working Paper No. 24–22). Peterson Institute for International Economics.

Chaisse, J., & Su, X. (2025). Normative realignment in domestic trade barriers procedures: Driving unilateralism in the EU, US, and China. *World Trade Review*, 1–26.

Gnangnon, S. K. (2025). *Effect of the multilateral surveillance of trade policies on economic institutions, participation in global value chains and export upgrading in developing countries.* EconStor Preprints 313119, ZBW—Leibniz Information Centre for Economics.

Huang, J., Zhong, Y., & Zhang, Y. (2023). Does environmental regulation of cleaner production affect the position of enterprises in global value chains? A quasi-natural experiment based on the implementation of cleaner production. *Sustainability, 15*(13), 10492.

Kim, J. Y., Garri, M., Beynon, M., & Pickernell, D. (2025). Exploring South Korean foreign direct investment motives and state-level location decisions: US evidence 1995–2008. *Thunderbird International Business Review*, 1–22.

Leal-Arcas, R., Alsheikh, A., Maqtoush, J., Althunayan, N., Dal, H., Berto, L. A., Aldughaither, N., Bashiti, A., & Afaneh, B. (2024). Trade, geopolitics, and environment. *Journal of Infrastructure, Policy and Development, 8*(7), 5114.

Oyenuga, M. O., & Jeresa, S. (2025). Adaptation and resilience: Private, public, and individual change makers. In *Climate neutrality through smart eco-innovation and environmental sustainability* (pp. 21–36). Springer.

Peters, M. A. (2023). *Semiconductors, geopolitics and technological rivalry: The US CHIPS & Science Act, 2022* (Vol. 55, pp. 1642–1646). Taylor & Francis.

Walters, D., James, P., & Johnstone, R. (2024). Effects of economic drivers on work health and safety in global supply chains: A discussion of the effectiveness of regulatory strategies and their economic contexts. *The Economic and Labour Relations Review, 35*(3), 556–575.

Wood, D. A. (2024). The evolution of global liquefied natural gas supply chains: A review. In *Sustainable liquefied natural gas* (pp. 23–55). Elsevier.

8

RISK ASSESSMENT IN GLOBAL VALUE CHAINS

Renata Klafke, Imran Ali and Tage Andersson

Introduction

Global value chains (GVCs) have become central to modern international trade, enabling companies to tap into global efficiencies and expand into new markets. However, this globalization also introduces complex risks that businesses must manage across multiple borders and with different stakeholders. The increased interconnectivity and scope of GVCs expose companies to a wide range of risks, from geopolitical instability and regulatory shifts to natural disasters and technological disruptions. These risks are multifaceted and unpredictable, making risk assessment in GVCs a critical area of focus for both businesses and policymakers.

The importance of addressing such risks is underscored by recent events such as the Brexit referendum, which created uncertainty for businesses reliant on the UK-European Union (EU) trade, etc. of Russia's invasion of Ukraine in 2022, which caused significant disruptions in energy supplies and raw materials, especially in Europe, which severely disrupted global supply chains. These recent geopolitical developments have accelerated the transformation of supply chain designs from a focus on efficiency to one of responsiveness, reliability, and resilience.

These examples, alongside the ongoing impacts of the COVID-19 pandemic, illustrate how risks within GVCs can have significant downstream effects on production, market performance, business continuity, etc. Thus, developing strategies to assess and mitigate these risks has never been more urgent.

Risk assessment is crucial for managing GVCs effectively. It involves identifying, evaluating, and ranking risks based on their likelihood and potential

DOI: 10.4324/9781003468899-8

impact. The forces that drive GVCs today, such as global market pressures, technological advancements, and political and economic dynamics, remain valid (Dornier et al., 1998).

The automotive industry, for example, faced a severe semiconductor shortage, leading to delays, layoffs, and major revenue losses. This highlighted the fragility of globally interconnected supply networks, where local disruptions can trigger worldwide effects (Gereffi, 2020). Companies need to pay attention to elements that go beyond their own operations and consider the weaknesses in their suppliers' and partners' networks as well. Wieland and Wallenburg (2013) highlight that taking a proactive approach to risk management helps companies become more resilient by forecasting disruptions, developing contingencies, diversifying suppliers, and collaborating closely with key stakeholders. Additionally, firms must reconsider their risk identification, evaluation, and mitigation tools for GVCs considering changing global and geopolitical forces.

This chapter aims to provide a comprehensive overview of the various risks embedded within GVCs, focusing on their identification, assessment, and management. It will first delve into the different types of risks commonly encountered in GVCs, including operational, financial, and reputational risks. Following this, we will examine various risk assessment frameworks that businesses can employ to navigate these complexities. The chapter will also present real-world case studies of recent disruptions in GVCs, analyzing the lessons learned and the implications for future strategies. Finally, we will offer practical recommendations for mitigating these risks and building resilient supply chains, culminating in key insights and best practices for companies striving to adapt in an increasingly volatile environment.

The chapter is organized as follows: Section "Risks in GVCs" discusses the types of risks commonly found in GVCs. Section "Production Failures" explores the various risk assessment frameworks used in GVC management. Section "Process Inefficiencies" presents case studies of recent disruptions in GVCs. By looking at recent case studies and academic insights, it presents a comprehensive approach to evaluating these risks. Section "Workforce Challenges" offers strategies for mitigating these risks and building resilient supply chains. Finally, we conclude the chapter with key insights and lessons learned.

Risks in GVCs

GVCs are inherently complex, creating a network of interdependencies across various regions and actors. While this structure enables businesses to tap into global efficiencies, it also opens them up to numerous risks, including economic risks and geopolitical tensions.

In many ways, GVC management parallels domestic value chain management, although it operates over a larger geographical area. Firms' value chains can be categorized on a spectrum from primarily domestic with some international interactions to fully integrated GVCs of large multinational corporations. For companies aiming to succeed in the unpredictable global landscape, having a solid grasp of these risks is essential. This section delves into the impact of geopolitical forces on GVCs from a firm supply chain risk assessment and design perspective. Understanding both past and present global and geopolitical forces is crucial, as they shape today's GVCs and will significantly transform them in the future (Dornier et al., 1998).

The following subsections provide an exploration of these internal, external, and geopolitical risks, offering insights into how they impact GVCs and strategies for effective management.

Production Failures

One of the most common internal risks is production failure. A breakdown in manufacturing, caused by equipment malfunctions, raw material shortages, or human error, can halt operations and lead to costly delays. For instance, a machinery failure in a factory may stop production lines for days or even weeks, causing bottlenecks that ripple through the supply chain.

To address the issue of production failures, companies need to adopt proactive maintenance strategies and invest in reliable technology. As argued by Slack and Brandon-Jones (2018), preventive maintenance can significantly reduce the risk of equipment breakdowns by identifying potential issues before they lead to complete failure. This approach not only minimizes unplanned downtime but also extends the lifespan of machinery and reduces repair costs.

Process Inefficiencies

Process inefficiencies can seriously hinder a company's performance, leading to increased waste, higher costs, and missed opportunities. To address these issues, companies must focus on continuous improvement and process optimization.

According to Slack and Brandon-Jones (2018), implementing lean management techniques can help reduce waste and improve efficiency. Lean practices emphasize eliminating non-value-adding activities and ensuring that every part of the process contributes to delivering value to the customer. Regular training programs for employees also play a critical role in minimizing inefficiencies, as a well-trained workforce is better equipped to follow optimized workflows and adapt to technological advancements.

Additionally, it is important to recognize that process inefficiencies are often related to risks such as shipping delays, product quality issues, and operational problems. By focusing on these improvements, businesses can boost productivity, cut costs, and enhance the reliability of their supply chain.

Workforce Challenges

Managing the workforce can be critical at times. High turnover rates, labor shortages, or strikes can undermine a company's ability to maintain consistent production and service levels.

Competitive compensation and career development are core elements to managing workforce challenges, but recent studies highlight additional effective measures. For example, Ying et al. (2023) argue that flexible working conditions and professional development programs can significantly improve retention rates, especially in small- and medium-sized enterprises where flexibility may be more critical than financial incentives. Similarly, Ogedegbe (2023) emphasizes the role of recognition and reward systems, noting that nonmonetary incentives, like public recognition or career progression opportunities, can keep employees motivated and loyal.

In this context, workforce issues are crucial risks that can affect overall operational efficiency. While offering competitive pay is important, fostering a supportive environment through flexible work options, professional development, and recognition programs plays a critical role in reducing workforce challenges and maintaining a stable, satisfied workforce.

Data Security

With the growing reliance on digital platforms, data security has become a major internal risk for companies operating within GVCs. Businesses now manage vast amounts of sensitive information, including intellectual property, customer details, and supplier contracts, making them more vulnerable to cyber threats. A security breach can lead to significant financial losses, reputational damage, and potential legal repercussions, underscoring the need for robust data protection measures.

To mitigate these risks, organizations need to implement strong cybersecurity frameworks. According to Cha (2022), investing in multilayered security systems, including firewalls, encryption, and intrusion detection systems, is essential for safeguarding sensitive data. Additionally, training employees on best practices for data protection is critical, as human error often contributes to breaches.

Furthermore, collaborative approaches are becoming increasingly relevant. According to a study by Brown et al. (2015), companies that engage in information sharing with suppliers and partners about potential cyber threats tend to build more resilient GVCs. By working together and sharing threat intelligence, companies can strengthen their collective defenses and ensure a higher level of security across the chain.

External Risks in GVCs

External risks arise from factors outside a company's control and can significantly impact operations. A comprehensive view of general external risks includes natural disasters, wars, trade wars, epidemics, terrorist attacks, and various economic and technological factors, as outlined in the literature.

Geopolitical Tensions

Geopolitical tensions can create significant hurdles for global supply chains, making it essential for companies to adopt proactive measures. One effective way to navigate these risks is through diversification. By spreading suppliers and production facilities across different regions, companies can reduce their reliance on any single source and minimize the impact of political instability in one area (Brussel & Teller, 2017). Regularly following news and analysis from credible sources allows companies to anticipate shifts that could impact their operations. Additionally, building strong connections with local partners offers valuable insights and practical support in adjusting to new regulations or customs requirements, an approach often used by freight forwarders to navigate complex trade environments.

A well-known example of geopolitical tensions affecting global supply chains is the U.S.–China trade war that began in 2018. This conflict led to increased tariffs on hundreds of billions of dollars' worth of goods traded between the two nations (Zeng et al., 2022). Companies like Apple had to rethink their supply chain strategies due to the rising costs associated with tariffs. In response, Apple and other tech organizations began to diversify their manufacturing locations, exploring alternatives such as Vietnam and India to mitigate the impact of the trade war and reduce dependence on Chinese manufacturing. Companies that invest in scenario planning can better prepare for unexpected geopolitical shifts. By analyzing potential outcomes and developing strategic responses in advance, companies can enhance their resilience and agility in the face of geopolitical challenges.

Economic Risks

Economic risks can significantly disrupt GVCs, affecting everything from production costs to consumer demand. Factors such as economic recessions, inflation rates, and currency fluctuations create an unpredictable business environment. For example, during the COVID-19 pandemic, many companies faced sudden drops in demand, leading to inventory surplus and financial strain. Moreover, inflation rates and currency fluctuations can vary widely across different regions, complicating the planning process. These economic developments can create risks such as volatile energy prices and rising labor costs, further complicating operational strategies. This unpredictability emphasizes the importance of efficient supply chain strategies that can adapt to sudden changes (Ibrahim et al., 2021).

To effectively mitigate these economic risks, companies should develop a comprehensive risk management strategy. According to Pournader et al. (2020), businesses can enhance their resilience by diversifying suppliers and markets, implementing flexible pricing strategies, and investing in market research to better understand consumer behavior.

Environmental Risks and Natural Disasters

Environmental risks and natural disasters pose significant challenges to GVCs. These risks can arise from a variety of factors, including climate change, extreme weather events, and ecological degradation, which can disrupt supply chains and impact operational efficiency. For instance, hurricanes, floods, and wildfires can halt production, damage infrastructure, and delay transportation, leading to substantial economic losses. A recent example was the impact of Hurricane Harvey in 2017, which caused extensive flooding in Houston, a major hub for the oil and gas industry. The storm resulted in shutdowns of refineries and significant disruptions to supply chains across various sectors, demonstrating how environmental disasters can ripple through interconnected networks.

To overcome these challenges effectively, companies need to implement risk management strategies that take environmental factors into account. Sánchez-Flores et al. (2020) emphasize the importance of integrating sustainable practices and focusing on resilience-building efforts to reduce the effects of environmental risks. This could mean exploring multiple supply sources, establishing robust disaster recovery plans, and leveraging data analytics to enhance forecasting and quick responses to disruptions. Overall, a systematic approach to risk identification, including tools like SWOT analysis and brainstorming sessions with stakeholders, is essential for effective risk management in GVCs.

The risks in GVCs are diverse and complex, requiring companies to be proactive and flexible in their approach to risk management. While internal risks can often be mitigated through improved processes and technology, external risks are more challenging and unpredictable. Companies that can anticipate and adapt to these risks will be better positioned to maintain resilience and competitiveness in the global market.

Analytical Tools for Risk Assessment

Over the last two decades, GVCs have experienced substantial changes due to various risks, including geopolitical tensions, economic shifts, supply chain interruptions, and technological vulnerabilities. To navigate these challenges effectively, organizations need to implement structured risk management procedures that incorporate sophisticated analytical tools and decision-making methodologies. This section explores the evolution of GVC risk management strategies, focusing on essential parameters, assessment tools, and techniques that have developed between 2004 and 2024.

Evolution of Risk Management in GVCs

The growing intricacy of GVCs has made it imperative for organizations to establish strong governance frameworks and systematic risk management structures. Traditionally, businesses have depended on models like ISO 31000 and the supply chain operations reference (SCOR) framework to identify, evaluate, and mitigate risks. Nevertheless, the ever-changing landscape of modern supply chains necessitates ongoing adjustments to meet new challenges. Today's organizations must transcend conventional risk management frameworks and create dynamic processes that foster resilience and adaptability in an unpredictable global environment (Manners-Bell, 2017). Embracing digital transformation strategies, such as predictive analytics and blockchain technology, has further enhanced supply chain security and risk forecasting capabilities (Kouvelis et al., 2011).

Key Parameters in Risk Assessment

A comprehensive risk assessment in GVCs involves classifying risks according to their origin and nature. Initially, assessments primarily concentrated on two main parameters: the probability of occurrence and the severity of impact (Schauer & Mouratidis, 2019). However, as the complexity of supply chain risks has increased, additional parameters, including detectability, exposure, avoidance, impact duration, cost, and expected utility, have become significant.

Detectability pertains to the capacity to recognize risks prior to their emergence, underscoring the necessity for proactive monitoring. Exposure indicates the degree of vulnerability an organization faces concerning specific risks, often assessed through a set of key risk indicators. Risk avoidance evaluates the practicality of preventing risks through strategic measures, while risk impact intensity gauges the potential severity of disruptions (Talluri et al., 2013). Furthermore, impact duration assesses how long a disruption is likely to affect operations, emphasizing the importance of swift response and recovery strategies. These expanded parameters equip organizations with a comprehensive understanding of potential weaknesses, enabling the formulation of focused mitigation strategies.

Shifting Focus from Risk Elimination to Resilience

Historically, supply chain risk management aimed at eliminating failures and minimizing uncertainty. However, in the current volatile global climate, it is increasingly acknowledged that some risks are unavoidable. Consequently, organizations should emphasize resilience, developing the ability to swiftly recover from disruptions. This shift in perspective has led to a focus on embedding resilience within risk management frameworks, ensuring operational continuity amid external shocks (Cruz, 2013). The experiences of the COVID-19 pandemic and geopolitical tensions have highlighted the necessity for organizations to evolve from traditional risk mitigation techniques toward resilience-oriented strategies that enhance flexibility and responsiveness (Banwet & Shankar, 2007).

Risk Management Processes and Methodologies

A variety of risk management models have been crafted to tackle the changing challenges faced by GVCs. Conventional approaches concentrate on risk identification, assessment, and mitigation, while newer methodologies include resilience and recovery as fundamental aspects (Kumar et al., 2013). Effective risk management necessitates a balance between proactive strategies, such as diversification and early warning systems, and reactive approaches that facilitate prompt recovery from disruptions.

The increasing emphasis on resilience underscores the recognition that certain risks are inevitable. Organizations prioritizing contingency planning, scenario modeling, and adaptive supply chain tactics are better prepared to manage unforeseen interruptions. This forward-thinking strategy allows businesses to lessen the financial and operational repercussions of crises, thereby ensuring enduring stability and competitiveness.

Quantitative and Qualitative Risk Assessment Tools

The application of both qualitative and quantitative tools has become crucial in contemporary risk assessment. Traditionally, qualitative techniques were utilized for risk identification, while quantitative methods were employed for assessment and mitigation (Schauer & Mouratidis, 2019). The incorporation of advanced data analytics, machine learning, and real-time monitoring has improved the accuracy and efficacy of risk evaluations.

Quantitative models enable organizations to measure the likelihood and potential impact of risks, providing data-driven insights essential for strategic decision-making. These models assist in estimating financial consequences, assessing supply chain vulnerabilities, and evaluating the effectiveness of mitigation efforts (Kouvelis et al., 2011). As supply chains grow increasingly digitized, real-time data analytics will play a vital role in identifying and addressing emerging threats.

Decision-Making Techniques for Risk Assessment

A range of decision-making methodologies has been established to bolster risk assessment in GVCs. Multi-criteria decision-making (MCDM) techniques have gained traction as a popular method for simultaneously evaluating multiple risk factors (Manners-Bell, 2017). These methods facilitate prioritization of risks based on severity, probability, and mitigation feasibility, ensuring effective resource allocation.

One advanced approach utilized in risk assessment is fuzzy set theory, which quantifies uncertain and ambiguous variables to enhance decision-making. Fuzzy logic models enable organizations to analyze complex risk scenarios by incorporating multiple uncertainty factors. These techniques improve companies' capacities to evaluate potential threats and devise adaptable risk management strategies (Talluri et al., 2013).

The Future of Risk Management in GVCs

As global supply chains become increasingly interlinked, the demand for advanced risk assessment tools will continue to escalate. Organizations must adopt a multifaceted approach that integrates predictive analytics, artificial intelligence (AI)-driven risk modeling, and blockchain-enabled transparency (Cruz, 2013). Transitioning from reactive risk management to proactive resilience-building will be essential for navigating future disruptions.

Firms that invest in state-of-the-art risk assessment technologies and data-driven decision-making practices will be better equipped to endure external shocks. Future advancements in AI, predictive analytics, and supply chain visibility solutions will further enhance businesses' capabilities to foresee, mitigate, and address risks before they escalate (Banwet & Shankar, 2007).

Strategies for Risk Mitigation

The growing complexity of GVCs has resulted in heightened risks stemming from geopolitical conflicts, natural calamities, health crises, and technological advancements. Companies engaged in international commerce encounter substantial obstacles in sustaining operational stability and continuity. To navigate this unpredictable landscape effectively, organizations must adopt comprehensive risk mitigation strategies that allow them to endure and flourish (Okoye et al., 2024). These strategies include various components such as diversifying supply chains, leveraging technological innovations, utilizing insurance options, and employing proactive risk management approaches.

Supplier and Market Diversification

A primary method for firms within GVCs to mitigate risks is through diversifying their supplier and market bases. Relying heavily on a single supplier or market increases susceptibility to disruptions, potentially resulting in production delays, inventory deficits, or loss of revenue. By expanding their supplier networks across diverse regions and markets, businesses can distribute risks more effectively, ensuring operational continuity even when specific locations are disrupted. This strategy became particularly significant during the COVID-19 pandemic, as companies that depended on single-source suppliers faced considerable delays due to factory shutdowns.

Additionally, entering new markets aids in risk reduction by dispersing exposure across different geographical areas. This approach protects firms from local demand fluctuations or political instability. Companies that broaden their customer bases can sustain steady revenue flows, even if one market experiences a downturn. This stability is crucial for organizations operating in unpredictable environments where regulatory shifts or local economic conditions may adversely affect performance (Smorodinskaya et al., 2021).

Onshoring, Nearshoring, and Friend-Shoring

Strategies such as onshoring, nearshoring, and friend-shoring are increasingly being implemented to reorganize supply chains and reduce risks associated with an unstable global environment.

Onshoring refers to the practice of relocating production back to its country of origin. This method enhances operational oversight and minimizes risks tied to long-distance supply chains, such as shipping delays and trade tariffs, while also addressing uncertainties linked to foreign policies. The COVID-19 pandemic underscored the relevance of this approach as businesses aimed to lessen their reliance on distant suppliers during global disruptions (Srivastava & Rogers, 2022). Furthermore, rising trade tensions among major economies have accelerated this trend, prompting companies to bring manufacturing operations closer to home to avoid tariffs and geopolitical disruptions.

Nearshoring involves shifting production closer to the home country or into neighboring nations. This strategy reduces lead times and transportation costs, allowing businesses to strike a balance between proximity and cost-effectiveness by capitalizing on competitive labor rates in nearby areas. Moreover, nearshoring boosts supply chain resilience by facilitating faster adjustments during disruptions (Gurbuz et al., 2023).

Friend-shoring focuses on relocating supply chains to nations with stable political relations and aligned economic interests. This strategy minimizes exposure to geopolitical threats like sanctions or trade barriers by collaborating with countries that share similar values, thereby fostering long-term partnerships. Considering growing geopolitical tensions, friend-shoring has gained popularity as organizations seek to diversify their supply chains among trustworthy nations, reducing reliance on adversarial countries. Strengthening ties with politically aligned nations enhances supply chain security while mitigating the risks associated with sudden policy shifts that could impact operations (Manuj & Mentzer, 2008).

Technological Innovations: AI, Blockchain, and Data Analytics

Technological advancements play a vital role in reducing risks within GVCs. Innovations such as AI, blockchain technology, and data analytics improve visibility throughout the supply chain and enhance decision-making processes (Okoye et al., 2024).

AI is instrumental in forecasting potential disruptions within global supply chains by analyzing extensive datasets using machine learning algorithms that adapt based on historical trends—effectively predicting demand fluctuations and identifying emerging threats before they escalate. Additionally, AI aids in optimizing inventory management through improved forecasting capabilities (Gurbuz et al., 2023).

Blockchain technology significantly enhances transparency across supply chains through its decentralized ledger system, which securely and immutably records transactions. This enables all stakeholders, from producers to consumers, to trace goods throughout their journey from production to delivery, thereby reducing opportunities for fraud. This is particularly crucial for industries with stringent compliance requirements, such as pharmaceuticals or food products, where authenticity and regulatory adherence are paramount (Manuj & Mentzer, 2008).

Data analytics offers organizations valuable insights derived from comprehensive information regarding supplier performance metrics and market trends. These insights are essential for efficiently identifying operational vulnerabilities through predictive models designed to optimize inventory levels and support procurement strategies in challenging scenarios.

When combined, AI technologies integrated with blockchain applications, supported by robust analytical frameworks, create an innovative triad that enhances oversight across complex networks, enabling businesses to better prepare for uncertain environments (Smorodinskaya et al., 2021).

Insurance Products and Risk-Sharing Agreements

Integrating insurance products and risk-sharing agreements is another crucial strategy for addressing financial uncertainties stemming from disruptions in GVCs. These financial tools provide essential protection against unforeseen events that may impact operations (Srivastava & Rogers, 2022).

Supply chain insurance protects businesses from losses due to disruption incidents, including damages during transport or shortages resulting from natural disasters or cyber threats, which can impede seamless connectivity among partners in these ecosystems. Obtaining such insurance helps mitigate adverse financial impacts directly related to organizational sustainability efforts amid frequent external shocks in the current environment (Okoye et al., 2024).

Risk-sharing agreements promote collaborative approaches among stakeholders, distributing responsibilities for crises encountered collectively through negotiated arrangements among suppliers, customers, and logistics partners. These agreements foster joint ownership toward resilience, achieved collaboratively while alleviating the burden on any single entity (Manuj & Mentzer, 2008).

Trade credit insurance provides coverage for situations where buyers default on payments due to circumstances beyond sellers' control. This safeguard is particularly important in international trading environments, where payment complexities often arise from cross-border transactions (Gurbuz et al., 2023).

Continuous Monitoring and Crisis Management

Effectively implementing risk mitigation strategies in interconnected GVCs requires ongoing evolution, strategic development, and constant monitoring. Organizations must create comprehensive risk management frameworks, leverage digital transformation, and adopt proactive crisis management plans.

Developing thorough plans begins with detailed assessments of vulnerabilities, identifying not only key supplier dependencies but also potential failure points across entire networks. This enables organizations to forge tailored approaches that address identified weaknesses through diversification strategies, contingency planning, and the use of technological solutions to enhance operational transparency (Smorodinskaya et al., 2021).

Crisis management includes preparatory actions structured around prompt, actionable responses established in advance. These initiatives encompass clear communication channels, activation of predefined contingencies, and collaboration to resolve conflicts. Effective crisis management strengthens an organization's capability to navigate challenges and enhances preparedness, significantly improving recovery speed following disruptions (Srivastava & Rogers, 2022).

In summary, the combination of developing suitable tactical frameworks, maintaining continuous vigilance, and effectively managing crises forms the essential foundation for safeguarding business interests in today's increasingly volatile global trade environment.

Case Studies and Practical Insights

Understanding the complexities and risks involved in GVC is crucial for businesses seeking to thrive in an interconnected world. This section presents a collection of case studies and practical insights that illustrate how organizations have navigated various internal and external challenges within their supply chains.

These case studies offer practical lessons and actionable insights for professionals and scholars, helping them strengthen resilience, boost agility, and improve overall performance in managing their GVC.

Case Study 1: Supply Chain Disruptions in the Shipping Industry

The shipping sector serves as a fundamental component of international trade, responsible for the transportation of over 80% of global goods. As a vital element within GVCs, this industry is particularly susceptible to various external disturbances, such as geopolitical conflicts, economic fluctuations, cyber threats, and natural calamities. In recent years, significant disruptions have occurred due to issues like port congestion, a shortage of containers, and rising security risks along essential maritime routes. The COVID-19 pandemic highlighted the vulnerability of supply chains, and ongoing geopolitical strife, including tensions in the Red Sea and the conflict between Russia and Ukraine, has exacerbated delays and fluctuations in prices. Furthermore, increasing fuel expenses, environmental regulations, and the shift toward digitalization are altering the industry's operational framework, compelling companies to adapt to sustain resilience and efficiency (Supply Chain Brain, 2024).

Among the key entities in the global shipping arena, Maersk, recognized as the second-largest container shipping organization worldwide, has encountered notable supply chain challenges. In 2024, a rise in attacks on cargo vessels in the Red Sea compelled Maersk to alter its shipping routes to navigate around the Cape of Good Hope, leading to longer transit periods and elevated shipping expenses. This rerouting, combined with widespread trade bottlenecks globally, resulted in delays in cargo delivery and increased freight costs, affecting businesses that depend on maritime shipping. Additionally, congestion at ports in Europe and Asia, along with changing regulations concerning carbon emissions, presented further operational hurdles (World Cargo News, 2024).

To address these challenges, Maersk has made substantial investments in digital technologies such as real-time cargo tracking and predictive analytics, aimed at enhancing supply chain visibility and managing risks effectively. The company has also diversified its shipping routes and strengthened collaborations with alternative logistics providers to lessen reliance on high-risk trading pathways. Moreover, Maersk has incorporated blockchain technology into its logistics framework to improve transparency, curb fraud, and bolster data security throughout its supply chain network (Maersk, 2024). These initiatives reflect a broader trend in the industry toward technological advancement and strategic resilience, positioning Maersk as a frontrunner in addressing supply chain risks and fostering stability in global trade.

Case Study 2: Supply Chain Disruption: Automotive Industry

The global automotive sector is currently grappling with significant supply chain challenges prompted by geopolitical tensions, natural disasters, and economic instability. The ongoing semiconductor shortage, which began during the COVID-19 pandemic, has been intensified by persistent global conflicts and trade barriers. Consequently, automobile manufacturers like Ford, General Motors, and Volkswagen continue to encounter difficulties in stabilizing their supply chains. The semiconductor sector is predominantly reliant on Taiwan and South Korea, which together contribute over 70% of global chip production. However, rising tensions between China and Taiwan present a substantial threat to the availability of chips worldwide. A possible conflict or further trade restrictions could aggravate the semiconductor scarcity, thereby affecting the manufacturing of electric vehicles (EVs) and autonomous vehicles (Craft.co, 2024). Additionally, the Russia-Ukraine War has resulted in shortages of critical raw materials such as palladium and neon gas that are vital for chip production. With Russia accounting for 40% of global palladium output and Ukraine supplying 50% of semiconductor-grade neon gas, these shortages have led to increased prices and prolonged production timelines (Ship Green Line, 2024).

In response to these challenges, automakers are employing various strategies. Companies are relocating their semiconductor supply chains from China and Taiwan to alternative regions like the United States, Europe, and India. Governments have intervened to facilitate this transition; for instance, the U.S. CHIPS and Science Act (2023) provides incentives for domestic semiconductor manufacturing to lessen reliance on Asian suppliers. Furthermore, car manufacturers are increasingly moving their production facilities to politically stable allied nations to mitigate risks associated with geopolitical conflicts. Another significant approach involves integrating AI-driven tools for monitoring supply chains to anticipate and manage potential disruptions proactively before they escalate. By diversifying their sources of supply, boosting regional production capabilities, and utilizing advanced monitoring technologies, automakers can diminish vulnerabilities while enhancing their resilience against future disruptions. These initiatives reflect broader risk mitigation strategies discussed in the book chapter concerning supplier diversification and technological investments aimed at strengthening supply chain robustness.

Case Study 3: Pharmaceutical Industry

The pharmaceutical sector remains highly susceptible to geopolitical disturbances, regulatory hurdles, and supply chain limitations. The COVID-19 pandemic highlighted the fragility within pharmaceutical supply chains, especially regarding reliance on China and India for active pharmaceutical ingredients (APIs). Recent geopolitical developments have further complicated these global supply networks. China's export restrictions on pharmaceutical raw materials have triggered price increases and shortages of crucial medications. With China supplying more than 40% of antibiotics globally along with APIs, Western pharmaceutical companies face heightened uncertainty while sourcing essential components (KPMG, 2024). The U.S.-China trade disputes coupled with escalating regulatory scrutiny have compelled pharmaceutical firms to investigate alternative manufacturing locations in Europe, the Middle East, and Latin America. Moreover, the Russia-Ukraine conflict has disrupted transportation pathways for medical supplies, leading to escalated costs as well as delays in shipments destined for European and North American markets (Inspectorio, 2024).

To counteract these issues effectively, pharmaceutical companies are adopting measures aimed at reducing risks while cultivating more resilient supply chains. Firms such as Pfizer and Moderna are investing in reshoring or nearshoring their production processes to lessen dependence on Asia-based suppliers. The integration of blockchain technology is emerging as a pivotal strategy for enhancing transparency within supply chains while ensuring compliance with regulations; this aids in safeguarding medical supplies against counterfeiting efforts. Additionally, companies are broadening their API sourcing beyond China and India toward more politically stable regions, thereby minimizing exposure to trade barriers or political unrest risks. Strategic collaborations with governments, as well as local manufacturers, are being established to bolster resilience within pharmaceuticals, ensuring consistent access to essential medicines without interruption. By implementing these strategies actively throughout the industry, can better protect its supply chains and reduce reliance on high-risk

areas while augmenting its capacity for managing prospective future disruptions, effectively aligning closely with principles emphasized in the book chapter regarding risk identification assessment mitigation across GVCs, underscoring adaptability alongside strategic foresight during crises.

Conclusion and Recommendations

The intricacies of GVCs offer both potential benefits and risks for companies functioning in a more interconnected environment. The chapter emphasizes that challenges such as geopolitical disputes, economic instability, interruptions in supply chains, and technological weaknesses require thorough risk evaluation and mitigation plans. Incidents in the automotive and pharmaceutical sectors illustrate how external disturbances can lead to widespread repercussions on production processes, supply accessibility, and financial outcomes. The ongoing semiconductor shortage in the automotive industry and the reliance on APIs highlight the essential need for supplier diversification, nearshoring strategies, and advancements in technology to alleviate these risks.

As the geopolitical situation evolves, with factors like trade conflicts, warfare, and regulatory changes, businesses must implement proactive approaches such as digital monitoring of supply chains, blockchain technology adoption, and government-backed programs like the CHIPS Act. In addition, enhancing resilience within supply chains can be achieved through cooperative partnerships, scenario planning exercises, and interventions driven by policy. As organizations continue to maneuver through unpredictable conditions, it is crucial to promote adaptability, transparency, and responsiveness within GVCs. This chapter illustrates that firms combining risk anticipation with innovative risk management tactics will be more capable of sustaining their operations, navigating crises effectively, and preserving their competitive edge in a progressively unstable global economy.

References

Banwet, D. K., & Shankar, R. (2007). Information risk management in supply chains: An assessment and mitigation framework. *Journal of Enterprise Information Management, 20*(6), 713–732.

Brown, S., Gommers, J., & Serrano, O. (2015). From cyber security information sharing to threat management. In *Proceedings of the 2nd ACM workshop on information sharing and collaborative security* (pp. 43–49). The Association for Computing Machinery.

Brussel, X., & Teller, C. (2017). Supply chain capabilities, risks, and resilience. *International Journal of Production Economics, 184*, 59–68.

Cha, S. Y. (2022). The art of cyber security in the age of the digital supply chain: Detecting and defending against vulnerabilities in your supply chain. In *The digital supply chain* (pp. 215–233). Elsevier.

Craft.co. (2024). Geopolitical risks and their impact on supply chains. *Enterprise Craft.* https://enterprise.craft.co/post/geopolitical-risks-and-their-impact-on-supply-chains

Cruz, J. M. (2013). Mitigating global supply chain risks through corporate social responsibility. *International Journal of Production Research, 51*(13), 3995–4010.

Dornier, P. P., Ernst, R., Fender, M., & Kouvelis, P. (1998). *Global operations and logistics: Text and cases.* Wiley.

Gereffi, G. (2020). What does the COVID-19 pandemic teach us about global value chains? The case of medical supplies. *Journal of International Business Policy, 3*(3), 287.

Gurbuz, M. C., Yurt, O., Ozdemir, S., Sena, V., & Yu, W. (2023). Global supply chains risks and COVID-19: Supply chain structure as a mitigating strategy for small and medium-sized enterprises. *Journal of Business Research, 155*, 113407.

Ibrahim, S. E., Centeno, M. A., Patterson, T. S., & Callahan, P. W. (2021). Resilience in global value chains: A systemic risk approach. *Global Perspectives, 2*(1), 27658.

Inspectorio. (2024). State of supply chain report 2024. *Inspectorio Insights.* https://www.inspectorio.com/state-of-supply-chain-report-2024

Kouvelis, P., Dong, L., Boyabatli, O., & Li, R. (2011). *Handbook of integrated risk management in global supply chains.* Springer.

KPMG. (2024). Global supply chain fragility: Five trends and their impact. *KPMG Insights.* https://kpmg.com/us/en/articles/2024/2024-supply-chain-update.html

Kumar, S., Boice, B. C., & Himes, K. J. (2013). Risk assessment and operational approaches to managing risk in global supply chains. *Transportation Journal, 52*(3), 391–410.

Maersk. (2024). *Navigate supply chain disruptions with Maersk.* https://www.maersk.com/news/articles/2024/04/15/navigate-supply-chain-disruption-with-maersk

Manners-Bell, J. (2017). *Supply chain risk management: Understanding emerging threats to global supply chains.* Kogan Page.

Manuj, I., & Mentzer, J. T. (2008). Global supply chain risk management. *Journal of Business Logistics, 29*(1), 133–155.

Ogedegbe, G. (2023). Retention efforts and organizational effectiveness: A descriptive study. *Innovative Journal of Arts and Social Sciences, 5*(5), 145–155. ISSN: 2714-3317

Okoye, C. C., Ofodile, O. C., & Tula, S. T. (2024). *Risk management in international supply chains: A review with USA and African Cases.* Magna Scientia.

Pournader, M., Kach, A., & Talluri, S. (2020). A review of the existing and emerging topics in the supply chain risk management literature. *Decision Sciences, 51*(4), 867–919.

Sánchez-Flores, R. B., Cruz-Sotelo, S. E., Ojeda-Benitez, S., & Ramírez-Barreto, M. E. (2020). Sustainable supply chain management-a literature review on emerging economies. *Sustainability, 12*(17), 6972.

Schauer, S., & Mouratidis, H. (2019). MITIGATE: A dynamic supply chain cyber risk assessment methodology. *Journal of Transportation Security, 12*(1), 45–67.

Ship Green Line. (2024). *New disruptions, geopolitics hang over 2024 supply chains.* https://www.shipgreenline.com/new-disruptions-geopolitics-hang-over-2024-supply-chains/

Slack, N., & Brandon-Jones, A. (2018). *Operations management* (9th ed.). Pearson.

Smorodinskaya, N. V., Katukov, D. D., & Malygin, V. E. (2021). Global value chains in the age of uncertainty: Advantages, vulnerabilities, and ways for enhancing resilience. *Baltic Region, 13*(3), 78–107.

Srivastava, M., & Rogers, H. (2022). Managing global supply chain risks: Effects of the industry sector. *International Journal of Logistics Research and Applications, 25*(7), 1091–1114.

Supply Chain Brain. (2024). *Maersk sees global trade disruptions lasting throughout 2024.* https://www.supplychainbrain.com/articles/40144-maersk-sees-global-trade-disruptions-lasting-throughout-2024

Talluri, S., Kull, T. J., Yildiz, H., & Yoon, J. (2013). Assessing the efficiency of risk mitigation strategies in supply chains. *Journal of Business Logistics*, *34*(3), 209–226.

U.S. Department of Commerce. (2023). CHIPS and science act implementation. *U.S. Government.* https://www.commerce.gov/chipsact

Wieland, A., & Wallenburg, C. M. (2013). The influence of relational competencies on supply chain resilience: A relational view. *International Journal of Physical Distribution & Logistics Management*, *43*(4), 300–320.

World Cargo News. (2024). *Maersk lifts full-year forecast amid supply chain disruptions.* https://www.worldcargonews.com/news/2024/08/maersk-boosts-full-year-financial-projections-amid-supply-chain-disruptions/

Ying, L. Q., Senathirajah, A. R. S., Al-Ainati, S., Haque, R., Isa, M. B. M., Ramasamy, G., & Krishnasamy, H. N. (2023). Strategic human resource management factors influencing job satisfaction in Malaysian audit firms: Towards improving employment policy. *International Journal of Operations and Quantitative Management*, *29*(2), 316–339.

Zeng, K., Wells, R., Gu, J., & Wilkins, A. (2022). Bilateral tensions, the trade war, and US–China trade relations. *Business and Politics*, *24*(4), 399–429.

9

SUPPLY CHAIN RESILIENCE IN THE FACE OF GEOPOLITICAL TURMOIL

Anas Iftikhar and Ilias Vlachos

Introduction: Why Supply Chain Resilience Matters Now More than Ever

In today's highly interconnected global economy, supply chains have become the lifeblood of industries. However, with rising uncertainty due to geopolitical conflicts, disruptions seem to lurk around every corner. Companies now recognise that their ability to withstand and adapt to disruptions is no longer an operational concern but rather a matter of survival. In this fiasco, it has become clear that traditional supply chains are no longer fit for purpose. Historically, supply chains were designed for efficiency, streamlining operations to minimise costs, increase speed, and enhance profits. However, recent events have proven that this approach is fragile. Whether it's a global pandemic, trade wars, regional conflicts, or political upheaval, we've seen just how quickly the foundations of global supply chains can be shaken.

Supply chain resilience is the ability of a supply chain to prepare for, adapt to, and recover from disruptions, which is now recognised as a critical factor for survival. But resilience is not just about "bouncing back." It's about building systems that can adapt and evolve in the face of uncertainty. A resilient supply chain doesn't simply survive; it thrives and comes out stronger. Companies that fail to build resilience into their supply chains risk not only operational inefficiencies but also long-term damage to their brand and bottom line.

In this chapter, we explore why resilience has become the central focus of modern supply chain strategy. We'll look at how geopolitical turmoil is reshaping the business landscape, why companies can no longer afford to rely on old models, and the growing importance of creating agile, flexible,

DOI: 10.4324/9781003468899-9

and robust supply chains. Below, we will examine the turbulent geopolitical environment that is driving this shift.

Understanding the New Normal: Geopolitical Turbulence

Over the past decade, the world has experienced an increasing level of geopolitical instability that has disrupted global trade and supply chains. Trade wars, economic sanctions, political conflict, and shifting regulatory landscapes are no longer outliers—they have become part of the everyday business environment. Take the U.S.–China trade war, for example. What began as a series of tariffs on Chinese imports quickly escalated into a complex trade conflict, forcing businesses worldwide to rethink their supplier networks. Companies that relied heavily on Chinese manufacturers were suddenly hit with increased costs, supply shortages, and uncertainty about future trade regulations. Many organisations had to scramble to find alternative suppliers or risk major disruptions in their operations.

Furthermore, Brexit has resulted in new tariffs, customs regulations, and border delays for businesses operating in the UK and throughout Europe. For companies with complex logistics networks spanning across Europe, Brexit was a wake-up call, forcing them to reassess everything from warehouse locations to transportation routes. More recently, the Russia-Ukraine conflict has had a profound impact on supply chains, particularly in industries reliant on raw materials like energy, metals, and grains. The ripple effects have been felt far beyond Eastern Europe, affecting global markets and leading to significant price hikes, shortages, and logistical challenges.

What makes today's geopolitical turbulence particularly challenging is its unpredictability. Businesses can no longer rely on the assumption that trade agreements will hold steady or that political conflicts will be contained within a specific region. The modern geopolitical landscape is fluid, complex, and often volatile. This new normal requires companies to rethink their approach to supply chain management. It's no longer enough to focus solely on efficiency and cost-cutting. In a world where the rules of global trade are constantly shifting, businesses must build supply chains that can weather these storms, adapt quickly, and minimise the impact of disruptions. The consequences of geopolitical turbulence are not just hypothetical; they are being felt in real time. Companies that have built flexibility and adaptability into their supply chains are navigating these challenges with more ease. Those that haven't are struggling to keep up, experiencing delays, shortages, and skyrocketing costs.

The need for supply chain resilience is clearer than ever. But what exactly does it mean to build a resilient supply chain, and why is it so crucial for the future?

The Growing Importance of Resilient Supply Chains

Resilience has become a buzzword in the business world, but for good reason. At its core, supply chain resilience is about ensuring that a company's operations can withstand shocks, adapt to new circumstances, and continue delivering value in the face of disruption. It's not just about preparing for worst-case scenarios; it's about being ready to pivot and adapt whenever the unexpected happens.

The COVID-19 pandemic offered a sobering lesson in the importance of supply chain resilience. As global lockdowns took effect, supply chains that had long been optimised for efficiency and cost savings buckled under the pressure. Businesses that relied on single-source suppliers or just-in-time inventory models suddenly found themselves facing severe shortages and production stoppages. Many companies learned this lesson the hard way: when one part of a global supply chain fails, the entire operation can come to a standstill. Whether it's a critical component being delayed, a factory being shut down, or transportation routes being blocked, disruptions can ripple through the supply chain with devastating consequences.

But beyond the pandemic, the global landscape has changed in ways that demand more resilient supply chains. Companies that rely heavily on specific regions or suppliers for key materials are finding that political instability or natural disasters in those regions can halt their operations entirely. Even the weather has become an unpredictable force, with climate change leading to more frequent and severe natural disasters that can disrupt global logistics networks. Take the semiconductor industry, for example. The global chip shortage triggered by a combination of the pandemic, trade tensions, and supply-demand imbalances highlighted the fragility of supply chains in high-tech industries. Automotive companies, consumer electronics manufacturers, and even medical device producers found themselves scrambling for critical components, which in turn delayed production and drove up costs. The shortage underscored the need for companies to diversify their supplier base and build in redundancies to ensure continuity in supply.

In the past, many businesses hesitated to invest in resilience because it was seen as too expensive or unnecessary. The focus was on squeezing every possible cost out of the supply chain. But today, the conversation has shifted. Companies now recognise that the cost of not building resilience is far greater than the upfront investment. Supply chain disruptions can lead to lost revenue, customer dissatisfaction, damaged reputations, and even long-term financial harm. Resilience is no longer a luxury, it's a necessity. As global risks continue to rise, supply chains need to be flexible, responsive, and able to pivot quickly when faced with challenges. Companies that can build this kind of resilience into their operations will not only survive the next disruption but will also position themselves to thrive in an increasingly uncertain world.

The importance of resilience isn't just about avoiding disruption; it's about maintaining competitiveness. Businesses that can adapt quickly are more likely to keep their customers satisfied, sustain their revenue streams, and ultimately gain a competitive edge. In fact, companies that are perceived as reliable and able to deliver despite external challenges often see their market value increase during times of crisis. The growing importance of supply chain resilience isn't just a reaction to short-term challenges; it's a long-term shift in how businesses think about risk and opportunity. Building a resilient supply chain requires a proactive, forward-thinking approach that goes beyond simply reacting to disruptions. It means creating systems that are agile, adaptable, and robust enough to handle whatever comes next.

In an era defined by geopolitical turbulence, supply chain resilience has become a critical factor for businesses seeking to navigate uncertainty. No longer a "nice-to-have" feature, resilience is now a cornerstone of successful supply chain management. By understanding the shifting geopolitical landscape and recognising the growing importance of resilience, businesses can better prepare for the inevitable disruptions that lie ahead. The sections within this chapter that follow will explore the risks and common weaknesses, strategies, technologies, and collaborative efforts that can help companies build stronger, more resilient supply chains.

Identifying Risks in Global Value Chains

In the fast-paced world of international business, global value chains (GVCs) are the arteries through which goods, services, and information flow. These intricate networks connect suppliers, manufacturers, and consumers across multiple borders, creating opportunities for growth and efficiency. However, they also expose companies to a wide array of risks. Geopolitical upheavals, overreliance on specific regions, and the lack of real-time visibility into these sprawling supply chains can lead to catastrophic disruptions. Understanding these risks is the first step towards building resilience in GVCs.

Geopolitical Challenges that Disrupt Supply Chains

Supply chains do not operate in isolation from the political world. On the contrary, the political landscape plays an outsized role in determining how smoothly, or how chaotically, a supply chain functions. Geopolitical disruptions have become one of the most pressing risks facing GVCs today. From trade wars and sanctions to political instability and sudden regulatory shifts, businesses are finding themselves in the cross hairs of external forces that are largely beyond their control.

Trade Wars, Tariffs, and Sanctions

Few events in recent years have highlighted the vulnerability of supply chains to political decisions, quite like trade wars and tariffs. These economic skirmishes often begin as political bargaining chips but can quickly escalate into full-scale disruptions that ripple across industries. The U.S.–China trade war, for example, caused widespread upheaval as companies scrambled to adjust to new tariffs on hundreds of billions of dollars' worth of goods. Businesses that relied heavily on Chinese manufacturing suddenly found themselves facing skyrocketing costs or lengthy delays. Many were forced to pivot, either by reshoring production or by seeking out new suppliers in alternative regions, such as Vietnam or Mexico.

But it's not just tariffs. Sanctions, too, can have far-reaching consequences for GVCs. When sanctions are imposed on a country, companies doing business with suppliers or partners in that region must adapt quickly or face severe penalties. The Russia-Ukraine conflict is a stark reminder of how sanctions can upend entire industries, particularly in sectors like energy and agriculture. Western sanctions on Russia have left many companies struggling to secure critical raw materials such as oil, gas, and wheat, forcing them to rethink their sourcing strategies on short notice. In the face of such geopolitical risks, the lesson for companies is clear: flexibility and adaptability are no longer optional. Businesses need to diversify their supply chains, maintaining relationships with multiple suppliers across different regions to spread risk and minimise exposure to trade disputes or economic sanctions.

Political Instability and Regulatory Changes

The political landscape is constantly shifting, and these changes can introduce significant risks to GVCs. Political instability, whether through armed conflict, regime changes, or mass protests, has the potential to disrupt entire supply networks. Recent examples include the political protests in Hong Kong in 2019–2020, which shut down key transportation routes, and the 2021 military coup in Myanmar, which threw the country's entire manufacturing sector into disarray.[1] When a country experiences political unrest, it can lead to everything from temporary shutdowns of transportation hubs to long-term interruptions in production.

Adding another layer of complexity, regulatory changes are also becoming more frequent. New tariffs, environmental laws, and labour regulations can be imposed with little warning, leaving companies scrambling to comply. Brexit is a prime example of how such regulatory shifts can wreak havoc on supply chains. British companies that had once enjoyed seamless trade with the European Union (EU) suddenly found themselves burdened with new customs documentation, border delays, and expensive tariffs. Many were forced to relocate production or warehouse facilities to the EU to avoid these costly disruptions.

Political and regulatory risks are notoriously difficult to predict, but businesses can take proactive steps to mitigate their impact. The key is preparation, having contingency plans in place, maintaining close communication with partners in politically sensitive regions, and staying alert to regulatory changes that could affect operations.

Even as businesses face growing geopolitical challenges, many supply chains remain ill-equipped to handle disruptions. Several common weaknesses, ranging from an overreliance on specific suppliers to poor risk management practices, continue to expose companies to unnecessary risks. To build more resilient GVCs, it's critical to identify these vulnerabilities and address them head-on.

Overdependence on Specific Suppliers or Regions

One of the most glaring weaknesses in today's GVCs is overdependence on specific suppliers or regions. Many companies, in their pursuit of cost efficiency, have opted to concentrate production or sourcing in low-cost regions like China, Southeast Asia, or Eastern Europe. While this can yield short-term gains, it also creates a dangerous vulnerability. When disruptions such as natural disasters, political conflicts, or pandemics strike these regions, businesses that rely heavily on them can find themselves facing major supply shortages and production delays.

Additionally, understanding supply chain density is crucial in this context. Supply chain density refers to the concentration of suppliers and manufacturing facilities within specific geographic regions. When entities within a supply chain reside in close proximity to one another, that region can become vulnerable to disruptions. A single event, such as a natural disaster or political instability, can impact multiple suppliers simultaneously, leading to significant operational challenges. By diversifying their supplier base across various regions, organisations can reduce the risk associated with high-density areas, ensuring that if one location faces disruption, others can continue to operate and meet demand.

The global chip shortage that started in 2020 offers a prime example of how this overdependence can backfire. The semiconductor industry, concentrated primarily in East Asia, experienced widespread disruption due to COVID-19 lockdowns and increasing demand for electronics. This left industries reliant on chips like automotive, electronics, and medical devices, scrambling to secure critical components.[2] The lesson here is clear: diversification of suppliers is essential. Companies should avoid putting all their eggs in one basket, instead opting for multi-sourcing strategies that spread risk across different regions and suppliers.

Limited Visibility and Poor Risk Management

Another critical weakness that plagues many global supply chains is the lack of visibility. In a world where suppliers are often located halfway across the globe, businesses frequently lack real-time insight into what's happening within their supply networks. This lack of visibility makes it difficult to identify emerging risks, such as delays, shortages, or quality control issues, before they become full-blown crises.

Part of the problem is that many companies still rely on outdated or siloed technologies that don't provide a comprehensive view of the entire supply chain. Without this visibility, businesses are often caught off guard by disruptions, unable to respond quickly enough to mitigate the impact. Poor risk management practices further exacerbate the problem. Some organisations continue to treat risk management as an afterthought, with few processes in place to proactively identify and mitigate potential risks.

To address these shortcomings, companies need to invest in modern technologies that provide real-time supply chain visibility. Tools like advanced analytics, artificial intelligence (AI), and blockchain can help track shipments, monitor supplier performance, and even predict potential disruptions before they occur. By utilising these technologies, businesses can build a more responsive and resilient supply chain, better equipped to handle whatever challenges arise.

Building Resilient Supply Chains: Key Strategies

In today's dynamic business environment, the resilience of supply chains has emerged as a fundamental necessity rather than a mere luxury. As geopolitical tensions, natural disasters, and unforeseen events increasingly disrupt the flow of goods and services, organisations must adopt strategic measures to fortify their supply chains. This chapter outlines essential strategies that can help businesses enhance their resilience and thrive amid uncertainty.

Diversifying Supply Sources and Creating Redundancy

One of the cornerstones of building a resilient supply chain is diversification. The adage "Don't put all your eggs in one basket" resonates deeply in this context, as overreliance on a single supplier or geographical region can lead to catastrophic vulnerabilities. In today's interconnected world, disruption has many sources, from geopolitical conflicts to environmental catastrophes. By diversifying the supply sources, companies not only spread the risk and enhance their ability to respond to challenges swiftly but also exploit the unique strengths and capabilities of different suppliers and markets. This exposure can lead to improved operational performance and empower organisations to adapt to an ever-evolving business landscape.

How to Avoid Putting All Your Eggs in One Basket

To safeguard against potential disruptions, organisations must intentionally diversify their supply sources. This entails more than merely seeking multiple suppliers for critical materials; it involves exploring various geographical locations as well. For instance, companies that have relied solely on manufacturing in China should consider establishing relationships with suppliers in regions such as Southeast Asia, India, or Mexico. This approach not only mitigates the risk associated with regional disruptions but also enables businesses to tap into emerging markets with competitive advantages.

Furthermore, diversification extends to product lines and service offerings. Companies can create flexibility by introducing alternative products or services that can be quickly implemented in response to changes in demand. This dual approach to diversification allows businesses to adapt to shifting market conditions while ensuring a steady flow of goods.

Building Backup Plans into Your Supply Chain

Creating redundancy within the supply chain is another vital component of resilience. Organisations should establish comprehensive backup plans that outline alternative sourcing options and procedures for managing disruptions. This means not only identifying secondary suppliers but also developing processes like contractual agreements for capacity reservation to enable quick adjustments in response to unforeseen events.

Backup plans should include detailed contingency protocols that specify the steps to be taken when a disruption occurs, ensuring that all stakeholders understand their roles and responsibilities. Regularly testing these plans through simulations or drills can help identify gaps in preparedness and improve response times during actual crises.

For example, a manufacturer of electronic components might maintain a strategic relationship with multiple suppliers for essential parts. If one supplier encounters a disruption due to a natural disaster, political instability, or a supply shortage, the company can seamlessly pivot to an alternative supplier without significantly impacting production schedules. Such proactive strategies not only prepare organisations for major disruptive events but also foster a culture of resilience and adaptability throughout the organisation.

Case Study Example

A notable example of effective diversification and redundancy is Toyota's proactive approach to semiconductor inventory management, which proved invaluable during the semiconductor shortages caused by the COVID-19 pandemic.[3]

After the disruptions experienced during the 2011 earthquake and tsunami in Japan, Toyota shifted from a "just-in-time" inventory strategy to a "just-in-case" approach, maintaining higher stocks of critical components like semiconductors. Although this investment took nine years to pay off, it enabled Toyota to build a four-month stockpile of chips, allowing it to continue production smoothly while many competitors struggled with shortages. This proactive investment in redundancy ensured business continuity and highlighted the value of balancing efficiency with resilience, demonstrating that preparedness for future uncertainties can be a significant competitive advantage during times of global supply chain turmoil.

The lesson is clear that diversification and redundancy are not just strategic advantages; they are essential to surviving and thriving in a volatile global market. This case underscores the importance of not only diversifying sources but also continually assessing and updating strategies to adapt to new challenges as they arise. In an ever-changing landscape, the ability to pivot and respond swiftly can determine a company's long-term success.

Embracing Flexibility and Agility

In addition to diversification, embracing flexibility and agility within the supply chain is crucial for fostering resilience. The ability to adapt quickly to changing circumstances can make the difference between success and failure during a crisis. As businesses face an increasingly volatile environment, the need for rapid response mechanisms becomes significant, which enables them to adjust operations in real-time as circumstances evolve.

Agile supply chains are characterised by their ability to respond rapidly to fluctuations in demand and supply conditions. This requires not only flexible processes but also a cultural mindset that encourages innovation, collaboration, and quick decision-making. Organisations should consider implementing agile methodologies that facilitate rapid iterations and responsiveness to market changes. Companies, rather than relying solely on just-in-time inventory practices, should consider maintaining strategic inventory levels to buffer against uncertainties. This means identifying key products or components that are critical to operations and ensuring that sufficient stock is available to absorb short-term fluctuations in demand or supply. Additionally, businesses can implement flexible inventory management strategies, such as postponement and modular production, which allow them to delay final product assembly until customer demand is clearer. This not only minimises excess inventory but also enhances responsiveness to changing market conditions.

Furthermore, scenario planning is a valuable practice for building agility. By regularly conducting exercises that simulate various disruption scenarios, organisations can identify the weakest links and vulnerabilities in their supply chains and develop preemptive strategies. This proactive approach ensures that when real disruptions occur, companies are better equipped to respond quickly and effectively.

A remarkable instance of agility in action can be observed in the fashion industry's response to the COVID-19 pandemic. Many brands that traditionally operated on a seasonal production cycle swiftly adapted their supply chains to produce personal protective equipment (PPE) when demand surged. By reconfiguring production lines and collaborating with suppliers, these companies demonstrated the capacity to pivot and meet urgent market needs without sacrificing quality. This adaptability not only showcases operational flexibility but also reinforces the importance of maintaining strong relationships with suppliers, enabling businesses to shift gears when necessary. Such collaborations can lead to innovative solutions that enhance product offerings and streamline processes, thus fostering a more resilient supply chain in the long term.

Case Study Example

A pertinent case study is that of Zara, the fast-fashion giant renowned for its agile supply chain. Zara can design, produce, and deliver new products to stores in a matter of weeks. This remarkable speed is the result of a highly integrated supply chain that emphasises close collaboration with suppliers and rapid responsiveness to customer feedback. By maintaining a flexible supply chain that prioritises quick turnaround times and minimal lead times, Zara has positioned itself as a leader in an industry where consumer preferences can change almost overnight.

Zara's success underscores the value of agility and flexibility in supply chain management. Companies that embrace these principles will not only weather disruptions more effectively but will also seize new opportunities as they arise.

Why Collaboration Is Key to Supply Chain Resilience

Collaboration emerges as a cornerstone of resilient supply chains. In an increasingly interconnected world, no organisation can navigate disruptions alone. By working together, organisations can pool their knowledge and resources, allowing for quicker identification of potential disruptions and more effective contingency planning. Building strong partnerships across industries, governments, and communities is vital for fostering resilience. This interconnectedness enhances the ability to respond to unforeseen challenges, ensuring that partners can act swiftly and decisively in the face of adversity.

A collaborative approach enables organisations to share knowledge, resources, and best practices. Governments can play a pivotal role by providing support to industries during crises, while companies benefit from shared insights and pooled resources. For instance, during the pandemic, many governments collaborated with businesses to facilitate the rapid production of critical medical supplies. This collaboration included streamlining regulatory processes and providing financial incentives, thereby allowing businesses to shift their production lines more efficiently.

Moreover, collaboration extends to cross-sector partnerships that leverage diverse expertise. For example, technology companies can partner with manufacturers to develop innovative solutions that enhance supply chain efficiency and resilience. These collaborations create a synergistic effect, amplifying the collective capacity to respond to challenges. By harnessing the unique strengths of different sectors, organisations can implement creative solutions that would be difficult to achieve in isolation.

Additionally, engaging local communities can further strengthen collaborative efforts. Community involvement can provide valuable insights into local needs and capabilities, allowing organisations to tailor their responses more effectively. By fostering trust and communication at the grassroots level, companies can build a more robust support system that enhances their resilience during crises.

Establishing partnerships with supply chain players like suppliers, logistics providers, and even competitors can create a network of support that enhances resilience. Collaborative efforts can lead to shared resources, joint risk mitigation strategies, and innovative solutions to common challenges. These coordinative efforts enable organisations to swiftly adapt and reconfigure resources to collectively address uncertainties.

Furthermore, strategic alliances can provide access to new markets and customer bases, allowing partners to expand their reach while sharing the associated risks. By working together, companies can invest in research and development (R&D) initiatives that drive innovation, ensuring they remain competitive even in turbulent times. Ultimately, strong partnerships foster a sense of shared purpose, which can enhance commitment to mutual goals and outcomes.

Case Study Example

A notable example of effective collaboration is the Global Supply Chain Task Force formed during the COVID-19 pandemic. This coalition, comprising governments from various countries, private sector leaders, and international organisations such as the World Health Organization (WHO) and other United Nations agencies, aimed to streamline the production and distribution of critical medical supplies. By working together, these stakeholders were able to address supply chain disruptions and ensure that essential products reached those in need swiftly.

This case illustrates the power of collaboration in overcoming challenges that no single entity could address alone. By fostering strong relationships and open communication, businesses can create a resilient network that thrives in the face of uncertainty. The lessons learned from this collaborative effort can serve as a framework for future partnerships, emphasising the need for continuous dialogue and shared objectives in building a more resilient global supply chain.

Leveraging Digital Tools for Resilience

In today's digital age, technology plays a pivotal role in building resilient supply chains. Utilising digital tools can enhance visibility, streamline processes, and enable organisations to anticipate and respond to disruptions effectively. In today's dynamic business environment, adopting digital technologies holds immense significance. Through real-time information sharing, companies can proactively monitor market conditions, identify emerging opportunities, and transform their strategies to meet evolving objectives. This will not only strengthen their resilience but also position them to survive and thrive amid uncertainty.

Advanced technologies such as the Internet of Things (IoT), AI, and blockchain offer powerful solutions for improving supply chain visibility. These tools enable real-time monitoring of inventory, shipments, and supplier performance, allowing organisations to identify potential issues before they escalate into crises.

For example, IoT sensors can provide real-time data on the location and condition of shipments, while AI algorithms can analyse this data to predict potential delays or disruptions. This level of visibility empowers companies to make informed decisions and optimise their operations proactively. Additionally, the use of blockchain technology enhances transparency by providing an immutable record of transactions, enabling all parties involved to verify the authenticity and provenance of goods. This not only reduces the risk of fraud but also fosters trust among supply chain partners.

Predictive analytics also plays a crucial role in risk management within complex supply chains. Companies can utilise these tools to forecast demand fluctuations, identify potential risks, and navigate the complexities inherent in global operations. By harnessing big data and machine learning algorithms, organisations can make informed decisions, optimise operations, and respond proactively to emerging threats. For instance, by evaluating data from multiple points along the supply chain, companies can identify the weakest links (vulnerabilities), such as supplier delays or transportation bottlenecks, before they escalate into significant issues.

Case Study Example

A leading example of digital innovation in supply chain management is Unilever. The consumer goods giant employs advanced analytics and IoT technologies to gain real-time visibility into its supply chain. By monitoring everything from raw materials to end-consumer behaviour, Unilever can quickly adapt its production and distribution strategies to meet changing market demands. This proactive approach has not only improved efficiency but also significantly enhanced the company's resilience during disruptions.

Similarly, Amazon has leveraged technology to create a highly resilient supply chain, employing robotics, machine learning, and data analytics to optimise its logistics and inventory management. By investing in digital tools, Amazon has positioned itself to respond rapidly to consumer needs, further solidifying its status as a leader in e-commerce. This investment in technology not only supports operational efficiency but also fosters a customer-centric approach, ensuring that Amazon can meet the high expectations of its diverse customer base.

Building resilient supply chains is not merely a reactive measure; it is a proactive strategy that requires foresight, flexibility, and collaboration.[4] By diversifying supply sources, embracing agility, fostering collaboration, and leveraging digital tools, organisations can create supply chains that not only withstand disruptions but also thrive in an increasingly complex and unpredictable world. In this ever-evolving landscape, those who invest in resilience today will be the leaders of tomorrow.

Case Study Example

Huawei, a leading global telecommunication and technology company, has been significantly affected by the U.S.–China trade war and the subsequent sanctions imposed by the U.S. government. These sanctions limited Huawei's access to essential technologies, particularly semiconductors, which are crucial for its products, including smartphones and networking equipment. In response, Huawei implemented several strategies to mitigate these impacts.

The company intensified its efforts to develop a self-reliant supply chain by investing heavily in domestic semiconductor production and exploring alternative suppliers outside the United States. Huawei has also focused on enhancing its R&D capabilities to reduce its reliance on external technology. Furthermore, the firm diversified its product offerings to include more software and services, which lessened its dependence on hardware components subject to sanctions. This diversification helped Huawei mitigate some of the risks associated with international trade restrictions while simultaneously building new revenue streams less vulnerable to global supply chain disruptions.

This case highlights the importance of agility and adaptability in supply chain management. Companies facing geopolitical risks must invest in diversifying their supply bases and enhancing internal capabilities. Building a resilient supply chain often requires a shift towards self-sufficiency and innovation, particularly in industries heavily reliant on technology. As Huawei has shown, fostering partnerships with domestic suppliers and investing in R&D can mitigate risks associated with international tensions.

Case Study Example

During the COVID-19 pandemic, Pfizer faced significant challenges in manufacturing and distributing the vaccine globally. To overcome these hurdles, Pfizer activated its extensive global supply chain, which includes over 35 manufacturing sites and a network of more than 300 suppliers. The company established production capabilities across four continents, ensuring geographic diversification to mitigate risks associated with relying on a single region. To manage vaccine distribution, Pfizer utilised advanced cold chain logistics, including specially designed thermal shippers with dry ice, GPS-enabled tracking, and a combination of air and ground transport. These measures allowed Pfizer to maintain temperature integrity for up to 10 days, ensuring the vaccine reached even the most remote areas.

The company also used a "just-in-time" distribution system, shipping frozen vials directly to point of use (POU), such as hospitals and pharmacies, or leveraging its existing distribution centres in the United States and Germany. This flexibility was key to responding to rapidly changing demand across multiple regions, minimising waste, and maximising vaccine availability.

Pfizer's approach to manufacturing and distribution illustrates the power of comprehensive risk management, geographic diversification, and sophisticated cold chain capabilities. By leveraging multiple sites, utilising just-in-time distribution, and investing in thermal tracking technology, Pfizer managed to deliver a high-quality product to over 165 countries efficiently. Their strategy serves as an example of how end-to-end logistics, robust partnerships, and proactive preparedness can foster resilience in the face of complex global supply chain challenges.

References

1. Pennisi di Floristella, A. (2023). The everything but arms (EBA) scheme and the EU's normative dilemma: The case of Myanmar's garment sector. *Third World Quarterly*, *44*(11), 2404–2421.
2. Jackson, F. (2023). *Global chip shortage: Everything you need to know*. Retrieved October 15, 2024, from https://www.techrepublic.com/article/global-chip-shortage-cheat-sheet/
3. Rice, J. B., Klibi, W., & Trepte, K. (2022). Overcoming the financial barriers to building resilient supply chains. *Harvard Business Review*. https://hbr.org/2022/11/overcoming-the-financial-barriers-to-building-resilient-supply-chains
4. Sheffi, Y. (2007). Building a resilient supply chain. *Harvard Business Review*. Retrieved August 14, from https://hbr.org/2007/08/building-a-resilient-supply-ch

10

SUSTAINABILITY AND ESG IN GLOBAL VALUE CHAINS

Said Usman, Nasrin Asgari and Wantao Yu

Introduction

Global value chains (GVCs) are fundamental to modern economies, enabling the seamless production and distribution of goods and services across international borders. However, the integration of sustainability and ESG (environmental, social, and governance) principles into these value chains remains a pressing challenge. This is particularly crucial in light of increasing environmental concerns, social inequalities, and the necessity for ethical governance frameworks (Wang, 2023; Fang et al., 2022).

Sustainable supply chain management (SSCM) is pivotal in addressing these challenges by embedding environmental and social responsibilities into supply chain operations (Tran et al., 2023). Despite the growing political and industrial focus on sustainability, significant gaps remain in understanding how these principles can be effectively integrated, especially in emerging markets (Ngo et al., 2024). The COVID-19 pandemic has further exposed the vulnerabilities of global supply chains, highlighting the urgent need for resilience and sustainability (Khan et al., 2021; Chowdhury et al., 2021).

The manufacturing sector, particularly in emerging markets like Nigeria, is critical for sustainable development. Nigerian manufacturing firms face unique challenges in implementing SSCM practices, such as inadequate technology, unsustainable production methods, and limited institutional support (Bolaji et al., 2018; Orji & Ojadi, 2021). These challenges present significant risks not only to the environment and society but also to the economic stability of the region. With the Nigerian manufacturing sector contributing about 10% to the national gross domestic product (GDP), understanding and improving

DOI: 10.4324/9781003468899-10

SSCM practices in this context is vital for the country's economic and environmental future (National Bureau of Statistics [NBS], 2023).

Moreover, existing research has predominantly focused on developed economies, creating a critical void in understanding how SSCM can be effectively implemented in emerging markets like Nigeria. This gap is particularly pressing given that emerging markets often face more severe environmental and social challenges coupled with weaker institutional frameworks. By concentrating on the Nigerian context, this study seeks to fill this gap, providing empirical insights that can inform both local practices and broader global strategies for sustainable supply chains.

Objectives and Scope of the Chapter

In the pursuit of more sustainable supply chains, technological orientation (TO) and supply chain information integration (SCII) emerge as indispensable drivers of innovation and efficiency. TO, encompassing the adoption and utilisation of advanced technologies, is essential for unifying product development and sustainability, thereby enhancing efficiency, reducing waste, and fostering the development of sustainable products and processes (Ardito et al., 2021; Lei et al., 2019). However, the influence of TO on SSCM remains underexplored, particularly in emerging markets where the strategic implementation of TO can drive both ecological and economic gains (Silvestre, 2015; Orji et al., 2022). SCII, involving the seamless integration of information and processes, enhances efficiency and reduces operational costs by improving coordination among supply chain partners (SCPs). Despite its recognised importance for strategic communication, there is a notable gap in understanding how SCII affects SSCM practices, especially in technologically and regulatory-constrained environments (Silvestre, 2015; Huo et al., 2016; Yu et al., 2021). This study addresses these gaps by examining the roles of TO and SCII in facilitating SSCM practices within the Nigerian manufacturing sector, providing actionable insights for firms in similar contexts.

This chapter aims to explore the integration of sustainability and ESG principles within Nigerian manufacturing firms. By examining two detailed case studies, the chapter provides empirical evidence on the adoption of SSCM practices and analyses the roles of SCII and TO in enhancing business performance. The study also examines the influence of institutional forces such as government support (GS) and legal protections (LPs) on the adoption of these practices. The research is conducted with the objectives of examining the role of TO and SCII in enabling manufacturing firms to implement SSCM practices, investigating how the implementation of SSCM practices can improve business performance, and exploring the moderating role of institutional forces between TO and SSCM, as well as the relationship between SCII and SSCM.

Focusing on two Nigerian manufacturing firms, referred to as Company A and Company B for confidentiality, this chapter investigates the current implementation of SSCM practices, the impact of SCII and TO, and the influence of institutional forces. The analysis provides a nuanced understanding of the barriers and enablers of SSCM in an emerging market context. By highlighting the specific challenges and opportunities within Nigeria, this chapter contributes to the broader discourse on sustainable supply chains and offers practical insights for businesses and policymakers in similar emerging economies.

By addressing a critical research gap, this chapter aims to contribute significantly to the global discourse on sustainable supply chains. Highlighting the specific challenges and opportunities within the Nigerian manufacturing sector, it offers valuable lessons for other emerging economies. The findings can inform strategies that enhance the resilience and sustainability of GVCs, ensuring they are better equipped to face future disruptions and contribute to sustainable development goals.

Understanding the Landscape: SSCM and the Nigerian Manufacturing Context

Overview of SSCM and the Importance of GVCs

SSCM has gained prominence as a vital strategy for embedding ESG principles into traditional supply chain management. SSCM ensures that supply chain operations not only achieve economic objectives but also contribute to environmental protection and social equity (Fang et al., 2022). This shift towards sustainability is driven by increasing regulatory pressures, stakeholder demands, and the growing recognition of the long-term benefits of sustainable practices (Khan et al., 2021).

The COVID-19 pandemic has further highlighted the fragility of global supply chains and underscored the need for resilient and sustainable supply chain practices. The disruptions caused by the pandemic revealed significant vulnerabilities, prompting firms to re-evaluate and enhance their supply chain strategies to incorporate sustainability and resilience (Orji & Ojadi, 2021; Chowdhury et al., 2021).

In emerging markets, the importance of SSCM is particularly pronounced. These regions often struggle with severe environmental degradation and social inequalities, compounded by weaker regulatory frameworks and limited resources (Bolaji et al., 2018). For instance, in Nigeria, the manufacturing sector is crucial for economic development but poses significant environmental and social risks. Addressing these risks through SSCM practices is vital for sustainable economic growth and the well-being of the population.

GVCs involve the internationalisation of production processes, where different stages of the production process are located across different countries (Orji et al., 2022). For Nigerian manufacturing firms, participating in GVCs provides opportunities to access larger markets, acquire advanced technologies, and improve productivity and competitiveness (Orji & Ojadi, 2021). The integration into GVCs can help Nigerian manufacturers overcome some of the challenges they face, such as limited access to technology and capital. By collaborating with international partners, Nigerian firms can adopt best practices in sustainability and ESG, enhancing their capabilities to meet global standards. However, this integration also brings challenges, such as adhering to stringent environmental and social regulations imposed by global buyers and dealing with the complexities of coordinating activities across multiple countries.

Despite the critical importance of SSCM, there is a significant gap in the literature concerning its implementation in emerging markets. Most research focuses on developed economies, leaving a void in understanding how SSCM can be effectively integrated into the supply chains of developing countries. This research aims to fill this gap by providing empirical insights into the adoption of SSCM practices in the Nigerian manufacturing sector, offering valuable lessons for other emerging economies.

Manufacturing in Nigeria and SSCM Challenges in Emerging Economies

The manufacturing sector is vital to Nigeria's economic growth, contributing approximately 10% to GDP (National Bureau of Statistics [NBS], 2023). Despite its importance, the sector has historically been overshadowed by the focus on crude oil, resulting in slow industrialisation and limited contributions to national growth (Egbulonu & Duru, 2018). Manufacturing in Nigeria faces numerous challenges, including outdated technology, weak infrastructure, and limited institutional support (Uma et al., 2019). These challenges are exacerbated in developing economies where supply chain management is often hindered by economic inequality, rapid industrialisation, and a lack of environmental regulations. SSCM practices are gaining attention as a means of addressing these issues, but their adoption remains slow due to financial limitations, technological barriers, and institutional deficiencies (Sánchez-Flores et al., 2020). Nigerian firms are gradually recognising the importance of SSCM in mitigating these challenges and aligning with global sustainability standards (Orji et al., 2022).

The Role of TO in SSCM

TO refers to a firm's capacity to acquire, adopt, and utilise advanced technologies to innovate and improve processes (Gatignon & Xuereb, 1997). TO is essential for driving innovation enhancing efficiency. It also fosters the development of sustainable products and processes (Tseng et al., 2019). In the context of SSCM, TO plays a crucial role in unifying product development with sustainability goals, thus contributing to both ecological and economic gains (Ardito et al., 2021; Lei et al., 2019).

However, the relationship between TO and SSCM remains underexplored, particularly in emerging markets where technological capabilities may be limited. In Nigeria, for example, the strategic implementation of TO can significantly enhance SSCM practices by improving operational efficiency, reducing waste, and fostering innovation (Silvestre, 2015). Despite its potential benefits, few empirical studies have examined how TO impacts SSCM in the manufacturing sector (Lei et al., 2019; Tseng et al., 2019). This research aims to fill this gap by investigating the role of TO in SSCM implementation within Nigerian manufacturing firms, providing actionable insights for similar contexts.

Existing literature suggests that TO is vital for SSCM due to the increasing demand for information and innovation in driving sustainability. However, there is a scarcity of empirical evidence examining the relationship between TO and SSCM practices. This study attempts to fill this gap by exploring how TO as a firm-level resource can facilitate the implementation of SSCM practices in manufacturing firms, particularly in the Nigerian context.

The Role of SCII in SSCM

SCII involves the seamless integration of information and processes across the supply chain, enhancing coordination, communication, and joint decision-making (Huo et al., 2016). SCII is crucial for SSCM as it enables firms to manage sustainability-related information effectively, reducing uncertainty and improving overall supply chain performance (Busse et al., 2017).

Despite its recognised importance, the impact of SCII on SSCM is not fully understood, especially in environments with technological and regulatory constraints like Nigeria (Silvestre, 2015; Yu et al., 2021). Effective SCII can significantly enhance SSCM practices by facilitating the exchange of relevant and accurate information, enabling firms to make informed decisions and respond promptly to changes in the business environment (Yu et al., 2021).

SCII is typically divided into internal information integration (III) and external information integration (EII). III refers to the extent to which a firm creates a fully integrated information system within the organisation, facilitating information sharing across all functions. EII, on the other hand, involves the extent to which a firm collaborates with key external partners, integrating information and processes to enhance inter-organisational coordination (Huo et al., 2016).

Research on SCII has shown that higher levels of information integration led to better supply chain performance. For example, firms that effectively integrate information with their SCPs can reduce operational costs, improve customer satisfaction, and enhance overall supply chain efficiency (Tsai & Lasminar, 2021). However, there is limited empirical evidence on how SCII impacts SSCM practices, particularly in the context of developing economies. This study aims to explore the role of SCII in facilitating SSCM practices in the Nigerian manufacturing sector, providing insights that can guide businesses in similar contexts.

Institutional Forces Shaping SSCM Practices

Institutional forces, including GS, LP, and business networks (BNs), play a significant role in shaping firm strategies and practices related to SSCM (Cai et al., 2010). These forces can either facilitate or hinder the adoption of SSCM practices, depending on the regulatory and institutional environment.

GS encompasses the financial assistance and business-friendly policies provided by various government agencies. Governments can indirectly influence corporate operations by fostering environments conducive to business or directly through economic policy measures. In Nigeria, GS for SSCM is essential for promoting regulatory frameworks and infrastructure that encourage sustainable practices (Ilyas et al., 2020).

LP refers to the extent to which the rights of individuals and organisations are safeguarded by the legal system (Shou et al., 2016). A robust legal framework reduces transaction uncertainty, lowers costs associated with reputation building, and enhances trust in market dealings (Hemmert et al., 2016). Effective LP is particularly important in emerging economies like Nigeria, where underdeveloped legal systems can hinder the effective implementation of SSCM practices (Yang et al., 2018; Okafor et al., 2024).

BNs are essential for fostering trust, mutual aid, and efficient information sharing among SCPs (Hemmert et al., 2016). Stable BNs lead to longer-lasting partnerships and enhanced cooperation, which are crucial for the implementation of SSCM practices. In Nigeria, where formal institutions may be weak, BNs can play a significant role in facilitating the adoption of sustainable practices by providing informal support and information.

By examining the roles of these institutional forces, this research aims to provide a comprehensive understanding of the factors that influence the adoption of SSCM practices in the Nigerian manufacturing sector. The findings can inform strategies that enhance the resilience and sustainability of GVCs, ensuring they are better equipped to face future disruptions and contribute to sustainable development goals.

This literature review highlights the critical importance of SSCM in integrating ESG principles into supply chains, particularly in emerging markets. It underscores the need for a comprehensive understanding of how TO and SCII can facilitate the adoption of SSCM practices and the role of institutional forces in shaping these practices. By addressing these gaps, this research aims to provide valuable insights into the implementation of SSCM in the Nigerian manufacturing sector, contributing to the broader discourse on sustainable supply chains and offering practical strategies for businesses and policymakers in similar emerging economies.

Case Studies in Nigerian Manufacturing

Introduction to the Selected Case Studies

To gain empirical insights into the integration of sustainability and ESG principles within Nigerian manufacturing firms, this chapter examines two detailed case studies. The selected companies, referred to as Company A and Company B for confidentiality, represent illustrative examples of firms in the Nigerian manufacturing sector. These companies were chosen based on their significant market presence, commitment to sustainability practices, and availability of detailed data.

Company A: Within-Case Analysis

Company A is a manufacturing firm established in Lagos, Nigeria, in 2009. Company A operates in the manufacturing sub-sector of food and beverages and specialises in the production of indigenous food products such as seasoning cubes. Company A currently employs more than 500 people. Company A is also a member of the Manufacturers Association of Nigeria (MAN). Through the use of modern machinery, a well-motivated workforce, and maintaining a solid partnership with their customers, it seeks to be one of the most efficient manufacturers of food products in Nigeria.

TABLE 10.1 Results of company A's interview data

Dimension	*Findings*
TO	Provide new and innovative products regularly Operate more cost-effectively Develop an innovative culture to promote staff innovation
SCII	Effective communication using digital technologies to process relevant information Develop market intelligence through information sharing Access to additional information from suppliers using digital software Regular information sharing with SCPs to address specific issues Standardised certification from relevant suppliers
Institutional forces	Insufficiency of government assistance Ineffective laws and regulations Establish good BNs to reduce risk and foster SSCM collaboration Weak legal structure Insufficient incentive to encourage the adoption of SSCM Limited interest in sustainability objectives within BNs
Barriers to implementing SSCM practices/business performance	Financial limitations Difficulties monitoring suppliers' activities Reluctance to change and focus on conventional practices Infrastructure limitations Uncertainty over advantages and drawbacks The dearth of qualified professionals Limited awareness of environmentally friendly products among customers Mitigate uncertainty and reduce excessive waste in the production line Currency exchange fluctuation The difficulty of measuring sustainability Enhanced productivity

Source: Authors

Company B: Within-Case Analysis

With its headquarters in Lagos, Nigeria, Company B was established in 2007 and has grown into a key manufacturing firm in the fast-moving consumer goods (FMCG) sector. More specifically, company B specialises in the foods and beverages manufacturing sub-sector. Company B has many brands in its catalogue, ranging from nutritious corn-based snacks to high-quality biscuits. Company B has more than 500 full-time employees. Company B is a member of the MAN. Company B puts particular emphasis on corporate social responsibility (CSR) efforts. It seeks to touch all aspects of CSR in its sustainability efforts and has conducted many community programmes and supported many groups and individuals.

TABLE 10.2 Findings of the interview for the SCII, TO, institutional forces, SSCM practices, and business performance

Dimension	*Findings*
TO	Develop an innovative culture to promote staff innovation
	Diversify and enhance product offerings
	Improve their methods of production
	Constant improvement and taking part in innovative projects
SCII	Use of automated integration to monitor SCPs that have access to required information
	Establish communication with customers to tackle environmental problems
	Provide relevant training for employees on environmental and social responsibility
	Regular information sharing with SCPs to address specific issues
	Standardised certification from relevant suppliers
Institutional forces	Increased pressure from the government
	Ineffective laws and regulations
	Decrease transaction costs through BNs
	Government bureaucracy
	Insufficient government funding for innovation and research and development
	Limited interest in sustainability objectives within BNs
Barriers to implementing SSCM practices/ business performance	Financial limitations
	Reluctance to change and focus on conventional practices
	The dearth of qualified professionals
	Insufficient supplier awareness
	Limited awareness of environmentally friendly products among customers
	Enhance productivity and minimise labour costs
	Infrastructure limitations
	Currency exchange fluctuation

Source: Authors

Cross-Case Analysis: Uncovering Patterns and Trends

Introduction

The cross-case analysis section aims to identify and examine patterns and trends that emerged from the detailed examination of Company A and Company B. This analysis helps in understanding commonalities and differences in their approach to sustainability and ESG practices (Table 10.3).

TABLE 10.3 Summary of cross-case findings

Company A	*Company B*
TO	
Provide new and innovative products regularly	Provide new and innovative products regularly
Operate more cost-effectively	Diversify and enhance product offerings
Develop an innovative culture to promote staff innovation	Improve their methods of production
	Develop an innovative culture to promote staff innovation
SCII	
Information sharing with SCPs to address specific issues	Information sharing with SCPs to address specific issues
Effective communication using digital technologies to process relevant information	Establish communication with customers to tackle environmental problems
Develop market intelligence through information sharing	Provide relevant training for employees on environmental and social responsibility
Access to additional information from suppliers using digital software	Use of automated integration to monitor SCPs with access to required information
Standardised certification from relevant suppliers	Standardised certification from relevant suppliers
Institutional Forces	
Ineffective laws and regulations	Ineffective laws and regulations
Insufficiency of government assistance	Increased pressure from the government
Weak legal structure	Insufficient government funding for innovation and research and development
Establish good BNs to reduce risk and foster SSCM collaboration	Government bureaucracy
Insufficient incentive to encourage the adoption of SSCM	Decrease transaction costs through BNs
Limited interest in sustainability objectives within BNs	Limited interest in sustainability objectives within BNs

(*Continued*)

TABLE 10.3 (Continued)

Company A	*Company B*
Barriers to implementing SSCM practices/business performance	
Financial limitations	Financial limitations
Reluctance to change and focus on conventional practices	Reluctance to change and focus on conventional practices
The dearth of qualified professionals	The dearth of qualified professionals
Currency exchange fluctuation	Currency exchange fluctuation
Difficulties monitoring suppliers' activities	Insufficient supplier awareness
Limited awareness of environmentally friendly products among customers	Limited awareness of environmentally friendly products among customers
Infrastructure limitations	Infrastructure limitations
Mitigate uncertainty and reduce excessive waste in the production line	Enhance productivity and minimise labour cost

Source: Authors

Unlocking Insights: Deep Dives into Key Themes

SCII in Case Companies

In line with the research objective concerning the role of SCII in enabling the implementation of SSCM practices within manufacturing firms in Nigeria, this section provides an in-depth analysis of SCII practices in Companies A and B. Interestingly, a number of those interviewed from Company B suggested that the failure to communicate strategic information with critical SCPs was influenced by an unwillingness to share information. In spite of the long-standing relationships that existed between firms within the supply chains, there was competition and worries about confidentiality among the partners. Due to the presence of conflicting interests among the companies, the risk of information leaking was present.

Concerns were expressed when asked about the III. The limited level of information sharing was highlighted as a hindrance to the implementation of SSCM and as organisational culture. Contrary to Company B, Company A exhibited mutual trust by exchanging strategic information and collaborating with suppliers and customers on new product development initiatives for eco-friendly materials. Due to the limited life cycle of certain product categories, Company A relies on collaboration with its most important suppliers to prevent interruptions in its production operations.

While concerns remained, participants from Company B argued that sharing vital information with major suppliers was a matter of economic necessity and exhibited signs of information systems integration. Some of the participants still acknowledged the importance of information integration. Interviewees from Companies A and B emphasised the importance of certification for external information processing.

Upon closer examination of the interview data, it becomes increasingly evident that the role of SCII in the implementation of SSCM practices is nuanced and exhibits considerable variation across companies. Company B's reluctance for transparent information sharing can be construed as a significant barrier to the effective implementation of SSCM. The lack of transparency hinders the firm's ability to corroborate sustainability claims, thereby making the collaboration on SSCM practices problematic.

On the other hand, Company A's approach towards SCII serves as an exemplar for fostering SSCM. Their willingness to transparently share strategic information with SCPs underlines a beneficial model that enables the firm to integrate sustainability practices more efficaciously. Company A's transparent and collaborative approach offers a clear pathway to implementing SSCM practices, serving as empirical evidence supporting the idea that SCII is indeed instrumental for SSCM. Therefore, the data shows that SCII enables SSCM practices in Company A, whereas the lack of SCII hinders SSCM in Company B. This finding directly answers the main research question and emphasises that the extent to which SCII enables SSCM can vary greatly depending on a company's culture and level of information sharing.

Furthermore, the data points towards an additional layer of complexity: the role of III in shaping SSCM practices. Company B's tendency for limiting the flow of critical information to upper management poses an inherent challenge to SSCM implementation. It is inferred that for SCII to serve its full purpose in facilitating SSCM, comprehensive internal information sharing is paramount. Engaging personnel across hierarchical levels ensures a unified approach to sustainability, thus corroborating the argument that SCII serves as an essential facilitator for effective SSCM practices. This in-depth exploration and thematic analysis of the interview data not only enriches the understanding of the nuanced roles and mechanisms of SCII but also offers a comprehensive answer to the role of SCII in implementing SSCM practices in Nigerian manufacturing companies. The rich insights gathered from both Company A and Company B demonstrate the pivotal role of SCII in either enabling or constraining SSCM practices in manufacturing sectors in Nigeria.

TO of Case Companies

The research explores respondents' perspectives on how TO impacted their organisation. Two divergent and often conflicting discourses emerged. A small number of those respondents felt that their TO had enabled their firms to enhance their manufacturing processes, which significantly reduces their impact on the environment, increases their operational efficiency, and improves customer satisfaction. Some interviewees argued that TO creates new business channels that did not exist previously, and their organisations sought to embrace new technologies to meet global standards. The participants further stated that their manufacturing methods have evolved over time, and they have aggressively adopted production technologies to enhance production quality.

However, it is important to highlight that there was a sense among interviewees that technology for improving manufacturing and operational flexibility was prioritised above those enabling inter-firm procedures across their supply chains. Equally, some suppliers were restricted by manufacturers that gave short-term contracts, making it difficult for the suppliers to invest in costly systems without certainty of continuation.

Some of the respondents also highlighted certain technological barriers affecting the Nigerian business environment. More specifically, a common view among interviewees was that the lack of a robust database and poor technology infrastructure hinder the implementation of SSCM practices within the Nigerian manufacturing sector. Overall, these results provide important insights into the role of TO in implementing SSCM practices.

In line with the research objective concerning the role of TO in implementing SSCM practices, it is essential to delve deeper into the diverging strategies employed by Companies A and B. Company B, for example, has made substantial technological investments aimed at internal improvements and meeting international standards. However, the interview data suggests that this TO does not translate into a holistic approach that encompasses SSCM across the supply chain. While Company B has prioritised cutting-edge technologies to streamline internal manufacturing processes, these technologies are not geared towards enhancing communication or operational efficiencies with SCPs. Furthermore, these technologies do not explicitly support SSCM practices within the supply chain, thereby illustrating a crucial gap. This detailed observation directly speaks to the research question by emphasising that TO alone, without a specific focus on supply chain integration and sustainability, is insufficient in effectively enabling the implementation of SSCM practices.

The comments from Company A's chief operating officer underscore a systemic issue that impacts both TO and SSCM. The reluctance of suppliers to invest in technology due to short-term contracts not only hampers production but also has a direct bearing on SSCM. When suppliers are uncertain about their future business and are unwilling to invest in technologies that could enhance sustainable practices, the entire supply chain suffers.

Lastly, another critical layer that came to light during the interviews is the issue of poor technological infrastructure within the Nigerian business environment. This inadequacy is not merely a roadblock to efficient operations but also poses a formidable challenge to the implementation of SSCM practices. When businesses are grappling with basic technological issues, the idea of integrating sophisticated, sustainability-centered technologies into their operations becomes far-fetched. Therefore, the findings underscore that while TO has the potential to greatly enable SSCM practices, the current state of technological infrastructure in Nigeria significantly limits this potential.

Barriers to Implementing SSCM Practices/Business Performance in Case Companies

SSCM is still a nascent concept, particularly in emerging markets such as Nigeria. Overall, the participants commented on the challenges that affected their implementation of SSCM practices and business performance. Financial limitations, reluctance to change and focus on conventional practices, the dearth of qualified professionals, and infrastructure limitations were commonly highlighted. Currency exchange fluctuation, difficulties in monitoring suppliers' activities, and limited awareness of environmentally friendly products among customers also posted significant challenges.

Some participants felt that management did not fully enforce SSCM practices despite being aware of their importance. The lack of knowledge and experience with SSCM in the industry was another significant issue, with suppliers from developed countries being more knowledgeable about the subject.

Infrastructure limitations were also a significant challenge, with issues such as the distribution of water and power, poor quality of roads and rail networks, and traffic congestion affecting logistics operations. Currency exchange fluctuation was another barrier, impacting the purchase process for raw materials from global suppliers.

Despite these barriers, the interviews revealed a growing commitment to SSCM practices driven by CSR strategies and stakeholder demands. The adoption of sustainability practices was seen as providing a competitive advantage, enhancing reputation, and aligning with global business practices.

The interviews also shed light on the potential positive impacts of successfully implementing SSCM practices. Most participants indicated that despite the various challenges they face, there is an overarching belief that SSCM practices could offer a competitive advantage. These views correlate strongly with the objective of examining how SSCM practices could improve business performance. They indicate that when these barriers are addressed, there is a strong potential for firms to not only contribute positively to sustainability but also to enhance their competitive position in the market. While barriers exist, the benefits of adopting SSCM practices are manifestly clear in the participants' responses. Companies A and B both recognised the increasing importance of SSCM in global business practices, citing efforts to align with sustainability standards as part of their competitive strategy.

The managing director of Company A emphasised their commitment to a CSR strategy responsive to the growing demands of stakeholders for sustainable practices. Company B's logistics manager elucidated further on the business benefits, noting their enhanced reputation with customers due to their ethical stance. Overall, participants agreed that navigating and overcoming the aforementioned barriers could translate to notable advantages in a fiercely competitive market landscape. These views resonate strongly to examine how these practices could directly impact business performance. Furthermore, the findings offer multiple perspectives that enrich the discourse, especially concerning the local context and dynamics of emerging markets like Nigeria.

In addressing the core objectives of the study, it is evident that the barriers to SSCM practices are multifaceted but overcoming them aligns directly with the overarching goals of manufacturing companies in emerging markets. As both Companies A and B have demonstrated, aligning with SSCM practices, whether driven by competitive pressure, stakeholder demands, or ethical considerations, correlates directly with improved business performance. The data and insights drawn from the participants serve as a crucial foundation, allowing us to understand the nuanced interplay between SSCM practices, business performance, and the specific challenges and opportunities in the Nigerian manufacturing context.

Institutional Forces (GS, LP, BNs) in Case Companies

A recurrent theme in the interviews regarding LP was the weak legislation and ineffective laws. Another recurring theme was the lack of GS and delays caused by government bureaucracy. Participants highlighted the delays caused by system complexity and the lack of financial assistance for companies from the government in the form of incentives or tax discounts. While the majority emphasised the lack of GS, some respondents acknowledged that the government had made efforts to promote the implementation of SSCM practices, including regulatory pressure to adhere to environmental and labour safety legislation.

Opinions differed concerning the role of BNs. Some interviewees stated that businesses lacked faith in the system, which may be linked to system delays and bureaucracy. Despite this, BNs played an important role in providing information that helps in decision-making for better environmental results and gaining key market shares. However, there were concerns about the defensiveness against the implementation of SSCM practices in BNs, slowing the adoption of SSCM practices, particularly when it did not directly impact their operations.

Corruption throughout the procurement process also emerged as an issue. Firm connections were impacted by corrupt practices in procurement, where procurement officials collect payments from suppliers to endorse future business deals and loyalty. This corruption compelled suppliers to raise their rates to account for bribes, affecting the overall integrity of the supply chain.

Their primary concerns were operational and financial, not legal, leading to questions about LP's role. While a more effective legal system could help foster an environment more conducive to SSCM, the existing LP mechanisms did not seem to influence firms to either adopt or resist new technologies. These additional layers of analysis suggest that the complexities of implementing SSCM and adopting new technologies in this setting might be driven by a different set of factors, ones that operate somewhat independently of the existing LP mechanisms.

BNs played a complex role concerning the implementation of SSCM practices. BNs can act as facilitators by allowing companies to share best practices and information, thereby helping them to implement SSCM practices more effectively. Strong and collaborative networks offer firms the ability to quickly adopt technologies that align with sustainability objectives, enhancing the positive aspects of a TO or SCII. However, these networks can also perpetuate a culture of corruption and short-term opportunism that diminishes the integrity of the supply chain. These negative elements within the BN seem to counteract the potential positive influences of TO and SCII on the implementation of SSCM practices. While they do not moderate the relationship, understanding their nuanced role helps to contextualise why implementing SSCM practices successfully remains a challenge in the Nigerian manufacturing sector.

Comparative Insights from Case Studies

The cross-case analysis of Companies A and B reveals several critical insights into the implementation of SSCM practices, the role of TO and SCII, and the impact of institutional forces on business performance. Both companies, operating within the Nigerian manufacturing sector, face unique challenges and opportunities in adopting SSCM practices.

Technological Orientation: Both companies demonstrate a strong commitment to technological advancement, though their focuses differ. Company A emphasises cost-effective operations and fostering an innovative staff culture, while Company B prioritises product diversification and production improvement. Both companies recognise the importance of cultivating an innovative culture to drive staff innovation.

Supply Chain Information Integration: SCII practices in both companies highlight the significance of information sharing with SCPs. Common themes include effective communication using digital technologies, regular information sharing to address specific issues, and the use of standardised certifications from suppliers. However, the extent of SCII implementation varies, with Company A showing a more collaborative and integrated approach compared to Company B.

Institutional Forces: Both companies encounter challenges related to insufficient government assistance, ineffective laws and regulations, and weak legal structures. There is a consensus on the need for stronger BNs to mitigate risks and promote SSCM collaboration. Despite these challenges, both companies strive to comply with existing regulations and make use of available support.

Barriers to SSCM Practices and Business Performance: Financial limitations, resistance to change, and infrastructural limitations are significant barriers for both companies. Additional challenges include currency exchange fluctuations and difficulties in measuring sustainability. Both companies acknowledge the importance of enhancing productivity and reducing waste in the production line as critical to improving business performance.

Future Outlook and Recommendations

The findings from the in-depth case studies of two manufacturing firms in Nigeria, referred to as Company A and Company B, offer substantial insights into the implementation of SSCM practices. These insights are analysed through the lenses of TO, SCII, and the impact of institutional forces.

Enhancing TO for SSCM

The findings reveal that TO plays a crucial role in enabling SSCM practices within Nigerian manufacturing firms. Company A and Company B illustrate that while TO can drive internal efficiency and environmental management, its benefits do not always extend to external collaborations. The adoption of new technologies, although beneficial for enhancing internal manufacturing processes, faces significant barriers when it comes to inter-firm communication and collaboration. These barriers are often exacerbated by short-term contracts and financial constraints, which discourage suppliers from investing in costly systems without assured returns.

Interviewees highlighted that while TO could create new business channels and meet global standards, the lack of robust technological infrastructure and a poor database hinder these efforts. This situation is particularly challenging in an emerging market context like Nigeria, where businesses already contend with unstable electricity, policy uncertainties, and a shortage of skilled technology personnel. To enhance TO, it is essential to invest in advanced technologies, foster a culture of innovation, and establish long-term contracts to encourage suppliers to invest in sustainable technologies. Policymakers should consider targeted interventions to enhance technological infrastructure and provide meaningful incentives for SSCM adoption. Digital technologies, such as Internet of Things (IoT) devices, can be employed in manufacturing facilities to continuously monitor and optimise energy use and reduce waste. Such technologies ensure that all stakeholders have access to unchangeable records of a product's lifecycle, which not only aids in regulatory compliance but also builds consumer trust by providing proof of SSCM practices.

Strengthening SCII

The role of SCII in SSCM practices is nuanced and varies significantly across companies. Company A demonstrated successful SCII characterised by mutual trust and strategic information sharing with suppliers and customers, which facilitated the development of eco-friendly materials. Conversely, Company B faced significant challenges due to a reluctance to share strategic information with critical SCPs, impeding SSCM implementation. Enhancing SCII requires fostering a culture of trust, improving technology systems for efficient information sharing, and implementing standardised certification processes to facilitate better collaboration and sustainability practices.

Addressing Institutional Barriers

Institutional forces, including GS, LPs, and BNs, play a pivotal role in shaping SSCM practices. The interview data revealed a mixed perception of GS, with some respondents acknowledging efforts by the government to promote sustainability through regulatory pressure and environmental protection regulations. However, the majority lamented the lack of substantial financial assistance and incentives. Bureaucracy and system complexities also emerged as significant barriers, causing operational delays and limiting the effectiveness of SSCM practices.

LPs were found to be weak, with ineffective laws and protracted environmental litigation processes undermining faith in the system. This lack of robust legal frameworks contributes to the defensiveness observed among businesses towards implementing SSCM practices. Additionally, BNs, while potentially beneficial for sharing best practices and information, were often tainted by corruption and short-term opportunism, further complicating the landscape for SSCM implementation.

To address these institutional barriers, there is a need for stronger GS, improved legal frameworks, and reduced bureaucracy. Combating corruption within BNs is also essential to fostering a conducive environment for SSCM. Policymakers should develop strategies to provide consistent and substantial support to create an environment conducive to SSCM practices.

Overcoming Financial and Operational Challenges

Financial limitations and operational challenges are significant barriers to implementing SSCM practices. Both companies faced challenges such as financial constraints, resistance to change, and infrastructural limitations. Addressing these challenges requires securing funding for sustainability initiatives, providing employee training on sustainability practices, and improving infrastructure to support sustainable operations. Additionally, companies should focus on enhancing productivity and reducing waste in the production line. Stakeholders, including industry leaders and policymakers, should collaborate to develop solutions that mitigate financial and operational barriers, thereby enhancing the overall implementation of SSCM practices.

Recommendations for Policy and Industry Stakeholders

The study highlights several actionable recommendations for policymakers and industry stakeholders. Policymakers should enhance technological infrastructure and provide incentives for SSCM adoption. Legal frameworks need to be strengthened to support environmental protection and reduce bureaucratic delays. Industry leaders should foster a culture of trust and collaboration both within and across firms, promoting transparent information sharing and strategic partnerships. Policymakers can look to successful models from other emerging markets, such as Brazil's Industrial Policy for Innovation, which offers tax incentives and subsidies for companies investing in sustainable technologies. South Africa's Green Supply Chain Programme, which provides financial support for adopting green practices, is another model that Nigeria could emulate. By implementing similar policies, the government can encourage firms to invest in technologies that could facilitate SSCM practices, helping to overcome financial and institutional barriers. These recommendations aim to create a supportive environment for the successful implementation of SSCM in the Nigerian manufacturing sector.

Conclusion

The cross-case analysis of Companies A and B offers substantial insights into the implementation of SSCM practices. Both companies demonstrate a strong commitment to technological advancement, though their approaches to TO and SCII differ significantly. While Company A emphasises collaboration and information sharing, Company B struggles with transparency and strategic information sharing. Institutional barriers, such as insufficient GS and weak LPs, further hinder SSCM implementation.

The findings highlight the necessity of a multifaceted approach to enhancing SSCM practices in Nigerian manufacturing. Technological advancements and better integration of supply chain information are critical, but these must be supported by stronger institutional frameworks and a collaborative industry culture. By addressing these areas, Nigerian firms can not only meet global ESG standards but also drive sustainable development within the region.

Despite these challenges, the study highlights the importance of fostering a culture of innovation, trust, and collaboration to enhance SSCM practices. The findings offer valuable implications for policymakers, industry leaders, and academics, highlighting the need for targeted interventions and strategic partnerships to drive SSCM in Nigeria. As the manufacturing sector continues to evolve, ongoing research and targeted interventions will be crucial to overcoming existing barriers and leveraging opportunities for sustainability. The insights from this chapter provide a foundation for policymakers, industry leaders, and academics to foster a more sustainable and resilient manufacturing industry in Nigeria.

References

Ardito, L., Raby, S., Albino, V., & Bertoldi, B. (2021). The duality of digital and environmental orientations in the context of SMEs: Implications for innovation performance. *Journal of Business Research*, *123*, 44–56.

Bolaji, B. O., Olanipekun, M. U., Adekunle, A. A., & Adeleke, A. E. (2018). An analysis of noise and its environmental burden on the example of Nigerian manufacturing companies. *Journal of Cleaner Production*, *172*, 1800–1806.

Busse, C., Meinlschmidt, J., & Foerstl, K. (2017). Managing information processing needs in global supply chains: A prerequisite to sustainable supply chain management. *Journal of Supply Chain Management*, *53*(1), 87–113.

Cai, S., Jun, M., & Yang, Z. (2010). Implementing supply chain information integration in China: The role of institutional forces and trust. *Journal of Operations Management*, *28*(3), 257–268.

Chowdhury, P., Paul, S. K., Kaisar, S., & Moktadir, M. A. (2021). COVID-19 pandemic related supply chain studies: A systematic review. *Transportation Research Part E: Logistics and Transportation Review*, *148*, 102271.

Egbulonu, K. G., & Duru, E. E. (2018). Diversifying the Nigerian economy: Role of small and medium scale enterprises. *African Journal of Economics and Sustainable Development, 1*(1), 33–46.

Fang, H., Fang, F., Hu, Q., & Wan, Y. (2022). Supply chain management: A review and bibliometric analysis. *Processes*, *10*(9), 1681. MDPI.

Gatignon, H., & Xuereb, J. M. (1997). Strategic orientation of the firm and new product performance. *Journal of Marketing Research*, *34*(1), 77–90.

Hemmert, M., Kim, D., Kim, J., & Cho, B. (2016). Building the supplier's trust: Role of institutional forces and buyer firm practices. *International Journal of Production Economics, 180*, 25–37.

Huo, B., Han, Z., & Prajogo, D. (2016). Antecedents and consequences of supply chain information integration: A resource-based view. *Supply Chain Management: An International Journal*, *21*(6), 661–677.

Ilyas, S., Hu, Z., & Wiwattanakornwong, K. (2020). Unleashing the role of top management and government support in green supply chain management and sustainable development goals. *Environmental Science and Pollution Research*, *27*(8), 8210–8223.

Khan, S. A. R., Yu, Z., Golpira, H., Sharif, A., & Mardani, A. (2021). A state-of-the-art review and meta-analysis on sustainable supply chain management: Future research directions. *Journal of Cleaner Production*, *278*, 123357.

Lei, L., Wu, X., & Fu, Y. (2019). Effects of sustainability and technology orientations on firm growth: Evidence from Chinese manufacturing. *Sustainability*, *11*(16), 4406.

National Bureau of Statistics. (2023). *Key statistics.* Retrieved July 19, 2023, from http://www.nigerianstat.gov.ng/

Ngo, V. M., Quang, H. T., Hoang, T. G., & Binh, A. D. T. (2024). Sustainability-related supply chain risks and supply chain performances: The moderating effects of dynamic supply chain management practices. *Business Strategy and the Environment*, *33*(2), 839–857.

Okafor, C. C., Sydney Ani, U., & Ugwu, O. (2024). Critical solutions to the lapses of supply chain management in Nigeria's construction industry. *International Journal of Building Pathology and Adaptation*, *42*(4), 768–787.

Orji, I. J., & Ojadi, F. (2021). Investigating the COVID-19 pandemic's impact on sustainable supplier selection in the Nigerian manufacturing sector. *Computers & Industrial Engineering*, *160*, 107588.

Orji, I. J., U-Dominic, C. M., & Okwara, U. K. (2022). Exploring the determinants in circular supply chain implementation in the Nigerian manufacturing industry. *Sustainable Production and Consumption*, *29*, 761–776.

Sánchez-Flores, R. B., Cruz-Sotelo, S. E., Ojeda-Benitez, S., & Ramírez-Barreto, M. E. (2020). Sustainable supply chain management—a literature review on emerging economies. *Sustainability*, *12*(17), 6972.

Shou, Z., Zheng, X., & Zhu, W. (2016). Contract ineffectiveness in emerging markets: An institutional theory perspective. *Journal of Operations Management*, *46*(1), 38–54.

Silvestre, B. S. (2015). Sustainable supply chain management in emerging economies: Environmental turbulence, institutional voids and sustainability trajectories. *International Journal of Production Economics*, *167*, 156–169.

Tran, D. T. M., Thai, V. V., Duc, T. T. H., & Nguyen, T. T. (2023). The role of organisational and contextual factors in supply chain collaboration and competitive advantage: The case of the garment industry in Vietnam. *The International Journal of Logistics Management*, *35*.

Tsai, Y. T., & Lasminar, R. G. (2021). Proactive and reactive flexibility: How does flexibility mediate the link between supply chain information integration and performance? *International Journal of Engineering Business Management*, *13*, 1–12.

Tseng, C. H., Chang, K. H., & Chen, H. W. (2019). Strategic orientation, environmental innovation capability, and environmental sustainability performance: The case of Taiwanese suppliers. *Sustainability*, *11*(4), 1127.

Uma, K. E., Obidike, P. C., Chukwu, C. O., Kanu, C., Ogbuagu, R. A., Osunkwo, F. O., & Ndubuisi, P. (2019). Revamping the Nigerian manufacturing sub-sector as a panacea for economic progress: Lessons from South Korea. *Mediterranean Journal of Social Sciences*, *10*(4), 111–123.

Wang, S. L. (2023). Digital technology-enabled governance for sustainability in global value chains: A framework and future research agenda. *Journal of Industrial and Business Economics*, 175–192.

Yang, D., Sheng, S., Wu, S., & Zhou, K. Z. (2018). Suppressing partner opportunism in emerging markets: Contextualizing institutional forces in supply chain management. *Journal of Business Research*, *90*, 1–13.

Yu, K., Qian, C., & Zhang, L. (2021). Understanding sustainable development flexibility: An information perspective. *Business Strategy and the Environment*, *30*(4), 2173–2183.

11

REGIONAL BLOCS AND ECONOMIC ALLIANCES

Impact on Global Value Chain Integration

David M. Herold

Introduction

Global value chains (GVCs) have been increasingly influenced by geopolitical uncertainties, trade tensions and unprecedented disruptions such as the COVID-19 pandemic. These influences challenged the stability and efficiency of GVCs, leading companies to rethink their global supply chain strategies to remain competitive and resilient. One deciding factor for competitive and resilient global supply chains can be the critical role of regional blocs and economic alliances that shape the complexity behind global supply chain networks and thereby enable businesses to tap into global markets and operate across borders. In this chapter, we elaborate on the role of regional blocs and economic alliances and their implications for supply chains. In the next two sections, we provide an overview of GVCs and the role of regional blocs and economic alliances in these GVCs.

Overview of GVCs

GVCs can be seen as both the cause and effect of globalization, that is, the interconnected processes through which goods and services are produced, distributed, and consumed across the world. The establishment of GVCs allows the fragmentation of production so that businesses can source inputs from multiple countries, leveraging the comparative advantages of different regions. Each stage of production, from the extraction of raw materials to the assembly of final products, involves various actors spread across national borders. This division of labour can be regarded as a major factor in enhanced efficiency and reduced costs, as well as a driver of economic growth,

DOI: 10.4324/9781003468899-11

particularly for developing economies that seek integration into global markets (Gereffi et al., 2005).

Historically, GVCs facilitated trade liberalization and economic integration, with companies increasingly relying on cross-border supply networks to maintain competitiveness by optimizing production processes and accessing global talent pools. The vast majority of global trade involves intermediate goods and services that are traded within GVCs, emphasizing their importance in the world economy. Multinational corporations are at the heart of these chains, outsourcing various tasks to suppliers across multiple countries to achieve cost efficiency and flexibility. One of the most significant advantages of GVCs is the ability to specialize in specific tasks rather than producing entire products. This specialization allows countries to participate in the global economy based on their strengths, such as low-cost labour, access to natural resources or technological expertise. As a result, GVCs have been credited with lifting millions out of poverty, particularly in emerging markets, by creating jobs and transferring knowledge and technology.

However, the current landscape of GVCs is not without its challenges. The disruptions caused by the COVID-19 pandemic exposed the vulnerabilities of highly interconnected supply chains. The sudden stop in production in one region had ripple effects on other parts of the chain, leading to shortages of essential goods and delays in production. Moreover, increasing geopolitical tensions such as trade wars, protectionist policies and the rise of nationalism have prompted businesses to reconsider their reliance on certain regions and have led many firms to diversify their supply chains or consider relocating production to other countries to mitigate risks (Ali et al., 2022).

Importance of Regional Blocs and Economic Alliances in GVCs

Regional blocs and economic alliances play a critical role in shaping the structure and functioning of GVCs. Regional blocs such as the European Union (EU), the North American Free Trade Agreement (NAFTA), now the United States-Mexico-Canada Agreement (USMCA), and the Association of Southeast Asian Nations (ASEAN), were established to facilitate trade, investment and economic cooperation among member countries. By reducing tariffs, harmonizing regulations and promoting cross-border collaboration, regional agreements foster deeper integration within GVCs, allowing firms to operate more efficiently across multiple jurisdictions (Pomfret, 2021).

The role of regional blocs in GVCs is particularly strong in industries with complex production processes, such as automotive manufacturing, electronics and pharmaceuticals. In these sectors, firms benefit from proximity to suppliers, access to regional markets and shared infrastructure. For example, the automotive industry in Europe relies heavily on the close collaboration between car manufacturers in Germany and component suppliers in countries like Poland, Hungary and the Czech Republic. The EU's single market, which allows for the free movement of goods, services, capital and labour, has been instrumental in the success of such integrated production systems (Pichler et al., 2021).

Regional economic alliances provide a buffer against external shocks by creating more resilient supply chains. In times of crisis, such as the COVID-19 pandemic or geopolitical conflicts, regional cooperation can help ensure the continuity of production and supply within the bloc. The Regional Comprehensive Economic Partnership (RCEP), signed in 2020 by 15 Asia-Pacific countries, exemplifies this trend. The RCEP aims to strengthen regional supply chains by reducing trade barriers and improving market access, positioning the region as a hub for global manufacturing (Zreik, 2024).

In addition to driving economic integration, regional blocs offer political and strategic advantages. As the global order becomes increasingly fragmented, regional alliances serve as a counterbalance to rising protectionism and isolationist policies. By negotiating as a bloc, countries can collectively respond to external pressure, such as trade disputes or sanctions, and protect their interests in global markets. The EU's coordinated response to the US–China trade war, including its push for multilateralism and open trade, demonstrates the importance of regional alliances in defending GVCs against geopolitical risks (Dadush & Prost, 2023).

However, regional blocs are not without limitations. The concentration of production within a particular region can increase vulnerability to localized disruptions. For instance, the reliance on East Asian countries for electronics and semiconductor components has been highlighted as a risk, given the region's susceptibility to natural disasters and political tensions. The diversification of supply chains across multiple regions, rather than overreliance on a single bloc, is increasingly seen as a strategy to enhance resilience in GVCs.

The remainder of this book chapter is structured as follows: in the first section, an overview of regional blocs and economic alliances will be provided, including their definitions and purposes. This is followed by an outline of the different types of regional blocs and economic alliances and their inherent challenges. The next section offers insight into four concrete examples or case studies to highlight the impact on specific industries and regions. We conclude with an overview and discuss the future of regional blocs and economic alliances.

Regional Blocs and Economic Alliances: An Overview

Definitions of Regional Blocs and Economic Alliances

To better understand the role of regional blocs and economic alliances within GVCs, it is essential to first establish clear definitions of these terms. Both regional blocs and economic alliances refer to institutionalized forms of economic cooperation among countries, but they differ in terms of their scope, objectives and structures.

Regional Blocs

A regional bloc refers to a group of geographically proximate countries that collaborate to achieve common economic, political or social objectives. These blocs are characterized by preferential trade agreements, which reduce or eliminate barriers to trade, such as tariffs, quotas and import/export restrictions, among member states. One of the primary goals of regional blocs is to foster deeper economic integration by facilitating the free flow of goods, services, capital and sometimes labour. Regional blocs can take various forms, ranging from free trade agreements (FTAs) to customs unions, common markets and economic unions, each representing different levels of integration.

The EU is one of the most well-known examples of a regional bloc, and it exemplifies a high level of integration. The EU operates as an economic and political union with its own single market, which allows for the free movement of goods, services, people and capital among its member states. It also has a common external tariff and a unified trade policy towards non-member countries, demonstrating the advanced stage of cooperation that can be achieved within a regional bloc (Bhalla, 2016; McCormick, 2020).

Regional blocs can be formed for a variety of reasons, including enhancing competitiveness, improving access to larger markets and promoting regional stability. Regionalism is often motivated by the desire to reduce economic dependence on more distant global powers and to enhance economic collaboration within a specific geographic area. Regional blocs can also serve as a tool for member countries to negotiate more effectively on the global stage by pooling their resources and presenting a unified front in trade negotiations.

Economic Alliances

Economic alliances, while similar to regional blocs, are broader in scope and less geographically confined. These alliances involve agreements between two or more countries to collaborate on economic matters such as trade, investment, infrastructure development and technological innovation. Economic alliances may span multiple regions and often involve partnerships between countries with complementary economic interests rather than strict geographical proximity. These alliances can be established to pursue specific economic objectives, such as enhancing market access or developing strategic industries (Davison, 2017).

One of the distinguishing features of economic alliances is their flexibility. Unlike regional blocs, which are often formalized through treaties and institutionalized structures, economic alliances can take the form of bilateral or multilateral agreements tailored to specific sectors or industries. For example, the Belt and Road Initiative led by China represents a large-scale economic alliance focused on infrastructure development and investment in Asia, Europe and Africa. The Belt and Road Initiative seeks to create a modern Silk Road by strengthening economic ties between participating countries, facilitating trade and improving connectivity (Rana et al., 2021).

While economic alliances tend to prioritize trade liberalization and economic cooperation, they are also often driven by strategic geopolitical considerations. Countries may form alliances to enhance their global influence or to secure access to critical resources, such as energy or raw materials. This has become particularly relevant in the context of the US-China rivalry, where both nations have sought to build alliances to strengthen their positions in global trade and geopolitics (Heiduk, 2022). As such, economic alliances are frequently used as a means of gaining leverage in multilateral trade negotiations, allowing countries to secure more favourable terms by negotiating as part of a collective rather than individually.

Both regional blocs and economic alliances serve as mechanisms for economic cooperation, but while regional blocs are typically defined by geographical proximity and deep levels of integration, economic alliances are more flexible, allowing countries from different regions to collaborate on shared economic goals.

Different Types (e.g., Free Trade Agreements, Customs Unions, Economic Unions)

Regional blocs and economic alliances come in various forms, each representing different levels of economic integration and cooperation among member states. They range from basic agreements aimed at reducing trade barriers to highly integrated unions with shared policies and institutions. This section will explore three primary types of regional economic agreements: FTAs, customs unions and economic unions.

Free Trade Agreements

An FTA is the most basic form of economic cooperation between countries, focused primarily on reducing or eliminating tariffs, quotas and other trade barriers for goods and services traded among member states. FTAs are designed to facilitate trade by creating a more favourable environment for cross-border transactions, often while allowing each country to maintain its own trade policies with non-member countries. One of the key features of an FTA is its limited scope in terms of integration. FTAs do not typically address the movement of labour or capital, nor do they harmonize domestic regulations or policies. Instead, they are focused on improving market access for goods and services between the countries involved. FTAs can be bilateral, involving just two countries, or multilateral, involving several nations.

The Comprehensive and Progressive Agreement for Trans-Pacific Partnership (CPTPP) is an example of a multilateral FTA that spans countries from multiple continents, including Asia, Oceania and the Americas. FTAs are particularly attractive to countries seeking to boost trade without committing to deeper forms of integration that would require ceding sovereignty over economic policies (Wu & Chadee, 2022). Despite their benefits, FTAs are sometimes criticized for fostering trade diversion, where trade is shifted from more efficient global suppliers to less efficient FTA members due to preferential treatment. This can undermine the broader goals of global free trade. However, in an era of increasing protectionism, FTAs continue to serve as critical tools for economic collaboration, especially when multilateral trade negotiations stall (Schott, 2004).

Customs Unions

A customs union represents a higher level of economic integration than an FTA because it involves not only the removal of internal barriers to trade but also the establishment of a common external tariff on goods imported from non-member countries. This means that all member states of a customs union apply the same tariffs and trade policies towards external countries, creating a more unified approach to international trade. As a consequence, customs unions offer the advantage of eliminating the need for complex rules of origin, which are necessary in FTAs to prevent non-members from routing their goods through the member country with the lowest tariff. With a common external tariff, goods can move freely between member states without the need for such regulations, simplifying trade and reducing administrative costs (Bickel, 2021).

The Southern Common Market (Mercosur), established in 1991, is an example of a customs union comprising Argentina, Brazil, Paraguay and Uruguay, with Venezuela's membership currently suspended. Mercosur aims to facilitate the free movement of goods, services and production factors among its members, while coordinating trade policies with external nations. However, customs unions are often challenging to maintain due to the need for member countries to agree on a common external trade policy, which can lead to tensions when national interests diverge (Coffey, 2013). Customs unions can also serve as stepping stones to deeper economic integration. The European Economic Community (EEC)—founded in 1957 as a customs union—later evolved into the EU, demonstrating how customs unions can lay the groundwork for more advanced forms of cooperation (Parsons, 2002).

Economic Unions

An economic union represents the most advanced form of economic integration, involving not only the free movement of goods and services but also the harmonization of economic policies among member states. Economic unions typically involve a single market, which allows for the unrestricted movement of labour, capital and services, as well as the adoption of common regulations, tax policies and, in some cases, a shared currency (Schütze, 2012).

Economic unions offer significant benefits, such as the elimination of barriers to investment and the creation of a larger, more efficient market. The EU is the most prominent example of an economic union. The EU's single market ensures that goods, services, capital and people can move freely among member states without restrictions. In addition, 19 of the 27 EU member countries have adopted the euro as their common currency, further integrating their economies. The EU also has centralized institutions, such as the European Commission and the European Central Bank, which oversee policy implementation and monetary regulation, illustrating the depth of integration achieved in an economic union. However, they also require member countries to cede a substantial degree of sovereignty, particularly in areas like fiscal and monetary policy. The eurozone crisis in the early 2010s highlighted the challenges of maintaining a unified economic policy across countries with varying economic conditions, demonstrating the risks associated with such deep integration (Quaglia, 2013).

Overarching Challenges Posed by Regional Blocs and Economic Alliances

While regional blocs and economic alliances are essential for facilitating trade along GVCs, they also face a set of significant challenges. These challenges stem from the complexities of coordinating policies across different countries, the risk of creating economic imbalances and potential geopolitical tensions, which will be discussed in detail in this section.

Diverging National Interests

One of the most fundamental challenges in maintaining regional blocs and economic alliances is managing the divergent interests of member countries. Countries often have different economic structures and levels of development as well as political priorities, which can make it difficult to align policies and strategies. For example, in the EU, there is often a tension between wealthier northern European nations, which prioritize fiscal austerity and competitiveness, and southern nations, which advocate for greater fiscal flexibility to support economic growth (Stockhammer, 2016). Another example is the Mercosur regional bloc, where differences in economic development and industrial capacity between member countries have led to disputes over trade policies and market access. Countries like Brazil and Argentina, the two largest economies in Mercosur, often have conflicting trade interests, which complicates negotiations and hinders deeper integration (Gómez-Mera, 2009).

Economic Imbalances and Dependency

Another challenge posed by regional blocs and economic alliances is the risk of creating or exacerbating economic imbalances between member countries. Economic integration may lead to uneven benefits, with wealthier or more competitive nations gaining disproportionately while less developed countries struggle to keep pace. Moreover, smaller or less developed countries within a regional bloc may become overly reliant on trade and investment from their more powerful counterparts, limiting their ability to pursue independent economic strategies. For instance, in the East African Community, smaller economies like Burundi and Rwanda are heavily dependent on the larger economies of Kenya and Tanzania. This dependency can lead to vulnerabilities, particularly if the dominant economies experience downturns or if trade relations deteriorate (Collier & Venables, 2012). The formation of regional blocs may lead to trade diversion, where trade is shifted away from more efficient global suppliers in favour of less efficient producers within the bloc due to preferential treatment. While this may benefit member states in the short term, it can reduce overall global welfare and lead to inefficiencies in the long run (Bhagwati, 2008).

Political and Geopolitical Risks

Regional blocs and economic alliances are also vulnerable to political and geopolitical risks. Because these alliances involve the pooling of economic and political resources, they can be subject to internal political instability or shifts in government priorities. Changes in leadership or political ideology within member states can lead to challenges in maintaining the coherence and stability of the alliance. A striking example of how domestic political shifts can disrupt regional integration is the United Kingdom's (UK) exit from the EU (Brexit). The UK's departure not only undermined the EU's cohesion but also created uncertainty around trade agreements, immigration and regulatory frameworks (Taggart & Szczerbiak, 2021). Geopolitical tensions also pose significant challenges. Regional blocs and economic alliances can sometimes become arenas for broader geopolitical struggles because member countries may be aligned with different global powers. The US-China rivalry, for instance, has created challenges for trade alliances such as the CPTPP because member countries have had to navigate the conflicting interests of these two global powers (Park et al., 2021).

Regulatory and Institutional Complexity

A further challenge is the regulatory and institutional complexity that often accompanies regional economic integration. Regional blocs aim to harmonize a wide range of regulations, including trade policies, labour standards, environmental regulations and competition laws. This can be a daunting task, particularly when member countries have different legal systems, regulatory frameworks and levels of economic development (Herold & Marzantowicz, 2023). For example, the EU has faced considerable challenges in harmonizing regulations across its member states. The implementation of EU-wide standards in areas such as product safety, environmental protection and financial regulation has often been met with resistance from member states that prefer to maintain their own national regulations (Schütze, 2012). Moreover, the institutional structure required to govern regional blocs and economic alliances can become cumbersome and inefficient. The need for consensus-based decision-making in organizations like the EU and the World Trade Organization can slow down policy responses and hinder the ability to adapt to rapidly changing economic conditions.

Case Studies

Case Study 1: NAFTA/USMCA

The NAFTA was a landmark trade accord between the United States, Canada and Mexico that came into effect in 1994, aiming to eliminate most tariffs on goods traded among the three countries. The NAFTA sought to promote cross-border trade and investment by reducing trade barriers and establishing rules on intellectual property, labour and environmental standards. It led to the creation of a highly integrated North American supply chain, particularly in industries like automotive manufacturing, where goods and components flowed freely across borders. In 2020, the NAFTA was replaced by the USMCA, which updated key provisions to address concerns about labour standards, trade imbalances and the impact on domestic industries. The USMCA introduced stricter rules of origin for automotive products, enhanced protections for labour and environmental standards and modernized intellectual property provisions, reflecting a more protectionist stance aimed at safeguarding North American industries while maintaining the benefits of regional trade integration (Arnaud, 2024).

Impact on the North American Automotive Industry

The North American automotive industry has been one of the sectors most impacted by NAFTA and its successor, the USMCA. When NAFTA came into effect in 1994, it significantly altered the landscape of the automotive industry by eliminating tariffs on automotive products traded between the United States, Canada and Mexico. This led to the creation of an integrated supply chain that spanned the three countries, allowing manufacturers to specialize in different stages of production based on their comparative advantages. Under NAFTA, Mexico emerged as a major hub for automotive production, thanks to its lower labour costs and favourable regulatory environment. The country attracted significant investment from global automakers, including Ford, General Motors and Chrysler, as well as major suppliers of automotive components. By 2016, Mexico had become the world's seventh-largest producer of vehicles, with the vast majority of its production destined for export, primarily to the United States (Dávalos, 2020).

However, the benefits of this arrangement were not evenly distributed. While consumers and firms in North America benefitted from lower costs, labour unions in the United States and Canada expressed concerns about job losses due to the relocation of manufacturing to Mexico. Critics argued that NAFTA contributed to the decline of the US manufacturing sector, particularly in regions that were heavily dependent on automotive production. Despite these criticisms, the automotive industry continued to thrive under NAFTA, with the agreement fostering innovation, efficiency and competitiveness across North America (Crossa, 2024).

Evolution from NAFTA to USMCA and Its Implications

The transition from NAFTA to the USMCA in 2020 marked a significant shift in the regulatory and economic framework governing trade in North America. The USMCA was negotiated in response to criticisms of the NAFTA, particularly concerning labour standards, environmental protections and the impact on the US manufacturing sector. One of the primary drivers of this renegotiation was the desire of the US government to reassert control over trade imbalances and address perceived flaws in NAFTA that led to job losses in the United States. One of the most important changes introduced by the USMCA was the new rules of origin requirements for the automotive industry: under the USMCA, 75% of a vehicle's components must be manufactured in North America to qualify for tariff-free trade, an increase from the 62.5% requirement under the NAFTA. This provision was designed to incentivize automakers to source more of their parts from within the region, thus boosting domestic production and supporting jobs in the United States and Canada (Álvarez Medina, 2021).

The transition to the USMCA has had mixed implications. On the one hand, the stricter rules of origin and labour provisions are expected to reduce the outsourcing of production to Mexico and encourage more domestic investment in the United States and Canada. However, some analysts argue that the increased regulatory burden may raise production costs, potentially making North American vehicles less competitive in global markets. Furthermore, the complexity of complying with the new rules may disrupt existing supply chains, which had become highly integrated under the NAFTA. Overall, the USMCA represents a recalibration of North American trade relations, with the goal of fostering a more equitable distribution of the benefits of regional economic integration (Ciuriak et al., 2020).

Case Study 2: EU

Influence on the Pharmaceutical Sector

The EU has played a significant role in shaping the pharmaceutical industry within its member states. As one of the world's largest markets for pharmaceuticals, the EU has implemented policies and frameworks that foster innovation, ensure safety and promote access to essential medicines. The creation of the European Medicines Agency (EMA) in 1995 was a key development, centralizing the evaluation and regulation of medicines ensuring that pharmaceutical products meet stringent safety, efficacy and quality standards before they reach the market. This has facilitated a streamlined approval process, enabling pharmaceutical companies to introduce new drugs more efficiently across the EU market (Mahalatchimy et al., 2012).

One of the EU's critical contributions to the pharmaceutical sector has been the harmonization of regulatory standards across member states, which has helped reduce fragmentation in drug approval processes. Before the establishment of the EMA, companies often faced complex and varying regulatory requirements in each country, which hindered their ability to quickly launch products across Europe. The EMA introduced a centralized procedure, allowing companies to submit a single application for the authorization of medicines, which is then valid across all member states. This harmonization not only reduces administrative burdens but also encourages investment in pharmaceutical research and development (R&D) because companies can more easily access the entire European market (Khanna, 2018).

Role of EU Regulations in Streamlining Production

EU regulations have been instrumental in streamlining pharmaceutical production across the region, with significant implications for efficiency, cost reduction and public health. One of the major accomplishments of the EU has been the creation of a single regulatory framework that applies to all member states, allowing for uniformity in production standards and processes. The harmonization of good manufacturing practices across the EU, enforced by the EMA, has been critical in ensuring that pharmaceutical products are produced under stringent quality controls, regardless of where they are manufactured within the EU (Khanna, 2018).

These regulatory frameworks reduce duplication of regulatory processes across borders, simplifying the production and distribution of medicines. For instance, manufacturers no longer need to comply with separate national regulations for each country within the EU, which has significantly lowered production costs and enhanced supply chain efficiency. The EU's regulatory regime has also been effective in safeguarding public health by setting rigorous safety and efficacy standards for medicines. Through the EMA's centralized procedure, manufacturers must adhere to high-quality production standards, which helps prevent the circulation of substandard or counterfeit drugs within the European market. This has made the EU a model of regulatory excellence in the pharmaceutical sector, with its stringent policies often serving as a benchmark for other regions globally (Mossialos, 2010).

Case Study 3: ASEAN Economic Community (AEC)

Integration of Electronics Manufacturing

The AEC has been instrumental in fostering the integration of electronics manufacturing in Southeast Asia, creating a cohesive regional production network. Electronics is one of the largest and most critical industries within the AEC, with countries like Singapore, Malaysia, Thailand, Vietnam and the Philippines playing significant roles in global supply chains. These nations specialize in various stages of electronics production, ranging from semiconductors and components to final assembly and exports. The AEC has provided a framework for facilitating this integration by reducing trade barriers, harmonizing standards and promoting investment across borders (Plummer, 2006).

One of the key factors driving the integration of electronics manufacturing within the AEC has been the region's comparative advantages. ASEAN countries benefit from a combination of low labour costs, strategic geographic positioning and infrastructure development, making them attractive destinations for multinational corporations. Global electronics firms such as Intel, Samsung and Foxconn have established manufacturing hubs in Southeast Asia, benefitting from the region's cost-effective production environment while leveraging the AEC's trade facilitation measures. By creating a more integrated and seamless production network, the AEC has helped reduce production costs and shorten lead times for companies operating within the region. This has allowed ASEAN countries to become key players in global electronics supply chains, with the region accounting for a significant share of global exports in electronics components and finished goods (Athukorala & Kohpaiboon, 2014).

Challenges and Opportunities in Southeast Asia

While the AEC has achieved notable successes in integrating Southeast Asia's economies, it also faces several challenges in realizing its full potential. One of the primary challenges is the disparity in economic development among ASEAN member states. Countries like Singapore and Malaysia have well-developed infrastructure and robust legal frameworks, making them attractive for foreign direct investment, while less-developed countries such as Laos, Myanmar and Cambodia face significant obstacles, including underdeveloped infrastructure and limited human capital. Moreover, AEC reliance on external demand, particularly from China, the United States and Europe, is a challenge. The electronics manufacturing sector is heavily dependent on exports to these markets. Fluctuations in global demand, trade tensions and disruptions in global supply chains, such as those seen during the COVID-19 pandemic, expose ASEAN countries to economic vulnerabilities (Menon & Fink, 2019).

Despite these challenges, the AEC presents significant opportunities for Southeast Asia. The region's young and growing population, coupled with increasing digitalization and rising consumer demand, provides fertile ground for economic expansion. These trends are expected to drive demand for electronics components, creating opportunities for ASEAN countries to further expand their role in global supply chains. Moreover, ASEAN's strategic location between major global markets provides opportunities for deeper integration with other regional trade agreements, such as the RCEP (Kimura & Obashi, 2016).

Case Study 4: African Continental Free Trade Area (AfCFTA)

Development of Textile and Apparel Industry

The AfCFTA, launched in 2021, represents a landmark achievement in Africa's pursuit of economic integration, with the potential to significantly boost industries such as textiles and apparel. Historically, Africa has struggled to develop a robust textile and apparel industry, primarily due to fragmented markets, high trade barriers and underdeveloped infrastructure. AfCFTA aims to address these challenges by creating the world's largest free trade area, encompassing 54 of Africa's 55 countries, thereby facilitating the free flow of goods, services and investments across the continent (Brenton & Hoppe, 2009).

The textile and apparel sector has been identified as one of the industries with the greatest potential to benefit from AfCFTA. With its abundant natural resources, including cotton, Africa has the raw materials necessary to support a thriving textile industry. By eliminating tariffs and harmonizing trade policies, AfCFTA can encourage intra-African trade, reduce production costs and enable economies of scale in textile and apparel manufacturing. Moreover, AfCFTA provides an opportunity to build regional value chains in textiles and apparel, allowing countries to specialize in different stages of production. For instance, cotton-producing countries like Burkina Faso can focus on raw material supply, while more industrialized nations such as South Africa can specialize in apparel production and export. This integration could reduce Africa's reliance on imported textiles and finished goods, fostering a more self-sufficient and competitive regional industry (Brenton & Hoppe, 2007).

Potential for Economic Growth and Challenges Faced

However, the successful implementation of AfCFTA is not without challenges. One of the primary obstacles is the lack of infrastructure, which hinders efficient trade and the development of regional supply chains. Poor transport networks, unreliable electricity and limited access to technology are significant barriers to the efficient production and distribution of goods. Countries must invest in infrastructure development to fully capitalize on the opportunities provided by AfCFTA. Another challenge lies in the wide disparity between the economic development levels of African countries. While countries like South Africa and Nigeria have more developed industries, many in Central and West Africa still lack industrial capacity and regulation. This uneven development could lead to unequal benefits from AfCFTA, with more developed countries potentially reaping the majority of the advantages. Moreover, non-tariff barriers, such as cumbersome customs procedures and varying regulatory standards across member states, could undermine the full realization of AfCFTA's benefits (Ekeocha et al., 2023).

Conclusion

In this book chapter, we set out to provide an introduction to the nature of regional blocs and economic alliances and their implications on GVCs as well as to offer insights into concrete examples of how these blocs and alliances have shaped our understanding of globalization. The history of regional blocs and economic alliances reflects the evolving nature of economic cooperation, driven by the desire to enhance trade, political stability and economic growth. With emerging geopolitical tensions and evolving regionalism, the formation of new regional blocs and economic alliances is increasingly uncertain, but they will remain central to shaping the future of international trade and cooperation.

References

Ali, I., Arslan, A., Chowdhury, M., Khan, Z., & Tarba, S. Y. (2022). Reimagining global food value chains through effective resilience to COVID-19 shocks and similar future events: A dynamic capability perspective. *Journal of Business Research*, *141*, 1–12.

Álvarez Medina, M. D. L. (2021). Impact of the United States-Mexico-Canada agreement (USMCA) rules of origin on the automotive sector in Mexico. *Norteamérica*, *16*(2), 403–430.

Arnaud, L. (2024). From NAFTA to USMCA: Revisiting the market access–policy space trade-off. *New Political Economy*, *29*(3), 356–369.

Athukorala, P.-C., & Kohpaiboon, A. (2014). Trade patterns in East Asia: Implications for the debate on mega-FTA initiatives. *Thailand and the World Economy*, *31*(4), 67–94.

Bhagwati, J. (2008). *Termites in the trading system: How preferential agreements undermine free trade*. Oxford University Press.

Bhalla, A. S. (2016). *Regional blocs: Building blocks or stumbling blocks?* Springer.

Bickel, F. (2021). *Customs unions in the WTO*. Springer.

Brenton, P., & Hoppe, M. (2007). *Clothing and export diversification: Still a route to growth for low-income countries?* (Vol. 4343). World Bank Publications.

Brenton, P., & Hoppe, M. (2009). Export competitiveness and regional integration in Africa. In *Beyond market access for economic development* (pp. 87–112). Routledge.

Ciuriak, D., Dadkhah, A., & Xiao, J. (2020). *Quantifying CUSMA: The economic consequences of the new North American trade regime* (Trade and International Policy Working Paper Issue). The C.D. Howe Institute.

Coffey, P. (2013). *Latin America: Mercosur* (Vol. 1). Springer Science & Business Media.

Collier, P., & Venables, A. J. (2012). Land deals in Africa: Pioneers and speculators. *Journal of Globalization and Development*, *3*(1).

Crossa, M. (2024). USMCA and uneven regionalized protectionism: Automotive industry in Mexico under US corporate control. *International Journal of Political Economy*, 1–14.

Dadush, U., & Prost, E. D. (2023). Preferential trade agreements, geopolitics, and the fragmentation of world trade. *World Trade Review*, *22*(2), 278–294.

Dávalos, E. (2020). Protectionism, USMCA and its possible effects on Mexico's automotive industry. *European Review of International Studies*, *7*(1), 81–104.

Davison, R. (2017). Building blocs: Regionalism and globalization in the Asia-Pacific. In *The new global politics of the Asia-Pacific* (pp. 214–246). Routledge.

Ekeocha, Q. O., Ubru, P. N., & Vincent, C. (2023). African continental free trade agreement (AfCFTA) and regional integration in Africa. In *African political economy in the twenty-first century: Theories, perspectives, and issues* (p. 181). Lexington Books.

Gereffi, G., Humphrey, J., & Sturgeon, T. (2005). The governance of global value chains. *Review of International Political Economy*, *12*(1), 78–104.

Gómez-Mera, L. (2009). Domestic constraints on regional cooperation: Explaining trade conflict in MERCOSUR. *Review of International Political Economy*, *16*(5), 746–777.

Heiduk, F. (2022). *Asian geopolitics and the US-China rivalry*. Routledge, Taylor & Francis.

Herold, D. M., & Marzantowicz, Ł. (2023). Supply chain responses to global disruptions and its ripple effects: An institutional complexity perspective. *Operations Management Research*, 1–12.

Khanna, B. (2018). Pharmaceutical regulations in European Union. In *Pharmaceutical medicine and translational clinical research* (pp. 175–213). Elsevier.

Kimura, F., & Obashi, A. (2016). *Production networks in East Asia: What we know so far*. Springer.

Mahalatchimy, A., Rial-Sebbag, E., De Grove-Valdeyron, N., Tournay, V., Cambon-Thomsen, A., Duguet, A.-M., & Taboulet, F. (2012). The European medicines agency: A public health European agency. *Medicine & Law*, *31*, 25.

McCormick, J. (2020). *Understanding the European Union: A concise introduction*. Bloomsbury Publishing.

Menon, J., & Fink, A. (2019). The fourth industrial revolution and its implications for regional economic integration in ASEAN. *Journal of Asian Economic Integration*, *1*(1), 32–47.

Mossialos, E. (2010). *Health systems governance in Europe: The role of European Union law and policy*. Cambridge University Press.

Park, C.-Y., Petri, P. A., & Plummer, M. G. (2021). The economics of conflict and cooperation in the Asia-pacific: RCEP, CPTPP and the US-China trade war. *East Asian Economic Review*, *25*(3), 233–272.

Parsons, C. (2002). Showing ideas as causes: The origins of the European Union. *International Organization*, *56*(1), 47–84.

Pichler, M., Krenmayr, N., Schneider, E., & Brand, U. (2021). EU industrial policy: Between modernization and transformation of the automotive industry. *Environmental Innovation and Societal Transitions*, *38*, 140–152.

Plummer, M. G. (2006). ASEAN–EU economic relationship: Integration and lessons for the ASEAN economic community. *Journal of Asian Economics*, *17*(3), 427–447.

Pomfret, R. (2021). 'Regionalism' and the global trade system. *The World Economy*, *44*(9), 2496–2514.

Quaglia, L. (2013). Financial regulation and supervision in the European Union after the crisis. *Journal of Economic Policy Reform*, *16*(1), 17–30.

Rana, P. B., Chia, W.-M., & Ji, X. (2021). The decentralizing international trade architecture: Perspectives from and role of Asia. *The Singapore Economic Review*, *66*(1), 59–84.
Schott, J. J. (2004). Free trade agreements: Boon or bane of the world trading system. *Free Trade Agreements: US Strategies and Priorities*, *3*(11).
Schütze, R. (2012). *European constitutional law*. Cambridge University Press.
Stockhammer, E. (2016). Neoliberal growth models, monetary union and the Euro crisis. A post-Keynesian perspective. *New Political Economy*, *21*(4), 365–379.
Taggart, P., & Szczerbiak, A. (2021). Putting Brexit into perspective: The effect of the Eurozone and migration crises and Brexit on Euroscepticism in European states. In *The politics and economics of Brexit* (pp. 106–126). Routledge.
Wu, T., & Chadee, D. (2022). Comprehensive and progressive agreement for trans-pacific partnership (CPTPP): Implications for the Asia-Pacific region. In *International business in the new Asia-Pacific: Strategies, opportunities and threats* (pp. 53–74). ISEAS Publishing.
Zreik, M. (2024). The regional comprehensive economic partnership (RCEP) for the Asia–Pacific region and world. *Journal of Economic and Administrative Sciences*, *40*(1), 57–75.

12

NAVIGATING THE PATH AHEAD

A Roadmap for Future Global Value Chains

Imran Ali, William Ho and Thanos Papadopoulos

Introduction

This book has explored the significant evolution of global value chains (GVCs) amid increasing geopolitical instability. From the initial chapter to the in-depth thematic discussions that followed, the primary aim has been to offer nuanced insight into how GVCs are changing in a more fragmented global context. Utilizing contemporary research, theoretical frameworks, and practical case studies, this volume has examined how various disruptions—such as trade conflicts, shifting power relations, and the rising emphasis on sustainability—are challenging conventional models of global production and supply.

At its essence, this work seeks to accomplish three main objectives: to assess the current state of GVCs through the prism of geopolitical turbulence; to provide illustrative case evidence demonstrating how businesses, regions, and institutions are addressing these challenges; and to propose forward-thinking strategies that can guide practice, inform policy decisions, and contribute to academic discourse. The interdisciplinary nature of this book enhances its value—integrating perspectives from international business, operations management, political economy, and technology studies. This blend caters to a varied readership, including scholars desiring rigorous analysis, practitioners searching for actionable insights, and policymakers navigating a changing global landscape.

The chapters indicate that the era of hyper-globalization—marked by fluid trade movements, offshoring practices, and just-in-time manufacturing—is experiencing significant stress. Events such as the COVID-19 pandemic, the conflict between Russia and Ukraine, and tensions between the United States and China regarding trade issues have revealed vulnerabilities within

DOI: 10.4324/9781003468899-12

many GVCs. A pivotal moment was marked by extensive tariffs imposed by the Trump administration that sparked retaliatory actions and led companies across different sectors to reassess their sourcing and manufacturing strategies. These tariffs particularly affected imports from China and disrupted established supply chains while encouraging firms to reconsider their reliance on specific markets—accelerating trends like nearshoring and diversification.

Contemporary GVCs are increasingly characterized as nonlinear rather than linear cost-optimized systems; they are influenced by political risks, complex regulations, as well as an escalating demand for transparency and sustainability. This transformation not only reshapes competitive advantages but also introduces new challenges related to resilience building, technological advancement adoption, workforce evolution.

Synthesis of Key Themes from Chapters 1 to 11

The preceding chapters in this volume have collectively illuminated the profound and multifaceted ways in which GVCs are being reshaped. Six dominant themes have emerged, offering a comprehensive understanding of the present disruptions and opportunities shaping the future of GVCs.

Geopolitical Disruptions and Trade Reconfigurations

Geopolitical uncertainty stands as a central force altering the structure and dynamics of GVCs. As explored in Chapters 1 through 3, rising tensions between global powers, including ongoing trade wars, the Russia-Ukraine conflict, and the recalibration of the China-US relationship, have generated significant friction in international trade. These shifts have led to strategic decoupling, reshoring, and friend-shoring initiatives. The global economic architecture, long predicated on cost-efficiency and interconnectedness, is now tilting toward strategic autonomy, regionalization, and risk diversification.

The reconfiguration of trade networks—particularly between developed and developing economies—has surfaced as a direct response to protectionist policies and national security concerns. Case studies throughout the book have shown how businesses are adapting their trade and sourcing strategies to mitigate exposure to geopolitical risk. The chapters advocate for a pragmatic yet forward-looking approach that balances economic openness with resilience-building measures.

Shifts in Labour, Employment, and Skills

Chapter 4 addresses the changing nature of work within GVCs. As GVCs become increasingly digitized and automated, the demand for traditional labor is declining in some sectors while new roles are emerging in others. The proliferation of digital tools has redefined job requirements, making digital literacy, adaptability, and analytical skills critical across all stages of the value chain.

Importantly, the chapter points out that these transformations are not geographically uniform. While advanced economies grapple with labour shortages and the ageing workforce, developing nations face challenges in skilling youth populations to participate meaningfully in modern GVCs. The need for massive investment in education, training, and upskilling is a recurring theme. Case studies show that firms that proactively invest in workforce development—particularly in tech-enabled skills—are better positioned to succeed in the evolving GVC landscape.

Technological Transformation and Digitalization of GVCs

Chapters 5 and 6 underscore the accelerating role of technology in shaping the future of GVCs. Technologies such as artificial intelligence (AI), blockchain, the Internet of Things (IoT), and advanced robotics are revolutionizing production networks, logistics, and coordination across borders. Digital twins, predictive analytics, and automated warehouses are enabling firms to anticipate disruptions, optimize operations, and enhance responsiveness.

This digital transformation is not merely operational—it is strategic. Technology is creating new possibilities for decentralized manufacturing (e.g., through 3D printing) and fostering innovative business models, such as platform-based supply ecosystems. The book demonstrates that companies leveraging digital technologies are better positioned to manage complexity and volatility. However, the digital divide remains a challenge, particularly for small and medium enterprises (SMEs) and firms in emerging economies, highlighting the need for inclusive digital capacity-building initiatives.

Governmental Policies and Regional Alliances

Chapters 7 to 11 examine the influential role of governments and regional blocs in shaping the trajectory of GVCs. Policy instruments such as tariffs, subsidies, export controls, and strategic trade agreements are being wielded to secure national interests. At the same time, regional alliances—like Association of Southeast Asian Nations (ASEAN), the European Union (EU), and the African Continental Free Trade Area (AfCFTA)—are facilitating greater intra-regional integration and creating more predictable trade environments.

Government-Industry Collaboration as a Key Driver of Adaptive GVCs

The partnership between government and industry is acknowledged as a crucial element in developing adaptive GVCs. Successful examples demonstrate collaborative efforts aimed at improving local manufacturing capabilities and digital infrastructure. The chapters advocate for a balanced policymaking approach that encourages open, transparent, and rule-based trade systems while allowing nations to build strategic resilience.

Risk Assessment and Supply Chain Resilience

Chapters 8 and 9 highlight the increasing necessity for resilience within GVCs. The vulnerabilities revealed by the COVID-19 pandemic, natural disasters, and geopolitical conflicts have led companies to prioritize redundancy, diversification, and visibility within their supply chains. Organizations are increasingly utilizing advanced analytics and risk modeling tools to pinpoint potential threats, simulate different scenarios, and proactively mitigate disruptions.

Resilience encompasses more than just recovery; it involves preparedness. The chapters recommend a shift from reactive to proactive risk management strategies, including engaging multiple supplier tiers, employing dual sourcing tactics, and developing regional contingency plans. Firms that embed resilience into their fundamental operations are better equipped to withstand and thrive during future uncertainties.

Environmental, Social, and Governance, Sustainability, and Responsible Governance

Sustainability has transitioned from a secondary issue to a critical strategic priority. Chapter 10 emphasizes the growing importance of environmental, social, and governance (ESG) criteria within GVCs. Stakeholders increasingly demand transparency, traceability, and accountability in sourcing and production methods. Regulatory frameworks, such as the EU's due diligence laws for supply chains, require companies to adhere to strict environmental and social standards.

Embracing ESG principles is aligned with achieving a competitive edge. Organizations with credible sustainability credentials attract investment, bolster brand reputation, and mitigate reputational risks. The chapter's case studies demonstrate that adopting ESG-aligned strategies is not only feasible but also advantageous, especially when implemented through cross-sector partnerships supported by digital traceability systems.

Emerging Imperatives for Future GVCs

As we look to the future of GVCs, several key imperatives will play a significant role in shaping their evolution. In light of ongoing geopolitical tensions, environmental challenges, and technological advancements, businesses must fundamentally reassess the design, management, and execution of their value chains. Five strategic priorities emerge: resilience; technological innovation; sustainability; the reconfiguration of global versus local operations; and considerations regarding the future of human capital. Each of these areas demands active participation from both businesses and policymakers.

Resilience as a Strategic Priority

The COVID-19 pandemic, along with ongoing conflicts and trade disputes, has highlighted the fragility of global supply chains. As a result, resilience is increasingly perceived not just as a defensive measure but as a vital strategic capability. Resilient GVCs are defined by their capacity to effectively absorb shocks while continuing to deliver value during disruptions. Traditionally focused on cost-efficiency through lean operations, often at the expense of flexibility or redundancy, organizations now recognize that long-term competitiveness relies on resilience. This shift in perspective necessitates investments in multi-sourcing approaches, nearshoring practices, inventory buffers, and supplier diversity initiatives. Additionally, digital tools such as real-time tracking systems and predictive analytics are becoming essential for proactively identifying vulnerabilities before they develop into larger disruptions throughout the value chain. Enhancing resilience also requires collaboration among various stakeholders, including suppliers, customers, and governmental entities involved in these networks.

Technology as a Catalyst for Transformation

Technological advancements are significantly challenging traditional frameworks within GVCs and transforming operational capabilities. Innovations from Industry 4.0 technologies—including AI, the IoT, blockchain technology, robotics, and digital twins—are reshaping how goods are sourced, produced, and delivered. AI combined with machine learning facilitates more agile decision-making, while blockchain improves transparency and trust across complex supplier networks. IoT devices enable predictive maintenance and dynamic logistical optimization, while robotics enhance manufacturing efficiency and quality. These innovations not only increase operational effectiveness but also provide organizations with real-time responsiveness amid volatile market conditions. However, realizing successful digital transformation requires integrating these capabilities into broader business strategies and workforce development rather than relying solely on isolated technology implementations.

Sustainability and ESG Compliance: A Fundamental Requirement

ESG considerations can no longer be regarded as peripheral; they are fundamental elements that determine the legitimacy and long-term viability of

GVCs. Heightened regulatory scrutiny, stakeholder expectations, and investor vigilance have compelled firms to deeply embed sustainable and responsible governance practices into their international operations. Environmental responsibility involves minimizing emissions and waste while ensuring resource efficiency throughout the entire value chain. Social obligations include fair labor practices, community engagement, and supplier diversity, while governance emphasizes ethical sourcing, anti-corruption measures, and transparency. Future-ready GVCs recognize that ESG compliance is not merely about meeting legal requirements; it serves broader goals of creating shared value. Companies that prioritize these aspects typically enjoy stronger reputations, improved access to green financing, and enhanced loyalty among customers and employees. Aligning business objectives with ESG goals contributes to achieving larger global ambitions, such as the United Nations Sustainable Development Goals (SDGs). As climate change and social inequality remain pressing global challenges, prioritizing sustainability and ESG compliance will be essential for securing future success and fostering collaborative efforts worldwide.

Localization vs Globalization: Striking a Balance

The contrast between globalization and localization has evolved into a more nuanced discussion. Amid rising geopolitical tensions and nationalism, many companies are reassessing their global reach. However, a complete withdrawal from globalization is not the answer; instead, efforts should focus on achieving a balance. Localization strategies such as reshoring and regionalization offer proximity to key markets, reducing exposure to cross-border disruptions and allowing for greater control over supply chain dynamics. Conversely, extensive networks still provide advantages in scale, efficiency, and access to innovation. The future will likely consist of hybrid models characterized by "glocal" strategies that merge efficiencies derived from global frameworks with localized responsiveness, potentially requiring the establishment of regional hubs, adaptable production methods, and digitally facilitated cross-border transactions. Rather than viewing globalization as a liability, firms must learn to orchestrate diversified, modular, and adaptive GVCs that integrate the strengths of both global reach and local resilience.

Human Capital and Skills for the Future of Work

Amid the technological and strategic transformations, the human element remains critical. The future of GVCs relies significantly on the capabilities of individuals who design, manage, and innovate within them. As automation and AI increasingly handle routine tasks, the demand for human skills such as problem-solving, cross-cultural communication, ethical judgment, and digital literacy will rise. Reskilling and upskilling are vital to ensure that the workforce can adapt to the requirements of digitized and decentralized value chains. Furthermore, attracting and retaining talent necessitates a focus on employee well-being, career development, diversity, and inclusive leadership. Global talent shortages in logistics, data science, cybersecurity, and ESG compliance further underscore the urgency for proactive workforce development. Governments, educational institutions, and businesses must collaborate to create pathways for skilled professionals who can lead the next generation of GVCs. Essentially, the human aspect is not being displaced by technology—it is being redefined. Investing in people is a direct investment in the future competitiveness and resilience of GVCs.

Together, these five imperatives—resilience, technology, sustainability, localization, and human capital—will define the GVCs of the future. They are interconnected themes that require coordinated, long-term engagement from all stakeholders in the global economy.

A Multi-Stakeholder Roadmap for GVC Transformation

Business Strategies

In a climate marked by increasing geopolitical instability, pandemics, climate disruptions, and technological upheaval, the role of businesses in transforming GVCs is crucial. Private enterprises are no longer passive participants in global trade networks but are key architects in creating resilient, sustainable, and future-proof GVCs. This section outlines three interconnected strategic imperatives for businesses: (1) redesigning supply networks to enhance resilience and flexibility; (2) investing in technological innovation and predictive analytics; and (3) embedding ESG principles into the core of supply chain strategies. Collectively, these actions establish a robust corporate response to the evolving landscape of global risks.

Redesigning Supply Networks with Resilience and Flexibility

Traditional models of lean and cost-efficient supply chains are increasingly insufficient when confronted with systemic shocks such as trade disputes, political sanctions, and regional conflicts. The COVID-19 pandemic highlighted the vulnerabilities of highly optimized GVCs, prompting many companies to reassess their dependence on single-source suppliers and production hubs concentrated in specific regions. Consequently, businesses are now required to transition toward supply networks that emphasize both resilience—the ability to withstand and recover from disruptions—and flexibility—the capacity to swiftly adapt to changes.

A resilient supply network involves diversifying suppliers and manufacturing sites to mitigate reliance on high-risk areas. This strategy includes adopting a

"China Plus One" approach, relocating essential components closer to home, and establishing regional or multi-local supply hubs. Additionally, firms are increasingly implementing redundancy measures—such as maintaining safety stock, utilizing dual sourcing, and creating buffer capacities—to safeguard operational continuity.

Conversely, flexibility necessitates an agile supply chain design. Agile supply chains incorporate demand sensing, prompt decision-making, and modular production systems that can be rapidly scaled or reconfigured. Strategic alliances and horizontal collaborations are also crucial. By pooling resources, infrastructure, and market insights, companies can develop collaborative resilience ecosystems. Organizations like Toyota and Unilever have adopted such network-based resilience strategies, achieving notable improvements in their ability to endure supply disruptions and recover more swiftly.

It is essential to recognize that resilience and flexibility should be regarded not as costs but as competitive advantages that bolster long-term business continuity and bolster stakeholder confidence.

Investing in Technological Innovation and Predictive Analytics

Technology serves as the cornerstone of modern GVC transformation. Companies must invest in a range of digital technologies—including AI, the IoT, blockchain, and advanced analytics—to enhance visibility, foresight, and responsiveness in their supply chains.

Predictive analytics facilitates proactive supply chain management rather than reactive approaches. By harnessing big data from suppliers, customers, logistics providers, and geopolitical risk databases, companies can foresee potential disruptions and take preventive actions. For example, AI-driven risk modeling platforms can pinpoint hotspots of political instability, assess the likelihood of natural disasters, or evaluate the risks of supplier insolvency. Such insights enable businesses to adjust sourcing strategies, reroute shipments, or engage alternative vendors before disruptions occur.

IoT devices, such as Global Positioning System trackers and radio-frequency identification tags, provide real-time visibility into the movement and condition of goods, allowing for more precise coordination across supply chain nodes. Additionally, blockchain technology enhances traceability and trust by establishing immutable records of transactions, which is particularly critical in regulated sectors like pharmaceuticals and food.

Moreover, digital twins—virtual representations of physical supply chains—empower firms to simulate scenarios and optimize decision-making amid uncertainty. Companies like DHL and Siemens have been at the forefront of utilizing digital twins for inventory management, route optimization, and capacity forecasting, leading to reduced costs and improved resilience.

It is vital that technological innovation aligns with organizational capabilities. Upskilling the workforce, nurturing a culture of digital agility, and fostering cross-functional collaboration are crucial for maximizing the benefits of technological investments.

Embedding ESG into Core Supply Chain Strategy

Incorporating ESG factors into supply chain strategy has transitioned from being optional to becoming a fundamental business necessity. Stakeholders, including investors, regulators, consumers, and civil society, increasingly expect companies to exhibit ethical and sustainable practices throughout their value chains.

Environmental issues, particularly concerning carbon emissions, waste, and resource consumption, are central to sustainable supply chain strategies. Companies must embrace circular economy principles by designing processes that promote reuse, recycling, and reduction throughout production and logistics systems. Scope 3 emissions—those generated throughout the supply chain—need to be transparently measured and reported, accompanied by clear decarbonization pathways aligned with global targets such as the Paris Agreement.

Social considerations encompass labor rights, community engagement, and supplier diversity. Businesses must ensure that their suppliers—especially those in low-cost regions—comply with fair wage practices, safe working conditions, and antidiscrimination policies. Conducting supply chain audits, implementing supplier codes of conduct, and obtaining third-party certifications are vital tools for enforcing these standards.

Governance pertains to ethical procurement, anti-corruption measures, and responsible sourcing. A strong governance framework ensures compliance with international trade laws, sanctions, and ESG reporting requirements.

Integrating ESG into the core of supply chain strategies also enhances risk management. For instance, suppliers who do not adhere to environmental sustainability pose reputational and operational risks. Similarly, social unrest stemming from exploitative labor practices can disrupt production and harm brand reputation.

Leading companies such as Patagonia, IKEA, and Nestlé have incorporated ESG criteria into their supplier selection processes, performance evaluations, and investment decisions. These organizations demonstrate that supply chains aligned with ESG principles are not only ethically sound but also commercially advantageous, enhancing brand reputation and consumer trust.

In conclusion, the transformation of GVCs into resilient, flexible, and sustainable systems requires strategic actions from businesses. By redesigning supply networks, utilizing digital technologies, and embedding ESG at the core of their operations, organizations can thrive in uncertain environments while contributing to a more equitable global economy. These strategies are interconnected components of future-ready business models that align performance with purpose. The forthcoming era of competitiveness will hinge not solely on cost leadership but also on the ability to adapt, innovate, and lead responsibly in a geopolitically unstable world.

Government and Policy Recommendations

Balancing Open and Fair Trade with National Security Concerns

Governments are crucial in shaping the dynamics of GVCs, especially in a time characterized by increasing geopolitical uncertainties and economic fragmentation. As GVCs grow more complex and increasingly intertwined with national strategic interests, the scope for government policy has expanded beyond traditional trade facilitation to encompass national security, environmental sustainability, and social responsibility.

The foremost challenge is to uphold the principles of open and fair trade while addressing rising national security concerns. The resurgence of economic nationalism and the securitization of trade relationships have led to a surge in export controls, investment screening processes, and trade sanctions—particularly in high-tech sectors like semiconductors, AI, and critical minerals. Although these measures may be warranted under certain conditions, overreliance on them risks undermining the multilateral trading system and fragmenting global supply chains.

Governments must engage in transparent, evidence-based policymaking that acknowledges legitimate security concerns without turning trade into a weapon. This includes implementing narrowly targeted, proportionate trade restrictions supported by clear procedural guidelines and institutional safeguards. Furthermore, cooperation among like-minded nations is vital to minimize unintended consequences and ensure that national security measures do not devolve into systemic protectionism. Bilateral or plurilateral agreements with embedded security provisions offer a pragmatic approach to maintaining trade openness while addressing security needs.

Harmonizing Global Standards and Regulatory Frameworks

Alongside trade and security issues, harmonizing global standards and regulations remains an essential policy priority. Regulatory fragmentation increases compliance costs, creates uncertainty, and imposes disproportionate burdens on SMEs, particularly in developing countries. Harmonization facilitates smoother cross-border transactions, ensures interoperability of products and services, and enhances supply chain efficiency.

Efforts toward regulatory convergence should encompass a broad spectrum of domains—including product safety, digital governance, sustainability, labor rights, and ethical standards. Multilateral organizations such as the World Trade Organization (WTO), the Organisation for Economic Co-operation and Development (OECD), and international standard-setting bodies like the International Organization for Standardization (ISO) are pivotal in these endeavors. However, due to recent stalemates in multilateral negotiations, regional and bilateral initiatives have become increasingly important.

Trade agreements such as the Comprehensive and Progressive Agreement for Trans-Pacific Partnership (CPTPP), the AfCFTA, and the Regional Comprehensive Economic Partnership (RCEP) exemplify the potential of regional platforms to lead regulatory alignment. Additionally, regulatory sandboxes, pilot projects, and mutual recognition agreements (MRAs) can serve as practical tools to foster cross-border collaboration and support innovative practices without compromising regulatory integrity.

Incentivising Sustainable Innovation and Infrastructure Development

Governments can also serve as powerful catalysts for sustainable innovation and the development of resilient infrastructure—both of which are crucial for the future of GVCs. In light of climate change, increasing resource constraints, and evolving consumer expectations, traditional industrial policies must adapt to prioritize low-carbon technologies, circular economy models, and inclusive economic practices.

Public policy tools—such as green subsidies, tax incentives, concessional financing, and preferential procurement—can effectively direct investments toward sustainable business models and technologies. For instance, the EU's Green Deal and the United States' Inflation Reduction Act illustrate how national policies can encourage private sector investments in clean energy, sustainable manufacturing, and emission-reduction technologies. Importantly, these initiatives must adhere to international trade regulations to avoid causing distortions or retaliatory trade measures.

Simultaneously, investments in infrastructure should prioritize the enhancement of both the physical and digital components of GVCs. This encompasses improving port connectivity, modernizing logistics corridors, integrating various modes of transportation, and implementing smart trade platforms that facilitate real-time tracking, compliance, and analysis. In developing countries, blended finance models and global collaborations—particularly those involving development finance institutions and donor governments—can help address infrastructure shortfalls and ensure inclusive access to global markets.

Furthermore, governments should actively nurture innovation ecosystems. This entails promoting public-private partnerships (PPPs), funding research and development, encouraging collaboration between universities and industries, and fostering industry clusters that build local capabilities and enhance value-added production. Such strategic support for innovation ecosystems not only promotes economic diversification but also enables countries to ascend the value chain.

Toward a Coherent Policy Framework for GVC Transformation

Ultimately, governments function not only as regulators but also as architects of systemic change. Their involvement in facilitating the transformation of GVCs necessitates a cohesive policy framework that weaves together trade, security, innovation, and sustainability into a comprehensive strategic vision. This requires an all-encompassing governmental approach characterized by interministerial coordination and active collaboration with industry stakeholders.

By synchronizing domestic and international policies, governments can mitigate systemic risks, decrease policy uncertainty, and foster environments that enhance the competitiveness and resilience of businesses. Such alignment also guarantees that national economic objectives are pursued without compromising broader commitments to global cooperation, inclusive development, and environmental stewardship.

In conclusion, as the global environment becomes increasingly unstable and fragmented, governments must assume the role of architects for a new paradigm of GVCs—one that strikes a balance between openness and resilience, innovation and sustainability, and sovereignty and collaboration. The choices made today will shape the future global economic landscape, making government action both necessary and urgent.

Academic and Research Directions

As the global economy encounters heightened complexity and geopolitical challenges, the academic sector is crucial in shaping the future of GVCs. The research agenda must transcend traditional boundaries, adopting an interdisciplinary approach that aligns theory with practice, addresses emerging challenges, and supports the creation of inclusive, resilient, and sustainable value. This section delineates four strategic academic directions: interdisciplinary GVC research for geopolitical adaptation, development of theoretical frameworks focused on adaptive globalization, enhancement of practice-based knowledge transfer, and promotion of sustainable innovation and infrastructure.

Interdisciplinary GVC Research for Geopolitical Adaptation

Geopolitical disruptions—including trade conflicts, diplomatic tensions, sanctions, and political instability—have underscored the fragility of global supply chains. These events are complex and multifaceted, often intersecting with economics, international relations, environmental science, logistics, and digital technology. Thus, a fragmented approach to GVC research is inadequate. The way forward necessitates interdisciplinary research that synthesizes insights from political science, international business, economics, supply chain management, environmental studies, and technology.

Such collaborative research can yield a deeper understanding of how firms, industries, and nations can adjust their value chains in response to geopolitical changes. Political scientists, for example, can provide insights into state behavior and the implications of regulatory changes, while supply chain experts can analyze the operational impacts of these shifts. Environmental scholars can integrate sustainability considerations, particularly as GVCs increasingly incorporate ESG objectives alongside economic targets.

Moreover, interdisciplinary scholarship facilitates the creation of comprehensive risk assessment frameworks that take into account not only logistical and financial risks but also reputational, regulatory, and ethical dimensions. Universities and research institutions should establish structures that promote such cross-disciplinary collaboration, including joint research centers, cross-listed courses, and funding opportunities tailored for interdisciplinary endeavors. This collaborative research model will be vital in equipping businesses, policymakers, and civil society with the tools necessary to navigate an increasingly volatile and interconnected global environment.

Developing Theoretical Frameworks around Adaptive Globalization

Theoretical advancements are crucial for explaining and anticipating the new configurations of globalization. The previously dominant model of hyper-globalization is increasingly yielding to more fragmented and adaptable forms of global integration. Scholars need to reassess entrenched theories of international business and supply chains through the lens of today's dynamic global landscape.

Adaptive globalization refers to a flexible and responsive strategy for global integration that balances global efficiencies with local responsiveness. It acknowledges the necessity for firms to operate across borders while remaining sensitive to local economic, cultural, regulatory, and political contexts. Developing theoretical frameworks around adaptive globalization will enable researchers to conceptualize hybrid strategies, such as regionalization, friend-shoring, and strategic decoupling, which are becoming more pertinent.

These theoretical initiatives should integrate dynamic capabilities theory, institutional theory, resource dependency perspectives, and systems thinking to capture the relationship between external shocks and internal organizational responses. Researchers should also explore how digital technologies, such as AI and blockchain, facilitate new forms of decentralized and real-time coordination within GVCs. By crafting robust, empirically grounded theories of adaptive globalization, academia can enhance understanding of how GVCs evolve under pressure and inform managerial and policy decisions aimed at fostering resilience and sustainability.

Enhancing Practice-Based Knowledge Transfer

While theoretical knowledge is vital, its utility is amplified when translated into actionable insights for industry and policy stakeholders. Thus, enhancing practice-based knowledge transfer should be a strategic priority for academic institutions involved in GVC research. Universities must strengthen ties with industry partners, government entities, and international organizations to ensure their research addresses real-world challenges and is disseminated through accessible and impactful channels.

Research methodologies such as case studies, participatory action research, and industry-engaged doctoral projects are effective ways to bridge the gap between theory and practice. Academic journals should also promote the publication of practitioner-oriented insights, and business schools can incorporate experiential learning modules where students collaborate directly with firms facing disruptions in their GVCs.

Moreover, academics should engage in policy dialogues by participating in advisory boards, roundtables, and think tanks that focus on trade, innovation, and sustainability. This engagement ensures that academic insights influence public debate and policymaking processes. Knowledge hubs, both digital and physical, can facilitate ongoing interactions between scholars and practitioners, ensuring a continuous feedback loop between research and practical application.

Incentivizing Sustainable Innovation and Infrastructure

Sustainable innovation and infrastructure development are essential components of future-ready GVCs. As the global economy shifts toward low-carbon and inclusive growth models, research must concentrate on how GVCs can be restructured to align with climate objectives, ethical governance, and social well-being. Academia has a distinct role not only in analyzing these transitions but also in advocating for necessary policy frameworks, investment strategies, and educational initiatives.

Research should investigate how digital technologies can facilitate the greening of GVCs through enhanced traceability, energy efficiency, and waste reduction. Scholars should also examine the socioeconomic impacts of green GVCs, particularly in developing nations, to ensure that sustainable transitions are inclusive and equitable.

To support such research, universities must align incentives—such as funding, recognition, and career advancement—with sustainability outcomes. Government research funding organizations can catalyze efforts by prioritizing sustainability-focused projects and fostering collaborations with businesses engaged in renewable energy, circular economy, and low-carbon logistics. Establishing academic consortia centered on sustainable infrastructure, involving engineers, economists, data scientists, and supply chain specialists, can drive large-scale innovation.

In summary, academic institutions are uniquely positioned to lead in reimagining and restructuring GVCs for the future. By promoting interdisciplinary collaboration, developing adaptive theories, engaging deeply with practitioners, and advocating for sustainable innovation, the academic community can significantly contribute to a more resilient, equitable, and forward-looking global economy.

Civil Society and Global Institutions

Promoting Inclusive and Equitable Participation in GVCs

The evolution of GVCs in response to geopolitical uncertainties and changing economic paradigms cannot solely rely on the efforts of governments or private enterprises. Civil society organizations (CSOs) and global institutions must play a crucial role in ensuring that the development of GVCs does not worsen global inequality or marginalization. Promoting inclusive and equitable participation in GVCs necessitates intentional strategies to engage diverse voices from various regions, sectors, and socioeconomic backgrounds.

A significant concern in current GVC structures is the uneven distribution of benefits, where low- and middle-income countries often supply labor and resources without receiving proportionate influence or value. Civil society can help rectify this imbalance by advocating for enhanced transparency in value distribution, pushing for fair labor practices, and representing communities directly or indirectly affected by supply chain decisions. For instance, non-governmental organizations (NGOs) and labor unions have been pivotal in exposing exploitative working conditions within apparel and electronics supply chains. Their sustained advocacy has prompted changes in sourcing practices and encouraged large multinational corporations to modify their codes of conduct.

Additionally, civil society actors serve as essential intermediaries in connecting local producers and marginalized groups—including smallholder farmers, women-led businesses, and Indigenous communities—with global supply chains. By building local capacity and providing access to market information, financing, and compliance knowledge, CSOs can help ensure a more level playing field. Empowering these stakeholders to engage in and benefit from GVCs fosters not only economic development but also social cohesion and long-term sustainability.

Inclusive participation also encompasses the consideration of environmental concerns, Indigenous knowledge systems, and community resilience in value chain decisions. Through advocacy and partnerships, civil society can promote GVCs that reflect local development objectives and environmental stewardship. The increasing prominence of ESG reporting frameworks often stems from sustained advocacy efforts by civil society actors, underscoring their critical role in reshaping global economic dynamics.

Facilitating PPPs

The convergence of public policy, private enterprise, and civil society often leads to some of the most effective and transformative changes within GVCs. PPPs act as dynamic vehicles to harness the complementary strengths of each sector. Governments provide regulatory oversight and policy incentives, businesses contribute innovation and scalability, while civil society brings legitimacy, accountability, and grassroots insights.

In the context of GVCs, PPPs can be particularly effective in tackling systemic challenges such as skills development, infrastructure deficits, traceability, and sustainability. For example, collaborations between multinational retailers, local authorities, and NGOs have led to the establishment of training programs that enhance the skills of workers in developing economies, enabling them to adapt to technological advancements in production processes. Such collaborative initiatives not only address immediate workforce requirements but also contribute to the creation of more resilient and agile supply networks.

Moreover, PPPs play a vital role in promoting responsible sourcing and sustainability within GVCs. Governments can set ambitious targets or provide incentives, businesses can implement traceability and emissions reduction programs, and civil society can monitor and report progress. The success of the Better Cotton Initiative (BCI) exemplifies this collaborative framework, where industry stakeholders, governments, and NGOs worked collectively to improve farming practices, enhance livelihoods, and mitigate environmental impacts in cotton supply chains.

Importantly, PPPs that include civil society actors tend to be more accountable and transparent. This is particularly beneficial in regions where institutional trust is low or where the risk of regulatory capture by vested interests exists. The involvement of civil society ensures that development outcomes align with broader societal goals, rather than being overshadowed by commercial priorities.

Encouraging Multicountry Cooperation and Governance Frameworks

The interconnected nature of GVCs implies that disruptions, opportunities, and responsibilities rarely adhere to national boundaries. Therefore, fostering robust multicountry cooperation and governance frameworks is essential for shaping equitable, resilient, and sustainable GVCs. While national strategies are important, they must be supplemented by cross-border collaboration to address shared challenges such as data standardization, climate risk, human rights, and trade facilitation.

Global institutions such as the WTO, International Labour Organization (ILO), and United Nations Conference on Trade and Development (UNCTAD) are instrumental in enabling this collaboration. By establishing norms, offering technical support, and facilitating dialogue, these organizations aid in harmonizing approaches and reducing friction in the global trade ecosystem. For instance, the WTO's Trade Facilitation Agreement (TFA) aims to streamline customs procedures and lower trade barriers—especially for developing countries—thereby enhancing their capacity to engage in GVCs.

Civil society can serve as an effective conduit within these multilateral initiatives, helping to amplify community voices, advocate for equitable standards, and ensure that governance structures do not become overly bureaucratic or disconnected from local realities. Cross-border coalitions of NGOs, labor unions, and advocacy groups have successfully lobbied for the inclusion of social clauses in trade agreements and promoted compliance with international labor rights within supply chains.

Furthermore, governance across multiple countries is crucial for effectively managing transnational risks, including climate change, cyber threats, and political instability. Such systemic risks can significantly disrupt GVCs and often necessitate coordinated responses that transcend national borders. In today's unpredictable environment, governance structures that promote data sharing, collaborative contingency planning, and mutual accountability are increasingly important. Civil society and global institutions can fulfill a vital role by monitoring and facilitating these frameworks, ensuring they are inclusive, transparent, and focused on long-term resilience rather than immediate benefits.

In summary, the future of GVCs hinges not only on the adaptability of businesses and governments but also on the proactive involvement of civil society and global institutions. By fostering inclusive participation, establishing meaningful partnerships, and promoting multicountry collaboration, these entities can contribute to the development of GVCs that are more equitable, accountable, and resilient amidst ongoing geopolitical and economic uncertainties.

The Role of International Cooperation

In a time characterized by escalating geopolitical tensions and intricate interdependencies, international cooperation has become a fundamental element in shaping the future of GVCs. The resilience, sustainability, and competitiveness of GVCs cannot be secured through isolated national strategies alone; they require unified and coordinated responses at both bilateral and multilateral levels. The interconnected nature of today's economy indicates that disturbances in one region can create global repercussions. Consequently, international cooperation is vital for establishing shared standards, crisis response frameworks, and long-term development alignment among nations.

Bilateral and Multilateral Coordination Mechanisms

Bilateral and multilateral coordination frameworks are essential for managing the cross-border dynamics of GVCs. While bilateral agreements are more limited in scope, they enable countries to negotiate specific trade and investment arrangements that address particular geopolitical, economic, or industrial issues. Such agreements may involve customs facilitation, regulatory harmonization, mutual recognition of standards, and even collaborative infrastructure projects that are critical for supply chain continuity.

However, it is through multilateral coordination that effective global governance of value chains is truly achieved. Institutions like the WTO, UNCTAD, and OECD play critical roles in establishing common frameworks, mechanisms for dispute resolution, and transparent policy environments. For instance, the WTO's TFA has led to reduced trade costs by promoting streamlined customs processes and enhanced cross-border cooperation. Similarly, regional multilateral agreements such as the CPTPP and the AfCFTA illustrate how countries can work together to minimize barriers, improve supply chain connectivity, and diversify sourcing strategies.

Moreover, multilateral frameworks are increasingly significant in addressing nontariff issues such as environmental regulations, data privacy laws, and human rights standards. As GVCs extend into high-tech and service sectors, governance mechanisms must evolve beyond traditional tariff discussions to encompass the broader sociopolitical and technological landscape. Coordinated approaches to digital trade, carbon accounting, and responsible sourcing are now being incorporated into multilateral discussions, marking a shift toward comprehensive governance of value chains.

Learning from Best Practices Across Regions

Cross-regional knowledge sharing is crucial for fortifying GVCs against future disruptions. Events such as the COVID-19 pandemic, the Russia-Ukraine conflict, and US–China trade tensions have highlighted the vulnerabilities of global supply networks. However, these crises also offer valuable insights and innovations that, if disseminated and adopted, can enhance global preparedness and resilience.

For example, the EU's strategy for developing integrated regional value chains—with a strong focus on circular economy principles, green transitions, and coordinated industrial policies—provides a model for achieving sustainability and economic cohesion. Similarly, East Asia's achievement in creating manufacturing networks through digital infrastructure, interfirm collaboration, and supply chain financing underscores the significance of technology-driven coordination.

The function of cross-border special economic zones (SEZs), particularly between China and Southeast Asian nations, exemplifies how bilateral collaboration can yield scalable models for production integration and workforce development. Conversely, Latin American economies illustrate how PPPs and export promotion agencies can assist SMEs in engaging with GVCs.

Learning from these varied experiences necessitates structured platforms for knowledge exchange. Initiatives like the Global Alliance for Trade Facilitation and UNCTAD's eTrade for All initiative offer venues for sharing best practices, digital solutions, and capacity-building strategies among governments, businesses, and international organizations. These efforts highlight the importance of peer learning in developing adaptive and forward-thinking supply chain approaches.

Institutions as Anchors of Stability and Global Trust

The presence of credible institutions is essential for fostering and maintaining trust in global trade and investment systems. When nations and companies engage in cross-border value chains, they rely not only on logistics and infrastructure but also on predictable legal frameworks, transparent regulations, and impartial dispute resolution mechanisms. International institutions serve as arbiters, standard-setters, and enforcers that help lower transaction costs and reduce uncertainty.

Organizations such as the World Bank, International Monetary Fund (IMF), WTO, and regional development banks act as institutional pillars that facilitate the integration of developing economies into global markets. Their financial support, technical assistance, and policy guidance empower countries to enhance their capabilities in areas like customs modernization, quality assurance, and export competitiveness. Additionally, they provide platforms for addressing conflicts and grievances that could otherwise lead to larger disruptions.

Crucially, these institutions must continue to adapt to remain legitimate and effective in a rapidly changing environment. Challenges such as climate change, cybersecurity threats, and digital protectionism call for new institutional capabilities and governance models. The ability of global institutions to mediate between diverse national interests while promoting collective action is increasingly straining to, particularly in the face of rising nationalism and fragmented global leadership.

Nonetheless, revitalizing institutional trust and capacity is essential—it cannot be overlooked. Both businesses and governments benefit when they operate within a rules-based international system that guarantees accountability, transparency, and mutual advantage. The advancement of shared global standards on ESG reporting, due diligence, and ethical sourcing exemplifies the positive impact of institutional influence on supply chain sustainability.

In conclusion, the future of GVCs will not solely depend on individual firm strategies or national industrial policies but also on the strength and adaptability of international cooperation. Bilateral and multilateral frameworks provide critical avenues for harmonizing regulations and reducing friction. Learning from regional practices enables stakeholders to enhance resilience through the adaptation of proven strategies. Most importantly, international institutions must be bolstered to act as the foundation of global trust, delivering stability in an otherwise volatile landscape. Only through these interconnected efforts can we establish a GVC system that is robust, inclusive, and prepared for the uncertainties of the future.

Future Trends and Scenarios

As GVCs continue to navigate an age of persistent uncertainty, their future will be influenced by several converging trends. These include technological advancements, evolving regulatory and trade blocs, heightened urgency regarding climate issues, and the ongoing threat of geopolitical disruptions. Anticipating and understanding these trends is crucial for businesses, policymakers, and academics aiming to develop resilient, adaptable, and sustainable global supply networks. This section examines four interconnected trends likely to influence the future of GVCs: the integration of AI and automation in supply chain design and management, the rise of green and climate-resilient sourcing, the changing role of regional blocs, and the importance of scenario planning for mitigating future disruptions. Additionally, it focuses on the long-term effects of Donald Trump's tariff policies and their impact on the global trading landscape.

AI and Automation in GVC Design and Management

AI and automation technologies are no longer just concepts of the future; they are rapidly becoming integral components of GVC design and operation. From demand forecasting and real-time inventory management to automated procurement and predictive maintenance, AI-driven tools are revolutionizing the efficiency, visibility, and responsiveness of global supply chains. Machine learning algorithms are increasingly employed to analyze complex interdependencies within supply networks, enabling firms to foresee bottlenecks and dynamically allocate resources.

The implementation of AI is particularly vital for achieving end-to-end visibility across geographically dispersed production networks. Companies are now utilizing AI-powered platforms to monitor shipments in real time, assess supplier performance, and even forecast potential political or environmental disruptions. Automation, especially in warehousing and manufacturing, is diminishing reliance on manual labor and reducing operational costs. However, this technological transition also presents challenges, including the need for substantial investments in digital infrastructure, cybersecurity measures, and workforce reskilling. Countries and firms that fall behind in digital readiness may find themselves increasingly marginalized within the global supply chain hierarchy.

Green GVCs and Climate-Resilient Sourcing

Climate change is no longer a distant threat; it is an immediate and escalating disruptor of global trade and supply networks. Rising temperatures, extreme weather events, and changing rainfall patterns are already affecting agricultural production, transportation reliability, and factory operations across various regions. In light of this, there is a growing push for "green" GVCs—supply chains that are not only environmentally sustainable but also resilient to climate shocks.

Green GVCs emphasize carbon reduction, circularity, and sustainable resource management. Businesses are increasingly evaluating the carbon footprints of their suppliers, incorporating eco-design principles in product development, and transitioning to renewable energy sources in their operations. Sourcing strategies are evolving to prioritize suppliers with strong ESG profiles, while climate-resilient sourcing entails mapping supply chain vulnerabilities to climate risks and diversifying inputs accordingly.

Moreover, regulatory pressures are increasing. For instance, the EU's Carbon Border Adjustment Mechanism (CBAM) and mandatory ESG disclosures in various regions are prompting companies to weave climate considerations into their supply chain strategies. Green GVCs not only mitigate risks but also enhance reputational value and long-term competitiveness, particularly as sustainability becomes a central expectation among investors and consumers.

Trump's Tariffs and Their Impact on GVCs

The trade policies enacted during Donald Trump's presidency, especially the introduction of tariffs on imports from China, represented a pivotal shift for GVCs. Adhering to the "America First" doctrine, the United States imposed tariffs on hundreds of billions of dollars of Chinese products, which resulted in retaliatory measures from Beijing and initiated a prolonged trade conflict. This escalation notably disrupted established supply chains, particularly for sectors dependent on intermediate goods from China.

In response, numerous companies, especially in the electronics, automotive, and consumer goods industries, began to shift parts of their supply chains to alternative countries, such as Vietnam, Mexico, and India. This trend, often termed the "China Plus One" strategy, reflects a broader movement toward decoupling driven by concerns over geopolitical risks. The tariffs introduced by Trump highlighted the vulnerabilities of overly concentrated sourcing strategies, prompting a reevaluation of trade dependencies.

The ongoing ramifications of these policies continue to shape global trade structures. Even with changes in the US administration, there exists a bipartisan agreement on the need to decrease reliance on Chinese manufacturing, indicating that this transition is more structural than temporary. The impact of Trump's tariffs has led to a more politically aware approach to supply chain management—one that necessitates consideration of not just economic factors but also regulatory and geopolitical alignments.

Evolving Roles of Regional Blocs

Simultaneously, as global multilateralism becomes increasingly fragmented, regional economic blocs have risen to prominence as key facilitators of trade and coordination of supply chains. Organizations such as the EU, the ASEAN, and the AfCFTA are playing increasingly strategic roles in shaping regional production and trade landscapes.

The EU continues to take the lead in establishing global standards related to sustainability, data protection, and product compliance, effectively extending its influence on GVCs through its regulatory framework. ASEAN has emerged as a vibrant center for the reconfiguration of GVCs, drawing manufacturing investments as companies diversify their operations away from China. The RCEP, which includes ASEAN countries and other key economies in the Asia-Pacific region, is anticipated to further enhance regional integration.

On the other hand, AfCFTA has substantial potential to boost intra-African trade and industrial development, fostering the creation of regional value chains while diminishing reliance on outside markets. However, realizing this potential will necessitate investments in infrastructure, regulatory alignment, and strengthening institutional capacities. Overall, regional blocs are acting as both shields against global uncertainties and catalysts for the establishment of restructured, regionally focused value chains.

Scenario Planning for Disruptive Geopolitical Shocks

In light of the volatile geopolitical climate, scenario planning has become a crucial skill for navigating the future of GVCs. This process involves identifying plausible future scenarios—such as military conflicts, pandemics, cyber-attacks, or economic decoupling—and evaluating their potential impacts on supply networks. It encourages organizations to transcend linear forecasting and prepare for various contingencies.

Innovative companies are creating digital replicas of their supply chains to model responses to different shocks. Governments and international organizations are increasingly participating in horizon scanning initiatives to anticipate disruptions and develop protective policies. Scenario planning fosters agility, enhances collaboration among stakeholders, and shortens recovery times during unexpected crises.

In summary, the future trajectory of GVCs will be influenced by a combination of digital, environmental, political, and regional dynamics. To succeed amid this uncertainty, stakeholders must actively pursue innovation, resilience, and collaboration. The trends discussed are interconnected and collectively delineate the strategic priorities for the next generation of GVCs.

Call to Action: A Collective Responsibility for the Future of GVCs

The responsibility for the future of GVCs extends beyond just corporations or governments; it encompasses a diverse range of stakeholders, including industry leaders, policymakers, academics, civil society, and international organizations. The disruptive influences of geopolitical tensions, pandemics, and economic nationalism have exposed weaknesses in global supply networks, revealing an overdependence on specific regions, single-source strategies, and rigid operational frameworks. These challenges highlight the need for a collective rethinking of GVC operations.

To achieve long-term sustainability, resilience, and equity, stakeholders must transition from reactive strategies to proactive, collaborative approaches. Businesses can no longer separate their decision-making from the broader global political and environmental landscape. Instead, they should engage with governments to advocate for policies that promote transparency, multilateral cooperation, and inclusive trade systems. Likewise, governments must refrain from implementing shortsighted protectionist measures that can fragment global trade, instead focusing on regulatory harmonization, fostering technological innovation, and supporting equitable development.

The disruptions to GVCs during the COVID-19 pandemic served as a wake-up call, and subsequent geopolitical tensions—such as the Russia-Ukraine conflict, escalating US-China relations, and protectionist trends in various countries—have further emphasized the vulnerabilities of the interconnected global trade system. These circumstances present a distinct opportunity for stakeholders to recognize their interdependence and take coordinated steps to secure the future of global commerce.

Engaging All Stakeholders to Co-Create Resilient and Sustainable Systems

Achieving resilience and sustainability in GVCs requires coordinated and inclusive efforts that leverage the strengths of all participants in the value chain. Multinational corporations play a crucial role, as they possess the scale and resources to redesign global operations with an emphasis on redundancy, diversification, and flexibility. This includes rethinking sourcing strategies, investing in real-time visibility technologies, and enhancing partnerships across different regions to mitigate risks.

SMEs, despite often facing resource limitations, are also essential players in GVCs. Policymakers should establish support mechanisms, such as targeted incentives, digital infrastructure, and capacity-building initiatives, to help SMEs integrate sustainably and competitively into international markets.

Academic institutions and research organizations must continue to explore the complexities of GVC disruptions and innovations. By providing data-driven insights and evidence-based recommendations, they can bridge the gap between theory and practice and support the development of effective and equitable policies.

Moreover, civil society, which is frequently overlooked in discussions about supply chains, must not be marginalized. As consumer preferences shift toward ethically and environmentally responsible production, CSOs can serve as watchdogs, ensuring accountability in sourcing practices, human rights, and environmental impacts. Their involvement enhances transparency and fosters public trust in the governance of GVCs.

Additionally, international institutions such as the WTO, UNCTAD, and regional trade blocs must take on more assertive leadership roles. They should function as neutral forums for dialogue, dispute resolution, and knowledge sharing—especially at a time when unilateral policies and nationalist agendas threaten the stability of the multilateral trading system.

Building a More Equitable Global Economy Through Strategic Adaptation

A defining characteristic of a resilient GVC system is its capacity to adapt to shocks while fostering equity among nations and sectors. Strategic adaptation goes beyond mere operational changes; it entails reevaluating the principles that dictate value distribution, risk management, and capacity-building across the chain.

A historical example of poorly aligned strategic adaptation occurred during the Trump administration's enforcement of punitive tariffs on a wide array of Chinese imports from 2018 to 2020. Although these tariffs were framed as measures to protect American jobs and industries, they resulted in widespread unintended consequences for GVCs. American manufacturers dependent on intermediate goods from China experienced soaring production costs, while retaliatory tariffs from China further disrupted agricultural exports and heightened trade tensions.

While these tariffs prompted a reconfiguration of GVCs, it did not necessarily lead to increased resilience or sustainability. Some companies relocated production to cheaper countries like Vietnam or Mexico, yet often without addressing fundamental vulnerabilities such as excessive cost-cutting or a lack of transparency in supply chains. Moreover, the fragmentation instigated by such protectionist policies eroded trust in the global trade system, diminished investment flows, and left SMEs in both exporting and importing countries facing uncertainty.

The takeaway is that protectionism, lacking a long-term strategy for inclusive growth and innovation, can lead to a zero-sum scenario. Moving forward, governments must embrace smarter, collaborative strategies—such as investing in domestic capabilities without undermining global integration and fostering regional cooperation that complements rather than supplants global trade.

Strategic adaptation also necessitates investments in sustainable and inclusive infrastructure. Climate-related disruptions, ranging from floods to wildfires, increasingly threaten GVCs. Consequently, firms need to incorporate climate risk assessments into their supply chain planning. Likewise, investment in upskilling and digital education, particularly in emerging markets, is crucial for enabling equitable participation in the evolving GVCs that are becoming increasingly data-driven and technology-intensive.

Finally, it is vital that adaptation strategies do not reinforce global inequalities. The future of GVCs must not solely focus on resilience for the affluent and powerful but should also create inclusive pathways for developing economies to enhance their roles within the value chain—from suppliers of raw materials to high-value producers and innovators.

As demonstrated throughout this book, GVCs are situated at the intersection of economic development, technological advancement, and geopolitical complexities. To effectively address the challenges ahead, it is essential for all stakeholders to adopt a unified vision that prioritizes resilience, sustainability, and equity—not merely as lofty ideals but as critical strategic necessities. The imperative is unequivocal: collaborative action is required across borders and industries to reconstruct a GVC system capable of not only enduring future disruptions but also fostering a more equitable and sustainable global economy.

Conclusion

Reaffirmation of the Need for Transformation

The previous chapters have provided a thorough examination of a world in which GVCs face unprecedented pressures from geopolitical tensions, technological advancements, and environmental challenges. The shifting trade dynamics between developed and emerging economies, technological disruptions, the rise of protectionist measures, and a growing emphasis on ESG criteria all underscore a critical message: the current state of affairs is unsustainable. The period characterized by stable, linear, and efficiency-focused supply chains has transitioned into a more fragmented, complex, and uncertain environment. In this volatile landscape, the necessity for transformation is not merely urgent; it is vital for survival.

This transformation must be comprehensive, integrated into every segment of the value chain. Attributes such as resilience, agility, sustainability, and inclusivity are no longer mere aspirations but have become essential strategic priorities. For GVCs to flourish, they need to be reenvisioned as adaptive networks that can respond effectively not only to immediate disruptions but also to long-term structural changes. Achieving this requires collaboration among businesses, governments, and international institutions, alongside a renewed emphasis on innovation, risk management, and cooperative efforts.

Furthermore, it is crucial to understand that the forces propelling this transformation are interconnected. Geopolitical tensions impact trade policies, which subsequently influence business decisions regarding sourcing and production. Technological advancements redefine how and where value is generated. Expectations surrounding environmental and social governance shape investment behaviors and consumer preferences. These shifts do not happen in isolation; rather, they evolve together, necessitating cohesive responses from all stakeholders involved.

Final Thoughts on Navigating GVCs in a Volatile World

The instability of the current global landscape is not a transient occurrence; it is a defining element of our era. The resurgence of nationalist sentiments, trade conflicts, and the disintegration of multilateral agreements have overshadowed international trade. A prominent example of this trend was the implementation of tariffs during Donald Trump's presidency in the United States. The US–China trade war, initiated under his administration, disrupted established supply chains, increased costs for businesses and consumers, and prompted companies to reconsider their reliance on single-country sourcing strategies.

Trump's tariffs on over $360 billion worth of Chinese imports compelled many multinational corporations to seek alternative production sites, such as Vietnam, India, or Mexico. Although some were successful in relocating production, the transition was neither smooth nor devoid of costs. These developments highlighted the vulnerabilities inherent in concentrated supply chains and the political risks associated with GVCs. They also revealed a lack of preparedness among numerous firms for rapid, policy-driven disruptions. For policymakers, these events emphasized the fragility of economic interdependence in a politicized global landscape.

More broadly, the tariffs enacted during the Trump administration ignited a larger discourse regarding economic sovereignty, the diversification of supply chains, and the significance of regional resilience. Even with shifts in US leadership, the underlying concerns that prompted those tariffs—issues surrounding strategic dependence, technological appropriation, and industrial competitiveness—continue to exert influence. This continuity suggests that businesses need to prepare for not only isolated disruptions but also an extended period of geopolitical fragmentation.

In this context, GVC governance must be restructured to reconcile efficiency with security and autonomy. Strategies such as risk-based segmentation, multi-shoring, nearshoring, and friend-shoring have emerged as practical means to navigate these uncertainties. These approaches extend beyond mere geographic diversification; they focus on fostering trust-based partnerships, leveraging local capabilities, and minimizing exposure to unpredictable geopolitical events.

Another vital aspect of future navigation within GVCs is the pivotal role of technology. Innovations such as digital twins, AI-driven demand forecasting, blockchain for traceability, and platform-based collaboration models present new avenues for enhancing transparency, speed, and risk mitigation. However, the implementation of these technologies must be inclusive and guided by ethical considerations to prevent exacerbating the digital divide between advanced and developing economies.

Equally significant is the role of global institutions in fostering a collaborative environment conducive to GVC resilience. The current fragmentation of trade regulations, disputes over subsidies and standards, and the lack of coordination in crisis response have undermined the foundational structures that initially allowed GVCs to thrive. Revitalizing multilateralism—through the

WTO, regional agreements, or issue-specific coalitions—is crucial for restoring trust and predictability in the global economy.

The path forward will not be devoid of challenges. There will be political resistance to relinquishing control, economic costs tied to redundancies and diversification efforts, and institutional inertia that hinders reform. However, these challenges are minor compared to the systemic risks posed by inaction. Without intentional and collective initiatives, GVCs will become increasingly vulnerable to shocks—whether climate-related, political, or technological—that could disrupt key sectors and regions.

A Call to Action

This book concludes with a resolute call to action. For businesses, the directive is to transcend short-term efficiency gains and incorporate resilience and sustainability into core strategies. For governments, the task is to foster enabling environments through stable policies, targeted investments, and international collaboration. Academics and thought leaders are called to enhance understanding and support evidence-based decision-making. Civil society is urged to advocate for transparency, fairness, and inclusivity in the creation and distribution of value.

In summary, the transformation of GVCs is both essential and achievable. It will demand courageous leadership, flexible thinking, and steadfast collaboration. As we navigate a period characterized by uncertainty, disruption, and transition, the decisions made today will define the resilience and inclusivity of the global economy for generations to come.

INDEX

Note: Page numbers in *italics* indicate figures; **bold** indicate tables in the text.

Kolibri 360 GmbH
Ferdinand-Jühlke-Straße 7
99095 Erfurt, Deutschland
produktsicherheit@kolibri360.de